THE QUESTIONS
OF THE BIBLE

*ARRANGED IN THE ORDER OF THE
BOOKS OF SCRIPTURE*

COMPILED BY

WILLIAM CARNELLEY

WITH A PREFACE BY

SAMUEL G. GREEN, D. D.

WITH CONNECTIVE READINGS AND TABLES

WIPF & STOCK · Eugene, Oregon

Wipf and Stock Publishers
199 W 8th Ave, Suite 3
Eugene, OR 97401

The Questions of the Bible
Arranged in the Order of the Books of Scripture
By Carnelley, William and Green, Samuel G.
Softcover ISBN-13: 978-1-7252-9940-5
Hardcover ISBN-13: 978-1-7252-9939-9
eBook ISBN-13: 978-1-7252-9941-2
Publication date 5/1/2021
Previously published by T. Fisher Unwin, 1889

This edition is a scanned facsimile of
the original edition published in 1889.

DEDICATED

TO

THE MEMORY OF

THE LATE

JOHN RYLANDS,

IN

TOKEN OF A FRIENDSHIP

OF NEARLY

FIFTY YEARS.

FALLOWFIELD,
    MANCHESTER.

PREFACE.

THE following collection of extracts from Holy Scripture has been compiled by a layman who has been accustomed for many years to notice the immense number and variety of QUESTIONS contained in the Sacred Volume, and the force and interest which they add to almost every page.

Many of the highest truths connected with the relations of GOD to man are conveyed in an interrogative form. The *commands* of the Most High appeal to man's sense of duty, His *promises* and *threatenings* to their fears and hopes; but His *questions* search the conscience, challenging the soul's most earnest consideration, and silencing those who would 'reply against God.' Of these questions, some were addressed with startling force to the individual transgressor, with a meaning for all time. The call to Adam, 'Where art thou?' and that to Cain, 'Where is Abel thy brother?' have still power to thrill the guilty soul. So to the reason and heart of all men comes the great appeal, 'To whom then will ye liken Me, or shall I be equal?' while the voice from heaven that can be so stern melts into tones of deepest tenderness in the appeal, 'Why sayest thou, O Jacob, and speakest, O Israel, My way is hid from the Lord, and my judgment is passed over from my God?'

Akin to solemn words like these are the questions which have been found, wherever the Gospel has been preached, most calculated to awaken reflection, and to lead to repentance: 'How shall we escape, if we neglect so great salvation?' 'If the righteous scarcely be saved, where shall the ungodly and the sinner appear?' Or, again, the appeal is made to the tenderest affections: 'Wilt thou not from this time cry unto Me, My Father, Thou art the Guide of My youth?' Words like these have always furnished to the evangelical preacher the material for his most earnest and effective pleadings; and, applied by the power of the HOLY GHOST, have proved mighty to win the souls of old and young.

The words of CHRIST JESUS, to His disciples and to the multitudes, were largely made up of questions, by turns heart-searching and heart-winning, solemn in rebuke, tender in appeal: 'What shall it profit a man, if he gain the whole world, and lose his own soul?' 'Do ye not therefore err, not knowing the Scriptures, and the power of God?' 'Will ye also go away?' 'Simon, son of Jonas, lovest thou Me?' 'O thou of little faith, wherefore dost thou doubt?' In His discourses and parables especially, He often points their meaning by a challenge to His auditors: 'Do men gather grapes of thorns, or figs of thistles?' 'Tell Me therefore, which of them will love him most?' 'Which now of these three, thinkest thou, was neighbour unto him that fell among the thieves?' In fact, the *Questions of Jesus to men*, in all their immense variety of application, might themselves well form a subject of study by themselves, at every turn revealing the insight, the power, and the love of Him who spake as never man had spoken.

Then, while these Divine utterances are thus significant, there is a wonderful interest in the questions and appeals of *man to God*. These are manifold. Sometimes there is the transgressor's cry, defiant yet despairing: 'Am I my brother's keeper?' 'What profit is it that we have kept His ordinances?' and the demons' question: 'What have we to do with Thee, Jesus, Thou Son of God? art Thou come hither to torment us before the time?' Very frequent also in the Psalms and the Prophets, as well as in the Book of Job, is the cry for light and help amid the mysteries of Providence and the troubles of life: 'Wherefore hidest Thou Thy face, and holdest me for Thine enemy?' 'How long wilt Thou forget me, O LORD? for ever?' 'O the hope of Israel, the saviour thereof in time of trouble, why shouldest Thou be as a stranger in the land, and as a wayfaring man that turneth aside to tarry for a night?' Often, indeed, have the saints of God thus lifted up their pleading voice to heaven, in the spirit of that great appeal of the Son to the Father, uttered in the Psalms and re-echoed from the Cross—the question of questions, in the answer to which lay the secret of the world's hope: 'MY GOD, MY GOD, WHY HAST THOU FORSAKEN ME?'

Often, again, men have 'enquired of the Lord' in other tones than these; sometimes in an eager desire to know: 'By whom shall Jacob arise? for he is small;' but oftener in wonder and adoration: 'What is man, that Thou art mindful of him? and the son of man, that Thou visitest him?' 'Art Thou not from everlasting, O LORD my God, mine Holy One? we shall not die;' 'Lord, to whom shall we go? Thou hast the words of eternal life.' Very impressive and sublime are the questions which often in the Old Testament, especially in the Books of Job and Isaiah, set forth the majesty of JEHOVAH. 'Is there any number of His armies? and upon whom doth not His light arise?' 'Hast thou an arm like God? or canst thou thunder with a voice like Him?' 'Who hath directed the Spirit of the LORD, or being His counsellor hath taught Him? With whom took He counsel, and who instructed Him, and taught Him in the path of judgment, and taught Him knowledge, and showed to Him the way of understanding?' As if in response to words like these, are some of the most exulting utterances of faith and hope put into the form of questions, as if to challenge reply from all the powers of the universe: 'If God be for us, who can be against us?'

Many impressive *proverbs* are clothed in the form of questions. Nor is this the case in the Book of Proverbs only: the same mode of speech pervades all Scripture; 'Is Saul also among the prophets?' 'Will God in very deed dwell with men on the earth?' 'Canst thou by searching find out God?' 'Can two walk together, except they be agreed?' 'What can the man do that cometh after the king?' 'Should not the shepherds feed the flocks?' 'Do men gather grapes of thorns, or figs of thistles?' These are but a few signal instances of the deep meanings clothed in terse interrogations, which all who search the Scriptures may find for themselves, discovering in them food for meditation, daily and inexhaustible.

In the *historical parts of Scripture* the question is often part of the narration, which it helps vividly to carry on. Instances of this are too numerous, as well as too obvious, to quote. The paragraphs of the present compilation in which such questions are given will often serve to recall to the reader a connected history, and will lead him, perhaps, with new interest to study the whole passage of which the interrogation forms so emphatic and suggestive a part.

It is natural that some questions, from their nature, should be *often repeated;* and the comparison of the often widely-differing circumstances in which the same enquiry is made will be found most interesting. Thus, the simple question, *What is thy name?* brings before us, first, the scene at Peniel, when Jacob wrestled with the angel until the breaking of the day; next, the appearance to Manoah of the heavenly visitant whose name was 'Secret' or 'Wonderful'; and then, the meeting of Jesus with the demoniac by the Galilean lake whom the 'legion' of evil spirits had darkly enslaved. Or again, the words, *Whither goest thou?* recall, first, the lovely narrative of the meeting between Jacob and Esau; next, the encounter of the Levite with an old Benjamite at Gibeah, in one of the most terrible stories of Scripture; next, the prophet Zechariah's vision of 'the man with the measuring-line' in the day when Jerusalem was to be restored; and lastly, the solemn meeting between Jesus and His disciples when He was about to pass from them into a mystery of suffering and glory which they could not understand. The appeal repeatedly made to the prophets, *What seest thou?* calls up before our view the various and significant emblems of the 'almond-tree,' the 'seething-pot,' the 'two baskets of figs,' the 'plumb-line,' the 'basket of summer fruit,' the 'candlestick all of gold,' and the 'flying scroll.' The phrases, *How long? How much more?* will guide the Bible-reader into almost innumerable channels of profitable study, both in History, Psalm, and Prophecy, in the Old Testament and the New. To compare the passages thus brought into view, with their differences and their parallelisms, will often throw the greatest light upon the meaning of the word which, although given 'at sundry times and in divers manners,' is still one consistent whole.

It must not be forgotten that some of the most cogent *arguments* of the Apostle Paul are put in the form of questions. Thus: Do we then make void the law through faith?' 'Shall we continue in sin, that grace may abound?' 'Nay but, O man, who art thou that repliest against God?' 'If Christ be preached that He rose from the dead, how say some among you that there is no resurrection of the dead?' To answer questions like these, clearly and adequately, would be to become a master in New Testament Theology. And finally, the very sublimest questions ever heard by mortal ears are those once uttered in heaven: 'Who is worthy to open the Book, and to loose the seals thereof?' and, 'What are these which are arrayed in white robes, and whence came they?'

To bring into prominence this element of Holy Scripture, at once so characteristic, so interesting, and so variously important, is the aim of the following compilation. The questions are given, as they occur in the Books of Scripture according to the usual order, and in the Received Translation. Sometimes, it is true, the Revised Version differs from that of 1611, both in turning affirmations into questions, and the contrary; but with such critical points it has not been judged necessary to trouble readers who will use this book. For the most part there is no difference in this respect between the two versions. The questions are printed in a bold type, for the sake of ready distinction, and so much of the connexion is generally given as to render them intelligible. A **paragraph** form has been adopted in preference to the **ordinary verse-separation**. Chapter and verse are indicated in the margin; the number of the verse which contains the question being noted. The

PREFACE. 7

small figures attached to many of the verse-numbers point out the number of questions in that particular verse. The intention of the Compiler has been to give *all* the questions, of whatever kind, that occur in Scripture, the number contained in every separate chapter and book being shown in the margin ; and a Table appended to the volume giving a summary of the whole.

It is suggested that, apart from private study, leading to comparison with the Scriptures themselves, the book may be found useful in family Bible-readings or in Bible-classes. The leader of the class might propose questions, without mentioning the place, for the rest to find, the most successful in the search being rewarded by marks or otherwise. A continuance of this plan would contribute immensely to an acquaintance with the Word of God. As it is, many are familiar with Bible texts and sentences who have never learned to assign them to their proper places, or to take account of their connexion. We might, for instance, write down a series of brief questions like the following, and ask our readers to test their knowledge of the Bible by finding the book, chapter, and verse where they occur.

1. What saith the Scripture?
2. Who is sufficient for these things?
3. Who hath known the mind of the Lord?
4. Are the consolations of God small with thee?
5. Have we not all one Father?
6. How long shall thy vain thoughts lodge within thee?
7. Watchman! what of the night?
8. A wounded spirit who can bear?
9. Wilt Thou not revive us again?
10. Who may abide the day of His coming?
11. Will ye contend for God?
12. Understandest thou what thou readest?

A Bible-reader who can without hesitation turn to these twelve passages may be assumed to have a fair knowledge of Scripture. It is almost needless to add that, suggestive as most of the questions are in themselves, their instructiveness becomes far greater when they are read in their connexion. In fact, apart from this, they cannot be said to be properly known.

Similar papers might be prepared, to an almost indefinite extent; and we can imagine few better occupations for young people—say on the Lord's day afternoon—than to search for such a series of questions in a (reference) Bible without the help of a Concordance. If the Compiler should succeed by this or other means in giving an impulse to the study of the Divine Oracles, his long labour in preparing the present work will be richly rewarded. His earnest prayer is that the SPIRIT, by whose holy inspiration the Scriptures were given, will influence the mind of every reader, not only to a better understanding of the letter, but to an acceptance of the Word of God in its living power upon the understanding, the heart, and the life. And to Him alone be the glory!

GENESIS.

	CHAP.	VER.

NOW the serpent was more subtil than any beast of the field which the LORD God had made. And he said unto the woman, **Yea, hath God said, Ye shall not eat of every tree of the garden?**   3   1

And the LORD God called unto Adam, and said unto him, **Where** *art* **thou?**   9

And He said, **Who told thee that thou** *wast* **naked? Hast thou eaten of the tree, whereof I commanded thee that thou shouldest not eat?**   11²

And the LORD God said unto the woman, **What** *is* **this** *that* **thou hast done?** And the woman said, The serpent beguiled me, and I did eat.   13

    5

And the LORD said unto Cain, **Why art thou wroth? and why is thy countenance fallen? If thou doest well, shalt thou not be accepted?**   4   6² / 7

And the LORD said unto Cain, **Where** *is* **Abel thy brother?** And he said, I know not: **Am I my brother's keeper?** And He said, **What hast thou done?** the voice of thy brother's blood crieth unto Me from the ground.   9² / 10

    6

And Pharaoh called Abram, and said, **What** *is* **this** *that* **thou hast done unto me? why didst thou not tell me that she** *was* **thy wife? Why saidst thou, She** *is* **my sister?**   12   18² / 19 / 3

And Abram said unto Lot, Let there be no strife, I pray thee, between me and thee, and between my herdmen and thy herdmen; for we *be* brethren. *Is* **not the whole land before thee?**   13   9 / 1

1**

CHAP.	VER.	
15	2	And Abram said, **Lord** God, **what wilt Thou give me, seeing I go childless, and the steward of my house** *is* **this Eliezer of Damascus?**
	8	And He said unto him, I *am* the Lord that brought thee out of Ur of the Chaldees, to give thee this land to inherit it. And he said, **Lord** God, **whereby shall I know that I shall inherit it?**
	2	
16	8²	And he said, **Hagar, Sarai's maid, whence camest thou? and whither wilt thou go?** And she said, I flee from the face of my mistress Sarai.
	13	And she called the name of the Lord that spake unto her, Thou God, seest me: for she said, **Have I also here looked after Him that seeth me?**
	3	
17	17²	Then Abraham fell upon his face, and laughed, and said in his heart, **Shall** *a child* **be born unto him that is an hundred years old? and shall Sarah, that is ninety years old, bear?**
	2	
18	9	And they said unto him, **Where** *is* **Sarah thy wife?** And he said, Behold, in the tent.
	12	Therefore Sarah laughed within herself, saying, **After I am waxed old shall I have pleasure, my lord being old also?** And the Lord said unto Abraham, **Wherefore did Sarah laugh, saying, Shall I of a surety bear a child, which am old? Is any thing too hard for the** Lord? At the time appointed I will return unto thee, according to the time of life, and Sarah shall have a son.
	13	
	14	
	17	And the Lord said, **Shall I hide from Abraham that thing which I do; seeing that Abraham shall surely become a great and mighty nation, and all the nations of the earth shall be blessed in him?**
	23	And Abraham drew near, and said, **Wilt Thou also**

GENESIS:—XVIII.-XX.   11

	CHAP.	VER.

destroy the righteous with the wicked ? Peradventure there be fifty righteous within the city: **Wilt Thou also destroy and not spare the place for the fifty righteous that** *are* **therein ?** That be far from Thee to do after this manner, to slay the righteous with the wicked: and that the righteous should be as the wicked, that be far from Thee: **Shall not the Judge of all the earth do right ?** And the LORD said, If I find in Sodom fifty righteous within the city, then I will spare all the place for their sakes. And Abraham answered and said, Behold now, I have taken upon me to speak unto the Lord, which *am but* dust and ashes : Peradventure there shall lack five of the fifty righteous : **Wilt Thou destroy all the city for** *lack of* **five ?** And He said, If I find there forty and five, I will not destroy *it*. | **18** | 24

25

28

9

But before they lay down, the men of the city, *even* the men of Sodom, compassed the house round, both old and young, all the people from every quarter : and they called unto Lot, and said unto him, **Where** *are* **the men which came in to thee this night ?** | **19** | 5

And the men said unto Lot, **Hast thou here any besides ?** son in law, and thy sons, and thy daughters, and whatsoever thou hast in the city, bring *them* out of this place. | | 12

Behold now, this city *is* near to flee unto, and it *is* a little one: Oh, let me escape thither, (*is* **it not a little one ?**) and my soul shall live. | | 20

3

But Abimelech had not come near her: and he said, **Lord, wilt Thou slay also a righteous nation ? Said he unto me, She** *is* **my sister ?** and she, even she herself said, He *is* my brother : in the integrity of my heart and innocency of my hands have I done this. | **20** | 4
5

Then Abimelech called Abraham, and said unto him, **What hast thou done unto us ? and what have** | | 9[2]

CHAP.	VER.	
20	10	I offended thee, that thou hast brought on me and on my kingdom a great sin? thou hast done deeds unto me that ought not to be done. And Abimelech said unto Abraham, **What sawest thou, that thou hast done this thing?**
	5	
21	7	And she said, **Who would have said unto Abraham, that Sarah should have given children suck?** for I have born *him* a son in his old age.
	17	And God heard the voice of the lad; and the angel of God called to Hagar out of heaven, and said unto her, **What aileth thee, Hagar?** fear not; for God hath heard the voice of the lad where he *is*
	29	And Abimelech said unto Abraham, **What** *mean* **these seven ewe lambs which thou hast set by themselves?**
	3	
22	7	And Isaac spake unto Abraham his father, and said, My father: and he said, Here *am* I, my son. And he said, Behold the fire and the wood: **but where** *is* **the lamb for a burnt offering?**
	1	
23	15	My lord, hearken unto me: the land *is worth* four hundred shekels of silver; **what** *is* **that betwixt me and thee?** bury therefore thy dead.
	1	
24	5	And the servant said unto him, Peradventure the woman will not be willing to follow me unto this land: **must I needs bring thy son again unto the land from whence thou camest?**
	23²	And it came to pass, as the camels had done drinking, that the man took a golden earring of half a shekel weight, and two bracelets for her hands of ten *shekels* weight of gold; and said, **Whose daughter** *art* **thou?** tell me, I pray thee: **is there room** *in* **thy father's house for us to lodge in?**

	CHAP.	VER.

And he said, Come in, thou blessed of the Lord; **wherefore standest thou without?** for I have prepared the house, and room for the camels. — 24 31

And I asked her, and said, **Whose daughter** *art* **thou?** And she said, The daughter of Bethuel, Nahor's son — 47

And they called Rebekah, and said unto her, **Wilt thou go with this man?** And she said, I will go. — 58

For she *had* said unto the servant, **What man** *is* **this that walketh in the field to meet us?** And the servant *had* said, It *is* my master: therefore she took a vail, and covered herself. — 65 / 7

And the children struggled together within her; and she said, **If** *it be* **so, why** *am* **I thus?** And she went to inquire of the Lord. — 25 22

And Esau said, Behold, I *am* at the point to die: **and what profit shall this birthright do to me?** — 32 / 2

And Abimelech called Isaac, and said, Behold, of a surety she *is* thy wife: **and how saidst thou, She** *is* **my sister?** And Isaac said unto him, Because I said, Lest I die for her. And Abimelech said, **What** *is* **this thou hast done unto us?** one of the people might lightly have lien with thy wife, and thou shouldest have brought guiltiness upon us. — 26 9 / 10

And Isaac said unto them, **Wherefore come ye to me, seeing ye hate me, and have sent me away from you?** — 27 / 3

And he came unto his father, and said, My father: and he said, Here *am* I: **who** *art* **thou, my son?** And Jacob said unto his father, I *am* Esau thy firstborn; I have done according as thou badest me: arise, I — 27 18

CHAP.	VER.	
27	20	pray thee, sit and eat of my venison, that thy soul may bless me. And Isaac said unto his son, **How** *is it* **that thou hast found** *it* **so quickly, my son?**
	24	And he said, *Art* **thou my very son Esau?** And he said, I *am*.
	32	And Isaac his father said unto him, **Who** *art* **thou?** And he said, I *am* thy son, thy firstborn Esau. And
	33²	Isaac trembled very exceedingly, and said, **Who? where** *is* **he that hath taken venison, and brought** *it* **me, and I have eaten of all before thou camest, and have blessed him?** yea, *and* he shall be blessed. And when Esau heard the words of his father, he cried with a great and exceeding bitter cry, and said unto his father, Bless me, *even* me also, O my father. And he said, Thy brother came with subtilty, and hath taken
	36²	away thy blessing. And he said, **Is not he rightly named Jacob?** for he hath supplanted me these two times: he took away my birthright; and, behold, now he hath taken away my blessing. And he said, **Hast thou not reserved a blessing for me?** And Isaac answered and said unto Esau, Behold, I have made him thy lord, and all his brethren have I given to him for servants; and with corn and wine have I sustained him:
	37	**and what shall I do now unto thee, my son?**
	38	And Esau said unto his father, **Hast thou but one blessing, my father?** bless me, *even* me also, O my father. And Esau lifted up his voice, and wept.
	45	Until thy brother's anger turn away from thee, and he forget *that* which thou hast done to him: then I will send, and fetch thee from thence: **why should I be deprived also of you both in one day?** And
	46	Rebekah said to Isaac, I am weary of my life because of the daughters of Heth: **if Jacob take a wife of the daughters of Heth, such as these** *which are* **of the daughters of the land, what good shall my life**
	12	**do me?**

GENESIS:—XXIX.-XXXI.

| | CHAP. | VER. |

And Jacob said unto them, **My brethren, whence** *be* **ye?** And they said, Of Haran *are* we. And he said unto them, **Know ye Laban the son of Nahor?** And they said, We know *him*. And he said unto them, *Is* **he well?** And they said, *He is* well. — 29 · 4, 5, 6

And Laban said unto Jacob, **Because thou** *art* **my brother, shouldest thou therefore serve me for nought? tell me, what** *shall* **thy wages** *be?* — 15²

And it came to pass, that in the morning, behold, it *was* Leah: and he said to Laban, **What** *is* **this thou hast done unto me? did not I serve with thee for Rachel? wherefore then hast thou beguiled me?** — 25³, 8

And Jacob's anger was kindled against Rachel: and he said, *Am* **I in God's stead, who hath withheld from thee the fruit of the womb?** — 30 · 2

And she said unto her, *Is it* **a small matter that thou hast taken my husband? and wouldest thou take away my son's mandrakes also?** And Rachel said, Therefore he shall lie with thee to night for thy son's mandrakes. — 15²

For *it was* little which thou hadst before I *came*, and it is *now* increased unto a multitude; and the Lord hath blessed thee since my coming: **and now when shall I provide for mine own house also?** And he said, **What shall I give thee?** And Jacob said, Thou shalt not give me any thing: if thou wilt do this thing for me, I will again feed *and* keep thy flock. — 30, 31, 5

And Rachel and Leah answered and said unto him, *Is there* **yet any portion or inheritance for us in our father's house? Are we not counted of him strangers?** for he hath sold us, and hath quite devoured also our money. — 31 · 14, 15

CHAP.	VER.	
31	26	And Laban said to Jacob, **What hast thou done, that thou hast stolen away unawares to me, and carried away my daughters, as captives** *taken*
	27	**with the sword?** Wherefore didst thou flee away secretly, and steal away from me; and didst not tell me, that I might have sent thee away with mirth, and with songs, with tabret, and with harp?
	28	**And hast not suffered me to kiss my sons and my daughters?** thou hast now done foolishly in *so* doing. It is in the power of my hand to do you hurt: but the God of your father spake unto me yesternight, saying, Take thou heed that thou speak not to Jacob either good or bad. And now, *though* thou wouldest needs be gone,
	30	because thou sore longedst after thy father's house, *yet* **wherefore hast thou stolen my gods?**
	36[2]	And Jacob was wroth, and chode with Laban: and Jacob answered and said to Laban, **What** *is* **my trespass? what** *is* **my sin, that thou hast so hotly pursued after me?** Whereas thou hast searched all my stuff, **what hast thou found of all thy**
	37	**household stuff?** set *it* here before my brethren and thy brethren, that they may judge betwixt us both.
		And Laban answered and said unto Jacob, *These* daughters *are* my daughters, and *these* children *are* my children, and *these* cattle *are* my cattle, and all that thou
	43	seest *is* mine: **and what can I do this day unto these my daughters, or unto their children which**
	10	**they have born?**
32	17[3]	And he commanded the foremost, saying, When Esau my brother meeteth thee, and asketh thee, saying, **Whose** *art* **thou? and whither goest thou? and whose** *are* **these before thee?** then thou shalt say, *They be* thy servant Jacob's; it *is* a present sent unto my lord Esau: and, behold, also he *is* behind us
	27	And he said unto him, **What** *is* **thy name?** And he said, Jacob.

	CHAP	VER.
And Jacob asked *him*, and said, Tell *me*, I pray thee, thy name. And he said, **Wherefore** *is* **it** *that* **thou dost ask after my name?** And he blessed him there.	32	29
		5
And he lifted up his eyes, and saw the women and the children, and said, **Who** *are* **those with thee?** And he said, The children which God hath graciously given thy servant.	33	5
And he said, **What** *meanest* **thou by all this drove which I met?** And he said, *These are* to find grace in the sight of my lord.		8
And Esau said, Let me now leave with thee *some* of the folk that *are* with me. And he said, **What needeth it?** let me find grace in the sight of my lord.		15
		3
Shall **not their cattle and their substance and every beast of theirs** *be* **ours?** only let us consent unto them, and they will dwell with us.	34	23
And they said, **Should he deal with our sister as with an harlot?**		31
		2
And his brethren said to him, **Shalt thou indeed reign over us? or shalt thou indeed have dominion over us?** And they hated him yet the more for his dreams, and for his words.	37	8²
And he told *it* to his father, and to his brethren: and his father rebuked him, and said unto him, **What** *is* **this dream that thou hast dreamed? Shall I and thy mother and thy brethren indeed come to bow down ourselves to thee to the earth?**		10²
And Israel said unto Joseph, **Do not thy brethren feed** *the flock* **in Shechem?** come, and I will send thee unto them. And he said to him, Here *am I*.		13

2

CHAP.	VER.	
37	15	And a certain man found him, and, behold, *he was* wandering in the field: and the man asked him, saying, **What seekest thou?**
	26	And Judah said unto his brethren, **What profit** *is it* **if we slay our brother, and conceal his blood?**
	30	And he returned unto his brethren, and said, The child *is* not; **and I, whither shall I go?**
	8	
38	16	And she said, **What wilt thou give me, that thou mayest come in unto me?** And he said, I will send
	17	*thee* a kid from the flock. And she said, **Wilt thou give**
	18	*me* **a pledge, till thou send** *it?* And he said, **What pledge shall I give thee?** And she said, Thy signet, and thy bracelets, and thy staff that *is* in thine hand.
	21	Then he asked the men of that place, saying, **Where** *is* **the harlot, that** *was* **openly by the way side?**
	29	And it came to pass, as he drew back his hand, that, behold, his brother came out: and she said, **How hast thou broken forth?** *this* breach *be* upon thee: therefore his name was called Pharez.
	5	
39	9	*There is* none greater in this house than I; neither hath he kept back any thing from me but thee, because thou *art* his wife: **how then can I do this great wickedness, and sin against God?**
	1	
40	7	And he asked Pharaoh's officers that *were* with him in the ward of his lord's house, saying, **Wherefore look ye** *so* **sadly to day?** And they said unto him, We have dreamed a dream, and *there is* no interpreter of it.
	8	And Joseph said unto them, *Do* **not interpretations**
	2	*belong* **to God?** tell me *them*, I pray you.

	CHAP.	VER.
And Pharaoh said unto his servants, **Can we find** such a one **as this** is, **a man in whom the Spirit of God** is?	41	38
		1
Now when Jacob saw that there was corn in Egypt, Jacob said unto his sons, **Why do ye look one upon another?**	42	1
And Joseph saw his brethren, and he knew them, but made himself strange unto them, and spake roughly unto them; and he said unto them, **Whence come ye?** And they said, From the land of Canaan to buy food.		7
And Reuben answered them, saying, **Spake I not unto you, saying, Do not sin against the child; and ye would not hear?** therefore, behold, also his blood is required.		22
And he said unto his brethren, My money is restored; and, lo, it is even in my sack: and their heart failed them, and they were afraid, saying one to another, **What** is **this** that **God hath done unto us?**		28
		4
And Israel said, **Wherefore dealt ye** so **ill with me,** as **to tell the man whether ye had yet a brother?** And they said, The man asked us straitly of our state, and of our kindred, saying, Is **your father yet alive? have ye** another **brother?** and we told him according to the tenor of these words: **could we certainly know that he would say, Bring your brother down?**	43	6
		7 3
And he asked them of their welfare, and said, Is **your father well, the old man of whom ye spake?** Is **he yet alive?**		27 2
And he lifted up his eyes, and saw his brother Benjamin, his mother's son, and said, Is **this your younger brother, of whom ye spake unto me?** And he said, God be gracious unto thee, my son.		29
		7

GENESIS :—XLIV.-XLVII.

CHAP.	VER.	
44	4	*And* when they were gone out of the city, *and* not yet far off, Joseph said unto his steward, Up, follow after the men; and when thou dost overtake them, say unto them, **Wherefore have ye rewarded evil for good?** *Is*
	5	not this *it* **in which my lord drinketh, and whereby indeed he divineth?** ye have done evil in so doing. And he overtook them, and he spake unto them these same words. And they said unto him,
	7	**Wherefore saith my lord these words?** God forbid that thy servants should do according to this thing: behold, the money, which we found in our sacks' mouths, we brought again unto thee out of the land of Canaan:
	8	**how then should we steal out of thy lord's house silver or gold?**
	15²	And Joseph said unto them, **What deed** *is* **this that ye have done?** **wot ye not that such a man as**
	16³	**I can certainly divine?** And Judah said, **What shall we say unto my lord? what shall we speak? or how shall we clear ourselves?** God hath found out the iniquity of thy servants: behold, we *are* my lord's servants, both we, and *he* also with whom the cup is found.
	19	My lord asked his servants, saying, **Have ye a father, or a brother?**
	34	**For how shall I go up to my father, and the lad** *be* **not with me?** lest peradventure I see the evil that shall come on my father.
	11	
45	3	And Joseph said unto his brethren, I *am* Joseph; **doth my father yet live?**
	1	
46	33	And it shall come to pass, when Pharaoh shall call you, and shall say, **What** *is* **your occupation?**
	1	
47	3	And Pharaoh said unto his brethren, **What** *is* **your occupation?** And they said unto Pharaoh, Thy servants *are* shepherds, both we, *and* also our fathers.

	CHAP.	VER.
And Pharaoh said unto Jacob, **How old** *art* **thou?**	47	8
And when money failed in the land of Egypt, and in the land of Canaan, all the Egyptians came unto Joseph, and said, Give us bread: **for why should we die in thy presence?** for the money faileth.		15
Wherefore shall we die before thine eyes, both we and our land? buy us and our land for bread, and we and our land will be servants unto Pharaoh.		19
		4
And Israel beheld Joseph's sons, and said, **Who** *are* **these?**	48	8
		1
Judah *is* a lion's whelp: from the prey, my son, thou art gone up; he stooped down, he couched as a lion, and as an old lion; **who shall rouse him up?**	49	9
		1
And Joseph said unto them, Fear not: **for** *am* **I in the place of God?**	50	19
		1

Genesis 149

EXODUS.

	CHAP.	VER.
AND the king of Egypt called for the midwives, and said unto them, **Why have ye done this thing, and have saved the men children alive?**	1	18
		1
Then said his sister to Pharaoh's daughter, **Shall I go and call to thee a nurse of the Hebrew women, that she may nurse the child for thee?**	2	7
And when he went out the second day, behold, two men of the Hebrews strove together: and he said to him that did the wrong, **Wherefore smitest thou thy fellow?** And he said, **Who made thee a prince and a judge over us?** intendest thou to kill me, as		13
		14[2]

CHAP.	VER	
		thou killedst the Egyptian? And Moses feared, and said, Surely this thing is known.
2	18	And when they came to Reuel their father, he said, **How** *is it that* **ye are come so soon to day?**
	20[2]	And he said unto his daughters, **And where** *is* **he? why** *is* **it** *that* **ye have left the man?** call him, that
	7	he may eat bread.
3	11	And Moses said unto God, **Who** *am* **I, that I should go unto Pharaoh, and that I should bring forth the children of Israel out of Egypt?**
	13[2]	And Moses said unto God, Behold, *when* I come unto the children of Israel, and shall say unto them, The God of your fathers hath sent me unto you; and they shall say to me, **What** *is* **His name?** **what shall I say**
	3	**unto them?**
4	2	And the LORD said unto him, **What** *is* **that in thine hand?** And he said, A rod.
	11[3]	And the LORD said unto him, **Who hath made man's mouth? or who maketh the dumb, or deaf, or the seeing, or the blind? have not I the** LORD?
	14	And the anger of the LORD was kindled against Moses, and He said, *Is* not **Aaron the Levite thy brother?** I know that he can speak well. And also, behold, he
	5	cometh forth to meet thee: and when he seeth thee, he will be glad in his heart.
5	2	And Pharaoh said, **Who** *is* **the** LORD, **that I should obey His voice to let Israel go?** I know not the LORD neither will I let Israel go.
	4	And the king of Egypt said unto them, **Wherefore do ye, Moses and Aaron, let the people from their works?** get you unto your burdens.

EXODUS:—V.-X.

	CHAP	VER.
And the officers of the children of Israel, which Pharaoh's taskmasters had set over them, were beaten, *and* demanded, **Wherefore have ye not fulfilled your task in making brick both yesterday and to day, as heretofore?** Then the officers of the children of Israel came and cried unto Pharaoh, saying, **Wherefore dealest thou thus with thy servants?**	5	14
		15
And Moses returned unto the LORD, and said, LORD, **wherefore hast Thou** *so* **evil entreated this people? why** *is* **it** *that* **Thou hast sent me?**		22²
		6
And Moses spake before the LORD, saying, Behold, the children of Israel have not hearkened unto me; **how then shall Pharaoh hear me, who** *am* **of uncircumcised lips?**	6	12
And Moses said before the LORD, Behold, I *am* of uncircumcised lips, **and how shall Pharaoh hearken unto me?**		30
		2
And Moses said unto Pharaoh, Glory over me: **when shall I intreat for thee, and for thy servants, and for thy people, to destroy the frogs from thee and thy houses,** *that* **they may remain in the river only?**	8	9
And Moses said, It is not meet so to do; for we shall sacrifice the abomination of the Egyptians to the LORD our God: **lo, shall we sacrifice the abomination of the Egyptians before their eyes, and will they not stone us?**		26
		2
As yet exaltest thou thyself against My people, that thou wilt not let them go?	9	17
		1
And Moses and Aaron came in unto Pharaoh, and said unto him, Thus saith the LORD God of the Hebrews, **How long wilt thou refuse to humble thyself before Me?** let My people go, that they may serve Me.	10	3

CHAP.	VER.	
10	7²	And Pharaoh's servants said unto him, **How long shall this man be a snare unto us?** let the men go, that they may serve the LORD their God: **knowest thou not yet that Egypt is destroyed?** And Moses and Aaron were brought again unto Pharaoh: and he said
	8	unto them, Go, serve the LORD your God: *but* **who** *are*
	4	**they that shall go?**
12	26	And it shall come to pass, when your children shall say unto you, **What mean ye by this service?**
	1	
13	14	And it shall be when thy son asketh thee in time to come, saying, **What** *is* **this?** that thou shalt say unto him, By strength of hand the LORD brought us out from Egypt, from the house of bondage.
	1	
14	5	And it was told the king of Egypt that the people fled. and the heart of Pharaoh and of his servants was turned against the people, and they said, **Why have we done this, that we have let Israel go from serving us?**
	11²	**Because** *there were* **no graves in Egypt, hast thou taken us away to die in the wilderness? wherefore hast thou dealt thus with us, to carry us forth
	12	out of Egypt?** *Is* not this the word that we did tell thee in Egypt, saying, Let us alone, that we may serve the Egyptians? For *it had been* better for us to serve the Egyptians, than that we should die in the wilderness.
	15	And the LORD said unto Moses, **Wherefore criest thou unto Me?** speak unto the children of Israel, that
	5	they go forward.
15	11²	**Who** *is* **like unto Thee, O** LORD, **among the gods? who** *is* **like Thee, glorious in holiness, fearful** *in* **praises, doing wonders?**
	24	And the people murmured against Moses, saying, **What
	3	shall we drink?**

	CHAP	VER.
And in the morning, then ye shall see the glory of the LORD; for that He heareth your murmurings against the LORD: **and what** are **we, that ye murmur against us?** And Moses said, *This shall be*, when the LORD shall give you in the evening flesh to eat, and in the morning bread to the full; for that the LORD heareth your murmurings which ye murmur against Him: **and what** are **we?** your murmurings *are* not against us, but against the LORD.	16	7
		8
And the LORD said unto Moses, **How long refuse ye to keep My commandments and My laws?**		28
		3
Wherefore the people did chide with Moses, and said, Give us water that we may drink. And Moses said unto them, **Why chide ye with me? wherefore do ye tempt the** LORD? And the people thirsted there for water; and the people murmured against Moses, and said, **Wherefore** is this that **thou hast brought us up out of Egypt, to kill us and our children and our cattle with thirst?** And Moses cried unto the LORD, saying, **What shall I do unto this people?** they be almost ready to stone me.	17	2²
		3
		4
And he called the name of the place Massah, and Meribah, because of the chiding of the children of Israel, and because they tempted the LORD, saying, **Is the** LORD **among us, or not?**		7
		5
And when Moses' father in law saw all that he did to the people, he said, **What** is **this thing that thou doest to the people? why sittest thou thyself alone, and all the people stand by thee from morning unto even?**	18	14²
		2
For that is his covering only, it is his raiment for his skin: **wherein shall he sleep?** and it shall come to pass, when he crieth unto Me, that I will hear; for I am gracious.	22	27
		1

CHAP.	VER	
32	11	And Moses besought the LORD his God, and said, LORD, **why doth Thy wrath wax hot against Thy people, which Thou hast brought forth out of the land of Egypt with great power, and with a mighty hand?**
	12	**Wherefore should the Egyptians speak, and say, For mischief did he bring them out, to slay them in the mountains, and to consume them from the face of the earth?** Turn from Thy fierce wrath, and repent of this evil against Thy people.
	21	And Moses said unto Aaron, **What did this people unto thee, that thou hast brought so great a sin upon them?**
	26	Then Moses stood in the gate of the camp, and said, **Who** *is* **on the** LORD's **side?** *let him come* unto me. And all the sons of Levi gathered themselves together unto him.
	4	
33	16[2]	**For wherein shall it be known here that I and Thy people have found grace in Thy sight?** *is it* **not in that Thou goest with us?** so shall we be separated, I and Thy people, from all the people that *are* upon the face of the earth.
	2	

Exodus 58

LEVITICUS.

CHAP.	VER.	
10	17	**WHEREFORE have ye not eaten the sin offering in the holy place, seeing** it *is* **most holy, and** *God* **hath given it you to bear the iniquity of the congregation, to make atonement for them before the** LORD?

	CHAP. VER
And Aaron said unto Moses, Behold, this day have they offered their sin offering and their burnt offering before the LORD; and such things have befallen me: and *if* I had eaten the sin offering to day, should it have been accepted in the sight of the LORD?	10 19
	2
	Leviticus 2

NUMBERS.

	CHAP. VER.
AND there were certain men, who were defiled by the dead body of a man, that they could not keep the passover on that day · and they came before Moses and before Aaron on that day: and those men said unto him, We *are* defiled by the dead body of a man: **wherefore are we kept back, that we may not offer an offering of the** LORD **in His appointed season among the children of Israel?**	9 7
	1
And the mixt multitude that *was* among them fell a lusting: and the children of Israel also wept again, and said, **Who shall give us flesh to eat?**	11 4
And Moses said unto the LORD, **Wherefore hast Thou afflicted Thy servant? and wherefore have I not found favour in Thy sight, that Thou layest the burden of all this people upon me? Have I conceived all this people? have I begotten them, that Thou shouldest say unto me, Carry them in thy bosom, as a nursing father beareth the sucking child, unto the land which Thou swarest unto their fathers? Whence should I have flesh to give unto all this people?** for they weep unto me, saying, Give us flesh, that we may eat.	11²
	12²
	13

NUMBERS:—XI., XII.

CHAP.	VER.	
11	18	And say thou unto the people, Sanctify yourselves against to morrow, and ye shall eat flesh: for ye have wept in the ears of the LORD, saying, **Who shall give us flesh to eat?** for *it was* well with us in Egypt: therefore the LORD will give you flesh, and ye shall eat. Ye shall not eat one day, nor two days, nor five days, neither ten days, nor twenty days; *but* even a whole month, until it come out at your nostrils, and it be loathsome unto you: because that ye have despised the LORD which *is* among
	20	you, and have wept before Him, saying, **Why came we forth out of Egypt?**
	22[2]	**Shall the flocks and the herds be slain for them, to suffice them? or shall all the fish of the sea be gathered together for them, to suffice**
	23	**them?** And the LORD said unto Moses, **Is the** LORD'S **hand waxed short?** thou shalt see now whether My word shall come to pass unto thee or not.
	29	And Joshua the son of Nun, the servant of Moses, *one* of his young men, answered and said, My lord Moses, forbid them. And Moses said unto him, **Enviest thou for my sake?** would God that all the LORD'S people were prophets, *and* that the LORD would put His spirit upon them!
12		
12	2[2]	And Miriam and Aaron spake against Moses because of the Ethiopian woman whom he had married: for he had married an Ethiopian woman. And they said, **Hath the** LORD **indeed spoken only by Moses? hath He not spoken also by us?** And the LORD heard *it*.
	8	My servant Moses *is* not so, who *is* faithful in all Mine house. With him will I speak mouth to mouth, even apparently, and not in dark speeches; and the similitude of the LORD shall he behold: **wherefore then were ye not afraid to speak against My servant Moses?**

	CHAP.	VER.

And the LORD said unto Moses, **If her father had but spit in her face, should she not be ashamed seven days?** let her be shut out from the camp seven days, and after that let her be received in *again*.   **12** 14

4

And wherefore hath the LORD brought us unto this land, to fall by the sword, that our wives and our children should be a prey? were it not better for us to return into Egypt?   **14** 3²

And the LORD said unto Moses, **How long will this people provoke Me? and how long will it be ere they believe Me, for all the signs which I have shewed among them?**   11²

And the LORD spake unto Moses and unto Aaron, saying, **How long** *shall I bear with* **this evil congregation, which murmur against Me?** I have heard the murmurings of the children of Israel, which they murmur against Me.   27

And they rose up early in the morning, and gat them up into the top of the mountain, saying, Lo, we *be here*, and will go up unto the place which the LORD hath promised: for we have sinned. And Moses said, **Wherefore now do ye transgress the commandment of the** LORD? but it shall not prosper.   41

6

And they gathered themselves together against Moses and against Aaron, and said unto them, *Ye take* too much upon you, seeing all the congregation *are* holy, every one of them, and the LORD *is* among them: **wherefore then lift ye up yourselves above the congregation of the** LORD?   **16** 3

And Moses said unto Korah, Hear, I pray you, ye sons of Levi: *Seemeth it but* **a small thing unto you, that the God of Israel hath separated you from the congregation of Israel, to bring you near**   9

CHAP	VER.	
16	10	to **Himself to do the service of the tabernacle of the** Lord, **and to stand before the congregation to minister unto them?** And He hath brought thee near *to Him*, and all thy brethren the sons of Levi with thee: **and seek ye the priesthood also?** For which cause *both* thou and all thy company *are* gathered together against the Lord:
	11	**and what** *is* **Aaron, that ye murmur against him?** And Moses sent to call Dathan and Abiram, the
	13	sons of Eliab: which said, We will not come up: *Is it* **a small thing that thou hast brought us up out of a land that floweth with milk and honey, to kill us in the wilderness, except thou make thyself altogether a prince over us?** Moreover thou hast not brought us into a land that floweth with milk and honey, or given us inheritance of fields and
	14	vineyards: **wilt thou put out the eyes of these men?** we will not come up.
	22	And they fell upon their faces, and said, **O God, the God of the spirits of all flesh, shall one man sin, and wilt Thou be wroth with all the congregation?**
	7	
17	13	And Moses did *so:* as the Lord commanded him, so did he. And the children of Israel spake unto Moses, saying, Behold, we die, we perish, we all perish. Whosoever cometh any thing near unto the tabernacle of the Lord shall die: **shall we be consumed with dying?**
	1	
20	4	And the people chode with Moses, and spake, saying, Would God that we had died when our brethren died before the Lord! **And why have ye brought up the congregation of the** Lord **into this wilderness, that we and our cattle should die there?**
	5	**And wherefore have ye made us to come up out of Egypt, to bring us in unto this evil place?** it *is* no place of seed, or of figs, or of vines, or of pomegranates; neither *is* there any water to drink.

NUMBERS:—XX.-XXIII.

	CHAP.	VER.
And Moses and Aaron gathered the congregation together before the rock, and he said unto them, Hear now, ye rebels; **must we fetch you water out of this rock?**	20	10
		3
And the people spake against God, and against Moses, **Wherefore have ye brought us up out of Egypt to die in the wilderness?** for *there is* no bread, neither *is there any* water; and our soul loatheth this light bread.	21	5
		1
And God came unto Balaam, and said, **What men** *are* **these with thee?**	22	9
And the LORD opened the mouth of the ass, and she said unto Balaam, **What have I done unto thee, that thou hast smitten me these three times?**		28
And the ass said unto Balaam, *Am* **not I thine ass, upon which thou hast ridden ever since** *I was* **thine unto this day? was I ever wont to do so unto thee?** And he said, Nay.		30[2]
And the angel of the LORD said unto him, **Wherefore hast thou smitten thine ass these three times?** behold, I went out to withstand thee, because *thy* way is perverse before me:		32
And Balak said unto Balaam, **Did I not earnestly send unto thee to call thee? wherefore camest thou not unto me? am I not able indeed to promote thee to honour?** And Balaam said unto Balak, Lo, I am come unto thee: **have I now any power at all to say any thing?**		37[3]
		38
		9
How shall I curse, whom God hath not cursed? or how shall I defy, *whom* **the** LORD **hath not defied?**	23	8[2]
Who can count the dust of Jacob, and the number of the fourth *part* **of Israel?**		10

CHAP.	VER
23	11

And Balak said unto Balaam, **What hast thou done unto me?** I took thee to curse mine enemies, and, behold, thou hast blessed *them* altogether. And he
12 answered and said, **Must I not take heed to speak that which the** LORD **hath put in my mouth?**

And when he came to him, behold, he stood by his burnt offering, and the princes of Moab with him. And
17 Balak said unto him, **What hath the** LORD **spoken?** And he took up his parable, and said, Rise up, Balak, and hear; hearken unto me, thou son of Zippor : God *is* not a man, that He should lie; neither the son of man,
19² that He should repent · **hath He said, and shall He not do** *it?* **or hath He spoken, and shall He not make it good?**

26 But Balaam answered and said unto Balak, **Told not I thee, saying, All that the** LORD **speaketh,
9 that I must do?**

He couched, he lay down as a lion, and as a great lion :
24 9 **who shall stir him up?** Blessed *is* he that blesseth thee, and cursed *is* he that curseth thee.

12 And Balaam said unto Balak, **Spake I not also to thy messengers which thou sentest unto me, saying, If Balak would give me his house full of silver and gold, I cannot go beyond the commandment of the** LORD, **to do** *either* **good or bad
2 of mine own mind;** *but* **what the** LORD **saith, that will I speak?**

27 4 **Why should the name of our father be done
1 away from among his family, because he hath no son?**

31 15 And Moses said unto them, **Have ye saved all the
1 women alive?**

And Moses said unto the children of Gad and to the

	CHAP.	VER.
children of Reuben, **Shall your brethren go to war, and shall ye sit here?** And wherefore discourage ye the heart of the children of Israel from going over into the land which the Lord hath given them?	**32**	6
		7
		2
Numbers 59		

DEUTERONOMY.

	CHAP.	VER.
How can I myself alone bear your cumbrance, and your burden, and your strife?	1	12
Whither shall we go up? our brethren have discouraged our heart, saying, The people *is* greater and taller than we; the cities *are* great and walled up to heaven; and moreover we have seen the sons of the Anakims there.		28
		2
For only Og king of Bashan remained of the remnant of giants; behold, his bedstead *was* a bedstead of iron; *is* **it not in Rabbath of the children of Ammon?** nine cubits *was* the length thereof, and four cubits the breadth of it, after the cubit of a man.	3	11
O Lord God, Thou hast begun to shew Thy servant Thy greatness, and Thy mighty hand: **for what God** *is there* **in heaven or in earth, that can do according to Thy works, and according to Thy might?**		24
		2
For what nation *is there so* **great, who** *hath* **God** *so* **nigh unto them, as the** Lord **our God** *is* **in all** *things that* **we call upon Him** *for?* **And what nation** *is there so* **great, that hath statutes and judgments** *so* **righteous as all this law, which I set before you this day?**	4	7
		8

CHAP	VER	
4	32	For ask now of the days that are past, which were before thee, since the day that God created man upon the earth, and *ask* from the one side of heaven unto the other, whether there hath been *any such thing* as this great thing *is*, or hath been
	33	heard like it? Did *ever* people hear the voice of God speaking out of the midst of the fire, as thou hast
	34	heard, and live? Or hath God assayed to go *and* take Him a nation from the midst of *another* nation, by temptations, by signs, and by wonders, and by war, and by a mighty hand, and by a stretched out arm, and by great terrors, according to all that the Lord your God did for you in Egypt
	5	before your eyes?
5	25	Now therefore why should we die? for this great fire will consume us: if we hear the voice of the Lord
	26	our God any more, then we shall die. For who *is there of* all flesh that hath heard the voice of the living God speaking out of the midst of the fire, as we
	2	*have*, and lived?
6	20	*And* when thy son asketh thee in time to come, saying, What *mean* the testimonies, and the statutes, and the judgments, which the Lord our God hath
	1	commanded you?
7	17	If thou shalt say in thine heart, These nations *are* more than I; how can I dispossess them?
	1	
10	12	And now, Israel, what doth the Lord thy God require of thee, but to fear the Lord thy God, to walk in all His ways, and to love Him, and to serve the Lord thy God with all thy heart and with all thy soul, to keep the commandments of the Lord, and His statutes, which I command
	1	thee this day for thy good?
11	30	*Are* they not on the other side Jordan, by the way where the sun goeth down, in the land of the
	1	

	CHAP.	VER.

Canaanites, which dwell in the champaign over against Gilgal, beside the plains of Moreh?

Take heed to thyself that thou be not snared by following them, after that they be destroyed from before thee; and that thou inquire not after their gods, saying, **How did these nations serve their gods?** even so will I do likewise. — **12** 30 / 1

But the prophet, which shall presume to speak a word in My name, which I have not commanded him to speak, or that shall speak in the name of other gods, even that prophet shall die. And if thou say in thine heart, **How shall we know the word which the** LORD **hath not spoken?** — **18** 21 / 1

And the officers shall speak unto the people, saying, **What man** is there **that hath built a new house, and hath not dedicated it?** let him go and return to his house, lest he die in the battle, and another man dedicate it. And **what man** is he **that hath planted a vineyard, and hath not** yet **eaten of it?** let him also go and return unto his house, lest he die in the battle, and another man eat of it. And **what man** is there **that hath betrothed a wife, and hath not taken her?** let him go and return unto his house, lest he die in the battle, and another man take her. And the officers shall speak further unto the people, and they shall say, **What man** is there that is **fearful and fainthearted?** let him go and return unto his house, lest his brethren's heart faint as well as his heart. — **20** 5 / 6 / 7 / 8 / 4

And that the whole land thereof is brimstone, and salt, and burning, that it is not sown, nor beareth, nor any grass groweth therein, like the overthrow of Sodom, and Gomorrah, Admah, and Zeboim, which the LORD overthrew in His anger, and in His wrath. even all nations shall say, **Wherefore hath the** LORD **done thus unto this land?** what meaneth **the heat of this great anger?** — **29** 24[2] / 2

CHAP.	VER.	
30	12	For this commandment which I command thee this day, it *is* not hidden from thee, neither *is* it far off. It *is* not in heaven, that thou shouldest say, **Who shall go up for us to heaven, and bring it unto us, that we may hear it, and do it?** Neither *is* it beyond the
	13	sea, that thou shouldest say, **Who shall go over the sea for us, and bring it unto us, that we may hear
	2	it, and do it?**
31	17	Then My anger shall be kindled against them in that day, and I will forsake them, and I will hide My face from them, and they shall be devoured, and many evils and troubles shall befall them; so that they will say in that day, **Are not these evils come upon us, because our God** *is* **not among us?**
	27	For I know thy rebellion, and thy stiff neck: **behold, while I am yet alive with you this day, ye have been rebellious against the** Lord; **and how much
	2	more after my death?**
32	6³	**Do ye thus requite the** Lord, **O foolish people and unwise?** *is* **not He thy father** *that* **hath bought thee? hath He not made thee, and established thee?**
	30	**How should one chase a thousand, and two put ten thousand to flight, except their Rock had sold them, and the** Lord **had shut them up?** For their rock *is* not as our Rock, even our enemies themselves *being* judges. For their vine *is* of the vine of Sodom, and of the fields of Gomorrah: their grapes *are* grapes of gall, their clusters *are* bitter: their wine *is* the
	34	poison of dragons, and the cruel venom of asps. *Is* **not this laid up in store with Me,** *and* **sealed up among My treasures?**
	38	And He shall say, **Where** *are* **their gods,** *their* **rock

DEUTERONOMY:—XXXII. JOSHUA:—I.-VII. 87

	CHAP.	VER.
in whom they trusted, which did eat the fat of their sacrifices, *and* drank the wine of their drink offerings? let them rise up and help you, *and* be your protection.	**32**	38
		6

Deuteronomy 33

JOSHUA

	CHAP.	VER
HAVE not I commanded thee? Be strong and of a good courage; be not afraid, neither be thou dismayed: for the LORD thy God *is* with thee whithersoever thou goest.	**1**	9
		1
That this may be a sign among you, *that* when your children ask *their fathers* in time to come, saying, **What** *mean* **ye by these stones?**	**4**	6
And he spake unto the children of Israel, saying, When your children shall ask their fathers in time to come, saying, **What** *mean* **these stones?**		21
		2
And it came to pass, when Joshua was by Jericho, that he lifted up his eyes and looked, and, behold, there stood a man over against him with his sword drawn in his hand: and Joshua went unto him, and said unto him, *Art* **thou for us, or for our adversaries?** And he said, Nay; but *as* captain of the host of the LORD am I now come. And Joshua fell on his face to the earth, and did worship, and said unto him, **What saith my lord unto his servant?**	**5**	13
		14
		2
And Joshua said, **Alas, O Lord** GOD, **wherefore hast Thou at all brought this people over Jordan, to deliver us into the hand of the Amorites, to**	**7**	7

CHAP.	VER.	
7	9	**destroy us?** would to God we had been content, and dwelt on the other side Jordan!
		For the Canaanites and all the inhabitants of the land shall hear *of it*, and shall environ us round, and cut off our name from the earth: and **what wilt Thou do unto Thy great name?** And the Lord said unto Joshua, Get
	10	thee up; **wherefore liest thou thus upon thy face?**
	25	And Joshua said, **Why hast thou troubled us?** the Lord shall trouble thee this day. And all Israel stoned
	4	him with stones, and burned them with fire, after they had stoned them with stones.
9	7	And the men of Israel said unto the Hivites, Peradventure ye dwell among us; and **how shall we make a league with you?** And they said unto Joshua, We
	8²	*are* thy servants. And Joshua said unto them, **Who** *are* **ye?** and **from whence come ye?**
	22	And Joshua called for them, and he spake unto them, saying, **Wherefore have ye beguiled us, saying, We**
	4	*are* **very far from you; when ye dwell among us?**
10	13	And the sun stood still, and the moon stayed, until the people had avenged themselves upon their enemies. *Is* **not this written in the book of Jasher?** So the
	1	sun stood still in the midst of heaven, and hasted not to go down about a whole day.
15	18	And it came to pass, as she came *unto him*, that she moved him to ask of her father a field: and she lighted off *her* ass; and Caleb said unto her, **What wouldest**
	1	**thou?**
17	14	And the children of Joseph spake unto Joshua, saying, **Why hast thou given me** *but* **one lot and one portion to inherit, seeing I** *am* **a great people, foras-**
	1	**much as the** Lord **hath blessed me hitherto?**

	CHAP.	VER.
And Joshua said unto the children of Israel, **How long** *are* **ye slack to go to possess the land, which the** LORD **God of your fathers hath given you?**	18	3
		1
Thus saith the whole congregation of the LORD, **What trespass** *is* **this that ye have committed against the God of Israel, to turn away this day from following the** LORD, **in that ye have builded you an altar, that ye might rebel this day against the** LORD? *Is* **the iniquity of Peor too little for us, from which we are not cleansed until this day, although there was a plague in the congregation of the** LORD, **but that ye must turn away this day from following the** LORD? and it will be, *seeing* ye rebel to day against the LORD, that to morrow He will be wroth with the whole congregation of Israel.	22	16
		17
Did not Achan the son of Zerah commit a trespass in the accursed thing, and wrath fell on all the congregation of Israel? and that man perished not alone in his iniquity.		20
And if we have not *rather* done it for fear of *this* thing, saying, In time to come your children might speak unto our children, saying, **What have ye to do with the** LORD **God of Israel?**		24
		4
	Joshua 21	

JUDGES.

	CHAP.	VER
NOW after the death of Joshua it came to pass, that the children of Israel asked the LORD, saying, **Who shall go up for us against the Canaanites first, to fight against them?**	1	1

CHAP.	VER.	
1	14	And it came to pass, when she came *to him*, that she moved him to ask of her father a field: and she lighted from off *her* ass; and Caleb said unto her, **What wilt thou?**
	2	
2	2	And ye shall make no league with the inhabitants of this land; ye shall throw down their altars: but ye have not obeyed my voice: **why have ye done this?**
	1	
4	6	And she sent and called Barak the son of Abinoam out of Kedesh-naphtali, and said unto him, **Hath not the Lord God of Israel commanded,** *saying*, **Go and draw toward mount Tabor, and take with thee ten thousand men of the children of Naphtali and of the children of Zebulun?**
	14	And Deborah said unto Barak, Up; for this *is* the day in which the Lord hath delivered Sisera into thine hand: **is not the Lord gone out before thee?** So Barak went down from mount Tabor, and ten thousand men after him.
	20	Again he said unto her, Stand in the door of the tent, and it shall be, when any man doth come and inquire of thee, and say, **Is there any man here?** that thou shalt say, No.
	3	
5	8	They chose new gods; then *was* war in the gates: **was there a shield or spear seen among forty thousand in Israel?**
	16	**Why abodest thou among the sheepfolds, to hear the bleatings of the flocks?** For the divisions of Reuben *there were* great searchings of heart. Gilead abode beyond Jordan: and **why did Dan remain in ships?** Asher continued on the sea shore, and abode in his breaches.
	17	
	28[2]	The mother of Sisera looked out at a window, and cried through the lattice, **Why is his chariot** *so* **long**

	CHAP.	VER.

in coming? why tarry the wheels of his chariots? Her wise ladies answered her, yea, she returned answer to herself, **Have they not sped? have they** *not* **divided the prey; to every man a damsel** *or* **two; to Sisera a prey of divers colours, a prey of divers colours of needlework, of divers colours of needlework on both sides,** *meet* **for the necks of** *them that take* **the spoil?**

5 30²

7

And Gideon said unto him, **Oh my Lord, if the** Lord **be with us, why then is all this befallen us? and where** *be* **all His miracles which our fathers told us of, saying, Did not the** Lord **bring us up from Egypt?** but now the Lord hath forsaken us, and delivered us into the hands of the Midianites. And the Lord looked upon him, and said, Go in this thy might, and thou shalt save Israel from the hand of the Midianites: **have not I sent thee?** And he said unto him, **Oh my Lord, wherewith shall I save Israel?** behold, my family *is* poor in Manasseh, and I *am* the least in my father's house.

6 13²

14
15

And they said one to another, **Who hath done this thing?** And when they inquired and asked, they said, Gideon the son of Joash hath done this thing. Then the men of the city said unto Joash, Bring out thy son, that he may die: because he hath cast down the altar of Baal, and because he hath cut down the grove that *was* by it. And Joash said unto all that stood against him, **Will ye plead for Baal? will ye save him?** he that will plead for him, let him be put to death whilst *it is yet* morning: if he *be* a god, let him plead for himself, because *one* hath cast down his altar.

29

31²

7

And the men of Ephraim said unto him, **Why hast thou served us thus, that thou calledst us not, when thou wentest to fight with the Midianites?** And they did chide with him sharply. And he said unto them, **What have I done now in comparison of**

8 1

2²

CHAP. VER	
8 3	you? *Is* not the gleaning of the grapes of Ephraim better than the vintage of Abi-ezer? God hath delivered into your hands the princes of Midian, Oreb and Zeeb and what was I able to do in comparison of you? Then their anger was abated toward him, when he had said that.
6	And the princes of Succoth said, *Are* the hands of Zebah and Zalmunna now in thine hand, that we should give bread unto thine army?
15	And he came unto the men of Succoth, and said, Behold Zebah and Zalmunna, with whom ye did upbraid me, saying, *Are* the hands of Zebah and Zalmunna now in thine hand, that we should give bread unto thy men *that are* weary?
18 7	Then said he unto Zebah and Zalmunna, What manner of men *were they* whom ye slew at Tabor? And they answered, As thou *art,* so *were* they; each one resembled the children of a king.
9 2	Speak I pray you, in the ears of all the men of Shechem, Whether *is* better for you, either that all the sons of Jerubbaal, *which are* threescore and ten persons, reign over you, or that one reign over you? remember also that I *am* your bone and your flesh.
9	But the olive tree said unto them, Should I leave my fatness, wherewith by me they honour God and man, and go to be promoted over the trees?
11	And the trees said to the fig tree, Come thou, *and* reign over us. But the fig tree said unto them; Should I forsake my sweetness, and my good fruit, and go to be promoted over the trees?
13	Then said the trees unto the vine, Come thou, *and* reign over us. And the vine said unto them, Should I leave my wine, which cheereth God and man, and go to be promoted over the trees?

JUDGES —IX.-XI.

	CHAP	VER
And Gaal the son of Ebed said, **Who** *is* **Abimelech, and who** *is* **Shechem, that we should serve him?** *is* **not** *he* **the son of Jerubbaal? and Zebul his officer?** serve the men of Hamor the father of Shechem: **for why should we serve him?**	9	28⁴
Then said Zebul unto him, **Where** *is* **now thy mouth, wherewith thou saidst, Who** *is* **Abimelech, that we should serve him?** *is* **not this the people that thou hast despised?** go out, I pray now, and fight with them.		38² 10
And the LORD said unto the children of Israel, *Did* **not** *I deliver you* **from the Egyptians, and from the Amorites, from the children of Ammon, and from the Philistines?**	10	11
And the people *and* princes of Gilead said one to another, **What man** *is* *he* **that will begin to fight against the children of Ammon?** he shall be head over all the inhabitants of Gilead.		18 2
And Jephthah said unto the elders of Gilead, **Did not ye hate me, and expel me out of my father's house? and why are ye come unto me now when ye are in distress?** And the elders of Gilead said unto Jephthah, Therefore we turn again to thee now, that thou mayest go with us, and fight against the children of Ammon, and be our head over all the inhabitants of Gilead. And Jephthah said unto the elders of Gilead, **If ye bring me home again to fight against the children of Ammon, and the** LORD **deliver them before me, shall I be your head?** And the elders of Gilead said unto Jephthah, The LORD be witness between us, if we do not so according to thy words. Then Jephthah went with the elders of Gilead, and the people made him head and captain over them: and Jephthah uttered all his words before the LORD in Mizpeh. And Jephthah sent messen-	11	7² 9

CHAP.	VER.	
11	12	gers unto the king of the children of Ammon, saying, **What hast thou to do with me, that thou art come against me to fight in my land?**
	23 24	So now the LORD God of Israel hath dispossessed the Amorites from before His people Israel, **and shouldest thou possess it? Wilt not thou possess that which Chemosh thy god giveth thee to possess?** So whomsoever the LORD our God shall drive out
	25	from before us, them will we possess. **And now** *art* **thou any thing better than Balak the son of Zippor,**
	26[2]	**king of Moab?** did he ever strive against Israel, or did he ever fight against them, while Israel dwelt in Heshbon and her towns, and in Aroer and her towns, and in all the cities that *be* along by the coasts of Arnon, three hundred years?
	9	why therefore did ye not recover *them* within that time?
12	1	And the men of Ephraim gathered themselves together, and went northward, and said unto Jephthah, **Wherefore passedst thou over to fight against the children of Ammon, and didst not call us to go with thee?** we will burn thine house upon thee with fire.
	3	And when I saw that ye delivered *me* not, I put my life in my hands, and passed over against the children of Ammon, and the LORD delivered them into my hand: **wherefore then are ye come up unto me this day, to fight against me?**
	5	And the Gileadites took the passages of Jordan before the Ephraimites: and it was *so*, that when those Ephraimites which were escaped said, Let me go over; that the men of Gilead said unto him, *Art* **thou an Ephraimite?** If he said, Nay; then said they unto
	3	him, Say now Shibboleth· and he said, Sibboleth: for he could not frame to pronounce it right.

JUDGES:—XIII, XIV

	CHAP	VER
And Manoah arose, and went after his wife, and came to the man, and said unto him, *Art* **thou the man that spakest unto the woman?** And he said, I *am*. And Manoah said, Now let thy words come to pass. **How shall we order the child, and** *how* **shall we do unto him?**	13	11
		12

And Manoah said unto the angel of the Lord, **What** *is* **thy name, that when thy sayings come to pass we may do thee honour?** And the angel of the Lord said unto him, **Why askest thou thus after my name, seeing it** *is* **secret?**

		17
		18
		4

| Then his father and his mother said unto him, *Is there* **never a woman among the daughters of thy brethren, or among all my people, that thou goest to take a wife of the uncircumcised Philistines?** And Samson said unto his father, Get her for me, for she pleaseth me well. | 14 | 3 |

And it came to pass on the seventh day, that they said unto Samson's wife, Entice thy husband, that he may declare unto us the riddle, lest we burn thee and thy father's house with fire **have ye called us to take that we have?** *is it* **not** *so?* And Samson's wife wept before him, and said, Thou dost but hate me, and lovest me not: thou hast put forth a riddle unto the children of my people, and hast not told *it* me. And he said unto her, **Behold, I have not told** *it* **my father nor my mother, and shall I tell** *it* **thee?** And she wept before him the seven days, while their feast lasted: and it came to pass on the seventh day, that he told her, because she lay sore upon him: and she told the riddle to the children of her people. And the men of the city said unto him on the seventh day before the sun went down, **What** *is* **sweeter than honey? and what** *is* **stronger than a lion?** And he said unto them, If ye had not plowed with my heifer, ye had not found out my riddle.

		15²
		16
		18²
		6

CHAP	VER	
15	2	And her father said, I verily thought that thou hadst utterly hated her; therefore I gave her to thy companion. *is* **not her younger sister fairer than she?** take her, I pray thee, instead of her.
	6	Then the Philistines said, **Who hath done this?** And they answered, Samson, the son in law of the Timnite, because he had taken his wife, and given her to his companion. And the Philistines came up, and burnt her and her father with fire,
	10	And the men of Judah said, **Why are ye come up against us?** And they answered, To bind Samson are we come up, to do to him as he hath done to us. Then three thousand men of Judah went to the top of the
	11²	rock Etam. and said to Samson, **Knowest thou not that the Philistines** *are* **rulers over us? what** *is* **this** *that* **thou hast done unto us?** And he said unto them, As they did unto me, so have I done unto them.
	18	And he was sore athirst, and called on the LORD, and said, Thou hast given this great deliverance into the hand of Thy servant : **and now shall I die for thirst, and fall into the hand of the uncircumcised?**
16	6	
	15	And she said unto him, **How canst thou say, I love thee, when thine heart** *is* **not with me?** thou hast mocked me these three times, and hast not told me wherein thy great strength *lieth.*
	1	
17	9	And Micah said unto him, **Whence comest thou?** And he said unto him, I *am* a Levite of Beth-lehem-judah, and I go to sojourn where I may find *a place*
	1	
18	3³	When they *were* by the house of Micah, they knew the voice of the young man the Levite. and they turned in thither, and said unto him, **Who brought thee hither?**

JUDGES:—XVIII.-XX.

	CHAP.	VER

and what makest thou in this *place*? and what hast thou here?

And they came unto their brethren to Zorah and Eshtaol: and their brethren said unto them, **What** *say* **ye?** And they said, Arise, that we may go up against them: for we have seen the land, and, behold, it *is* very good. **and** *are* **ye still?** be not slothful to go, *and* to enter to possess the land. | **18** | 8

| | | 9 |

Then answered the five men that went to spy out the country of Laish, and said unto their brethren, **Do ye know that there is in these houses an ephod, and teraphim, and a graven image, and a molten image?** now therefore consider what ye have to do. | | 14

And these went into Micah's house, and fetched the carved image, the ephod, and the teraphim, and the molten image. Then said the priest unto them, **What do ye?** And they said unto him, Hold thy peace, lay thine hand upon thy mouth, and go with us, and be to us a father and a priest: *is it* **better for thee to be a priest unto the house of one man, or that thou be a priest unto a tribe and a family in Israel?** | | 18

| | | 19 |

And they cried unto the children of Dan. And they turned their faces, and said unto Micah, **What aileth thee, that thou comest with such a company?** And he said, **Ye have taken away my gods which I made, and the priest, and ye are gone away: and what have I more?** and what *is* this *that* ye say unto me, **What aileth thee?** | | 23

| | | 24[2] |

| | | 11 |

And when he had lifted up his eyes, he saw a wayfaring man in the street of the city: and the old man said, **Whither goest thou? and whence comest thou?** | **19** | 17[2]

(Now the children of Benjamin heard that the children of Israel were gone up to Mizpeh.) Then said the children of Israel, **Tell** *us*, **how was this wickedness?** | | 2

| | **20** | 3 |

CHAP.	VER.	
20	12	And the tribes of Israel sent men through all the tribe of Benjamin, saying, **What wickedness** *is* **this that is done among you?**
	18	And the children of Israel arose, and went up to the house of God, and asked counsel of God, and said, **Which of us shall go up first to the battle against the children of Benjamin?** And the Lord said, Judah *shall go up* first
	23	And the children of Israel went up and wept before the Lord until even, and asked counsel of the Lord, saying, **Shall I go up again to battle against the children of Benjamin my brother?** And the Lord said, Go up against him
	28	Then all the children of Israel, and all the people, went up, and came unto the house of God, and wept, and sat there before the Lord, and fasted that day until even, and offered burnt offerings and peace offerings before the Lord And the children of Israel inquired of the Lord (for the ark of the covenant of God *was* there in those days, and Phinehas, the son of Eleazar, the son of Aaron, stood before it in those days), saying, **Shall I yet again go out to battle against the children of Benjamin my brother, or shall I cease?** And the Lord said, Go up; for to morrow I will deliver them into thine hand.
	5	
21	3	And the people came to the house of God, and abode there till even before God, and lifted up their voices, and wept sore; and said, **O Lord God of Israel, why is this come to pass in Israel, that there should be to day one tribe lacking in Israel?**
	5	And the children of Israel said, **Who** *is there* **among all the tribes of Israel that came not up with the congregation unto the** Lord? For they had made a great oath concerning him that came not up to the

	CHAP. VER.
LORD to Mizpeh, saying, He shall surely be put to death.	
How shall we do for wives for them that remain, seeing we have sworn by the LORD **that we will not give them of our daughters to wives?** And they said, **What one** *is there* **of the tribes of Israel that came not up to Mizpeh to the** LORD **?**	21 7 8
Then the elders of the congregation said, **How shall we do for wives for them that remain, seeing the women are destroyed out of Benjamin?**	16 —— 5

Judges 92

RUTH.

	CHAP. VER.
AND Naomi said, Turn again, my daughters : **why will ye go with me?** *are* **there yet** *any more* **sons in my womb, that they may be your husbands?** Turn again, my daughters, go *your way;* for I am too old to have an husband If I should say, I have hope, *if* I should have an husband also to night, and should also bear sons ; **would ye tarry for them till they were grown? would ye stay for them from having husbands?** nay, my daughters; for it grieveth me much for your sakes that the hand of the LORD is gone out against me.	1 11² 13²
So they two went until they came to Beth-lehem. And it came to pass, when they were come to Bethlehem, that all the city was moved about them, and they said, *Is* **this Naomi?**	19
I went out full, and the LORD hath brought me home	

CHAP	VER	
1	21	again empty: **why** *then* **call ye me Naomi, seeing the** LORD **hath testified against me, and the Almighty hath afflicted me?**
	6	
2	5	Then said Boaz unto his servant that was set over the reapers, **Whose damsel** *is* **this?**
	8	Then said Boaz unto Ruth, **Hearest thou not, my daughter?** Go not to glean in another field, neither go from hence, but abide here fast by my maidens: *let* thine eyes *be* on the field that they do reap, and go thou after them: **have I not charged the young men that they shall not touch thee?** and when thou art athirst, go unto the vessels, and drink of *that* which the young men have drawn. Then she fell on her face, and bowed herself to the ground, and said unto him, **Why have I found grace in thine eyes, that thou shouldest take knowledge of me, seeing I** *am* **a stranger?**
	9	
	10	
	19²	And her mother in law said unto her, **Where hast thou gleaned to day? and where wroughtest thou?** blessed be he that did take knowledge of thee. And she shewed her mother in law with whom she had wrought, and said, The man's name with whom I wrought to day *is* Boaz.
	6	
3	1	Then Naomi her mother in law said unto her, **My daughter, shall I not seek rest for thee, that it may be well with thee? And now** *is* **not Boaz of our kindred, with whose maidens thou wast?** Behold, he winnoweth barley to night in the threshing-floor.
	2	
	9	And he said, **Who** *art* **thou?** And she answered, I *am* Ruth thine handmaid: spread therefore thy skirt over thine handmaid; for thou *art* a near kinsman.
	16	And when she came to her mother in law, she said, **Who** *art* **thou, my daughter?** And she told her all that the man had done to her.
	4	

Ruth 16

FIRST SAMUEL.

	CHAP	VER
	1	8⁴

THEN said Elkanah her husband to her, **Hannah, why weepest thou? and why eatest thou not? and why is thy heart grieved?** *am* **not I better to thee than ten sons?**

And Eli said unto her, **How long wilt thou be drunken?** put away thy wine from thee.

		14
		5

And he said unto them, **Why do ye such things?** for I hear of your evil dealings by all this people.

	2	23

If one man sin against another, the judge shall judge him: **but if a man sin against the** LORD, **who shall intreat for him?** Notwithstanding they hearkened not unto the voice of their father, because the LORD would slay them.

		25

And there came a man of God unto Eli, and said unto him, Thus saith the LORD, **Did I plainly appear unto the house of thy father, when they were in Egypt in Pharaoh's house? And did I choose him out of all the tribes of Israel** *to be* **My priest, to offer upon Mine altar, to burn incense, to wear an ephod before Me? and did I give unto the house of thy father all the offerings made by fire of the children of Israel? Wherefore kick ye at My sacrifice and at Mine offering, which I have commanded** *in My* **habitation; and honourest thy sons above Me, to make yourselves fat with the chiefest of all the offerings of Israel My people?**

		27
		28²
		29
		6

And he said, **What** *is* **the thing that** *the* LORD **hath said unto thee?** I pray thee hide *it* not from me: God do so to thee, and more also, if thou hide *any* thing from me of all the things that He said unto thee.

	3	17
		1

CHAP.	VER.	
4	3	And when the people were come into the camp, the elders of Israel said, **Wherefore hath the** LORD **smitten us to day before the Philistines?** Let us fetch the ark of the covenant of the LORD out of Shiloh unto us, that, when it cometh among us, it may save us out of the hand of our enemies.
	6	And when the Philistines heard the noise of the shout, they said, **What** *meaneth* **the noise of this great shout in the camp of the Hebrews?** And they understood that the ark of the LORD was come into the camp.
	8	**Woe unto us! who shall deliver us out of the hand of these mighty Gods?** these *are* the Gods that smote the Egyptians with all the plagues in the wilderness.
	14	And when Eli heard the noise of the crying, he said, **What** *meaneth* **the noise of this tumult?** And the man came in hastily, and told Eli. Now Eli was ninety and eight years old; and his eyes were dim, that he could not see. And the man said unto Eli, I *am* he that came out of the army, and I fled to day out of the army. And he said, **What is there done, my son?**
	16	
	5	
5	8	They sent therefore and gathered all the lords of the Philistines unto them, and said, **What shall we do with the ark of the God of Israel?** And they answered, Let the ark of the God of Israel be carried about unto Gath. And they carried the ark of the God of Israel about *thither*.
	1	
6	2	And the Philistines called for the priests and the diviners, saying, **What shall we do to the ark of the** LORD? tell us wherewith we shall send it to his place
	4	Then said they, **What** *shall be* **the trespass offering which we shall return to him?** They answered, Five golden emerods, and five golden mice, *according to*

	CHAP.	VER.
the number of the lords of the Philistines: for one plague *was* on you all, and on your lords.		
Wherefore then do ye harden your hearts, as the Egyptians and Pharaoh hardened their hearts? when He had wrought wonderfully among them, did they not let the people go, and they departed?	6	6²
And the men of Beth-shemesh said, **Who is able to stand before this holy** Lord **God? and to whom shall He go up from us?**		20²
		6
Then said Saul to his servant, **But, behold,** *if* **we go, what shall we bring the man?** for the bread is spent in our vessels, and *there is* not a present to bring to the man of God **what have we?**	9	7²
And as they went up the hill to the city, they found young maidens going out to draw water, and said unto them, **Is the seer here?**		11
And as for thine asses that were lost three days ago, set not thy mind on them; for they are found **And on whom** *is* **all the desire of Israel?** *Is it* **not on thee, and on all thy father's house?** And Saul answered and said, *Am* **not I a Benjamite, of the smallest of the tribes of Israel? and my family the least of all the families of the tribe of Benjamin? wherefore then speakest thou so to me?**		20²
		21³
		8
Then Samuel took a vial of oil, and poured *it* upon his head, and kissed him, and said, *Is it* **not because the** Lord **hath anointed thee** *to be* **captain over His inheritance?** When thou art departed from me to day, then thou shalt find two men by Rachel's sepulchre in the border of Benjamin at Zelzah; and they will say unto thee, The asses which thou wentest to seek are found: and, lo. thy father hath left the care of the asses,	10	1

CHAP.	VER	
10	2	and sorroweth for you, saying, **What shall I do for my son?**

	11²	And it came to pass, when all that knew him beforetime saw that, behold, he prophesied among the prophets, then the people said one to another, **What** *is* **this** *that* **is come unto the son of Kish?** *Is* **Saul also among the prophets?** And one of the same place answered
	12²	and said, **But who** *is* **their father?** Therefore it became a proverb, *Is* **Saul also among the prophets?** And when he had made an end of prophesying, he came to the high place. And Saul's uncle said unto him and
	14	to his servant, **Whither went ye?** And he said, To seek the asses: and when we saw that *they were* no where, we came to Samuel.

	24	And Samuel said to all the people, **See ye him whom the** LORD **hath chosen, that** *there* **is none like him among all the people?** And all the people shouted, and said, God save the king.
	27	But the children of Belial said, **How shall this man save us?** And they despised him, and brought him no
	9	presents. But he held his peace.

11	5	And, behold, Saul came after the herd out of the field; and Saul said, **What** *aileth* **the people that they weep?** And they told him the tidings of the men of Jabesh.
	12	And the people said unto Samuel, **Who** *is* **he that said, Shall Saul reign over us?** bring the men, that
	2	we may put them to death.

12	3⁵	Behold, here I *am*: witness against me before the LORD, and before His anointed: **whose ox have I taken? or whose ass have I taken? or whom have I defrauded? whom have I oppressed? or of whose hand have I received** *any* **bribe to blind mine eyes therewith?** and I will restore it you.

FIRST SAMUEL:—XII.-XV.   55

	CHAP	VER
Is it **not wheat harvest to day?** I will call unto the Lord, and He shall send thunder and rain; that ye may perceive and see that your wickedness *is* great, which ye have done in the sight of the Lord, in asking you a king.	**12**	17
		6
And Samuel said, **What hast thou done?** And Saul said, Because I saw that the people were scattered from me, and *that* thou camest not within the days appointed, and *that* the Philistines gathered themselves together at Michmash, therefore said I, The Philistines will come down now upon me to Gilgal, and I have not made supplication unto the Lord: I forced myself therefore, and offered a burnt offering.	**13**	11
		1
How much more, if haply the people had eaten freely to day of the spoil of their enemies which they found? for had there not been now a much greater slaughter among the Philistines?	**14**	30²
And Saul asked counsel of God, **Shall I go down after the Philistines? wilt Thou deliver them into the hand of Israel?** But He answered him not that day.		37²
And the people said unto Saul, **Shall Jonathan die, who hath wrought this great salvation in Israel?** God forbid: *as* the Lord liveth, there shall not one hair of his head fall to the ground; for he hath wrought with God this day. So the people rescued Jonathan, that he died not.		5
		5
And Samuel said, **What** *meaneth* **then this bleating of the sheep in mine ears, and the lowing of the oxen which I hear?**	**15**	14
And Samuel said, **When thou** *wast* **little in thine own sight,** *wast* **thou not** *made* **the head of the tribes of Israel, and the** Lord **anointed thee king over Israel?**		17

CHAP.	VER	
15	19	**Wherefore then didst thou not obey the voice of the** LORD, **but didst fly upon the spoil, and didst evil in the sight of the** LORD?
	4	And Samuel said, **Hath the** LORD *as great* **delight in burnt offerings and sacrifices, as in obeying the voice of the** LORD? Behold, to obey *is* better than sacrifice, *and* to hearken than the fat of rams.
16	1	And the LORD said unto Samuel, **How long wilt thou mourn for Saul, seeing I have rejected him from reigning over Israel?** fill thine horn with oil, and go, I will send thee to Jesse the Beth-lehemite: for I have provided Me a king among his sons. And Samuel
	2	said, **How can I go?** if Saul hear *it*, he will kill me. And the LORD said, Take an heifer with thee, and say, I am come to sacrifice to the LORD.
	4	And Samuel did that which the LORD spake, and came to Beth-lehem. And the elders of the town trembled at his coming, and said, **Comest thou peaceably?**
	11	And Samuel said unto Jesse, **Are here all** *thy* **children?** And he said, There remaineth yet the youngest, and, behold, he keepeth the sheep. And
	4	Samuel said unto Jesse, Send and fetch him: for we will not sit down till he come hither.
17	8[2]	And he stood and cried unto the armies of Israel, and said unto them, **Why are ye come out to set** *your* **battle in array?** *am* **not I a Philistine, and ye servants to Saul?** choose you a man for you, and let him come down to me.
	25	And the men of Israel said, **Have ye seen this man that is come up?** surely to defy Israel is he come up: and it shall be, *that* the man who killeth him, the king will enrich him with great riches, and will give him his daughter, and make his father's house free in Israel.

	CHAP.	VER
And David spake to the men that stood by him, saying, **What shall be done to the man that killeth this Philistine, and taketh away the reproach from Israel? for who** is **this uncircumcised Philistine, that he should defy the armies of the living God?** And the people answered him after this manner, saying, So shall it be done to the man that killeth him. And Eliab his eldest brother heard when he spake unto the men, and Eliab's anger was kindled against David, and he said, **Why camest thou down hither? and with whom hast thou left those few sheep in the wilderness?** I know thy pride, and the naughtiness of thine heart, for thou art come down that thou mightest see the battle. And David said, **What have I now done?** *Is there* **not a cause?**	17	26[2]
		28[2]
		29[2]
And the Philistine said unto David, *Am* **I a dog, that thou comest to me with staves?** And the Philistine cursed David by his gods.		43
nd when Saul saw David go forth against the Philistine. he said unto Abner, the captain of the host, **Abner, whose son** *is* **this youth?** And Abner said, *As* thy soul liveth, O king, I cannot tell.		55
And Saul said to him, **Whose son** *art* **thou,** *thou* **young man?** And David answered, *I am* the son of thy servant Jesse the Beth-lehemite.		58
		12
And Saul was very wroth, and the saying displeased him; and he said, They have ascribed unto David ten thousands, and to me they have ascribed *but* thousands. **and** *what* **can he have more but the kingdom?**	18	8
And David said unto Saul, **Who** *am* **I? and what** *is* **my life,** *or* **my father's family in Israel, that I should be son in law to the king?**		18[2]

And Saul's servants spake those words in the ears of

CHAP.	VER.	
18	23	David. And David said, **Seemeth it to you** *a* **light** *thing* **to be a king's son in law, seeing that I** *am* **a poor man, and lightly esteemed?**
	4	
19	5	For he did put his life in his hand, and slew the Philistine, and the LORD wrought a great salvation for all Israel: thou sawest *it*, and didst rejoice: **wherefore then wilt thou sin against innocent blood, to slay David without a cause?**
	17²	And Saul said unto Michal, **Why hast thou deceived me so, and sent away mine enemy, that he is escaped?** And Michal answered Saul, He said unto me, Let me go, **why should I kill thee?**
	22	Then went he also to Ramah, and came to a great well that *is* in Sechu: and he asked and said, **Where** *are* **Samuel and David?** And *one* said, Behold, *they be* at Naioth in Ramah
	24	And he stripped off his clothes also, and prophesied before Samuel in like manner, and lay down naked all that day and all that night Wherefore they say, *Is* **Saul also among the prophets?**
	5	
20	1³	And David fled from Naioth in Ramah, and came and said before Jonathan, **What have I done?** what *is* **mine iniquity? and what** *is* **my sin before thy father, that he seeketh my life?** And he said unto him, God forbid; thou shalt not die: behold, my father will do nothing either great or small, but that he will shew it me: **and why should my father hide this thing from me?** it *is* not *so*.
	2	
	8	Therefore thou shalt deal kindly with thy servant, for thou hast brought thy servant into a covenant of the LORD with thee: notwithstanding, if there be in me iniquity, slay me thyself; **for why shouldest thou bring me to thy father?** And Jonathan said, Far be

FIRST SAMUEL:—XX., XXI.

	CHAP.	VER
it from thee. **for if I knew certainly that evil were determined by my father to come upon thee, then would not I tell it thee?** Then said David to Jonathan, **Who shall tell me? or what** *if* **thy father answer thee roughly?**	**20**	9
		10²
And it came to pass on the morrow, *which was* the second *day* of the month, that David's place was empty and Saul said unto Jonathan his son, **Wherefore cometh not the son of Jesse to meat, neither yesterday, nor to day?**		27
Then Saul's anger was kindled against Jonathan, and he said unto him, Thou son of the perverse rebellious *woman,* **do not I know that thou hast chosen the son of Jesse to thine own confusion, and unto the confusion of thy mother's nakedness?**		30
And Jonathan answered Saul his father, and said unto him, **Wherefore shall he be slain? what hath he done?**		32²
And when the lad was come to the place of the arrow which Jonathan had shot, Jonathan cried after the lad, and said, *Is* **not the arrow beyond thee?**		37
		13
Then came David to Nob to Ahimelech the priest: and Ahimelech was afraid at the meeting of David, and said unto him, **Why** *art* **thou alone, and no man with thee?** And David said unto Ahimelech the priest, The king hath commanded me a business, and hath said unto me, Let no man know any thing of the business whereabout I send thee, and what I have commanded thee: and I have appointed *my* servants to such and such a place. **Now therefore what is under thine hand?** give *me* five *loaves of* bread in mine hand, or what there is present. And the priest answered David, and said, *There is* no common bread	**21**	1
		3

CHAP.	VER	
		under mine hand, but there is hallowed bread; if the young men have kept themselves at least from women.
21	8	And David said unto Ahimelech, **And is there not here under thine hand spear or sword?** for I have neither brought my sword nor my weapons with me, because the king's business required haste.
	11²	And the servants of Achish said unto him, *Is* **not this David the king of the land?** did they not sing one to another of him in dances, saying, Saul hath slain his thousands, and David his ten thousands?
	14 15² 8	Then said Achish unto his servants, **Lo, ye see the man is mad: wherefore** *then* **have ye brought him to me? Have I need of mad men, that ye have brought this** *fellow* **to play the mad man in my presence? shall this** *fellow* **come into my house?**
22	8	Then Saul said unto his servants that stood about him, Hear now, ye Benjamites; **will the son of Jesse give every one of you fields and vineyards,** *and* **make you all captains of thousands, and captains of hundreds; that all of you have conspired against me, and** *there is* **none that sheweth me that my son hath made a league with the son of Jesse, and** *there is* **none of you that is sorry for me, or sheweth unto me that my son hath stirred up my servant against me, to lie in wait, as at this day?**
	13	And Saul said unto him, **Why have ye conspired against me, thou and the son of Jesse, in that thou hast given him bread, and a sword, and hast inquired of God for him, that he should rise against me, to lie in wait, as at this day?**
	14	Then Ahimelech answered the king, and said, **And who** *is so* **faithful among all thy servants as David, which is the king's son in law, and goeth at thy**

bidding, and is honourable in thine house? Did **22** 15
I then begin to inquire of God for him? be it far
from me: let not the king impute *any* thing unto his   4
servant, *nor* to all the house of my father: for thy
servant knew nothing of all this, less or more.

Therefore David inquired of the Lord, saying, **Shall** **23** 2
I go and smite these Philistines? And the Lord
said unto David, Go, and smite the Philistines, and save
Keilah And David's men said unto him, **Behold, we**   3
be afraid here in Judah: how much more then
if we come to Keilah against the armies of the
Philistines?

Will the men of Keilah deliver me up into his   11[2]
hand? will Saul come down, as Thy servant hath
heard? O Lord God of Israel, I beseech Thee, tell Thy
servant. And the Lord said, He will come down. Then
said David, **Will the men of Keilah deliver me and**   12
my men into the hand of Saul? And the Lord
said, They will deliver *thee* up.

Then came up the Ziphites to Saul to Gibeah, saying,
Doth not David hide himself with us in strong-   19
holds in the wood, in the hill of Hachilah, which
is **on the south of Jeshimon?**   6

And David said to Saul, **Wherefore hearest thou** **24** 9
men's words, saying, Behold, David seeketh thy
hurt?

After whom is the king of Israel come out?   14[2]
after whom dost thou pursue? after a dead dog,
after a flea.

And it came to pass, when David had made an end of
speaking these words unto Saul, that Saul said, *Is* **this**   16
thy voice, my son David? And Saul lifted up his
voice, and wept. And he said to David, Thou *art* more

CHAP.	VER	
24	19	righteous than I: for thou hast rewarded me good, whereas I have rewarded thee evil. And thou hast shewed this day how that thou hast dealt well with me. forasmuch as when the LORD had delivered me into thine hand, thou killedst me not. **For if a man find his enemy, will he let him go well away?** wherefore
	5	the LORD reward thee good for that thou hast done unto me this day.
25	10²	And Nabal answered David's servants, and said, **Who** is **David? and who** is **the son of Jesse?** there be many servants now a days that break away every man
	11	from his master. **Shall I then take my bread, and my water, and my flesh that I have killed for my**
	3	**shearers, and give** it **unto men, whom I know not whence they** be?
26	1	And the Ziphites came unto Saul to Gibeah, saying, **Doth not David hide himself in the hill of Hachilah,** which is **before Jeshimon?**
	6	Then answered David and said to Ahimelech the Hittite, and to Abishai the son of Zeruiah, brother to Joab, saying, **Who will go down with me to Saul to the camp?** And Abishai said, I will go down with thee.
	9	And David said to Abishai, Destroy him not **for who can stretch forth his hand against the** LORD's **anointed, and be guiltless?**
	14²	And David cried to the people, and to Abner the son of Ner, saying, **Answerest thou not, Abner?** Then Abner answered and said, **Who** art **thou** that **criest to**
	15³	**the king?** And David said to Abner, Art **not thou a** valiant **man? and who** is **like to thee in Israel? wherefore then hast thou not kept thy lord the king?** for there came one of the people in to destroy the king thy lord.

FIRST SAMUEL:—XXVI.-XXVIII.

	CHAP	VER.
And Saul knew David's voice, and said, *Is* **this thy voice, my son David?** And David said, *It is* my voice. my lord, O king. And he said, **Wherefore doth my lord thus pursue after his servant? for what have I done? or what evil** *is* **in mine hand?**	**26**	17
		18³
		12

And David said unto Achish, If I have now found grace in thine eyes, let them give me a place in some town in the country, that I may dwell there: **for why should thy servant dwell in the royal city with thee?** — **27** 5

And Achish said, **Whither have ye made a road to day?** And David said, Against the south of Judah, and against the south of the Jerahmeelites, and against the south of the Kenites. — 10 / 2

And the woman said unto him, Behold, thou knowest what Saul hath done, how he hath cut off those that have familiar spirits, and the wizards, out of the land · **wherefore then layest thou a snare for my life, to cause me to die?** And Saul sware to her by the LORD, saying, *As* the LORD liveth, there shall no punishment happen to thee for this thing. Then said the woman, **Whom shall I bring up unto thee?** And he said, Bring me up Samuel. And when the woman saw Samuel, she cried with a loud voice · and the woman spake to Saul, saying, **Why hast thou deceived me?** for thou *art* Saul And the king said unto her, Be not afraid: **for what sawest thou?** And the woman said unto Saul, I saw gods ascending out of the earth. And he said unto her, **What form** *is* **he of?** And she said, An old man cometh up, and he *is* covered with a mantle. And Saul perceived that it *was* Samuel, and he stooped with *his* face to the ground, and bowed himself. And Samuel said to Saul, **Why hast thou disquieted me, to bring me up?** And Saul answered, I am sore distressed; for the Philistines make war against me, and God is departed from me, and answereth me no more, neither by prophets, — **28** 9 / 11 / 12 / 13 / 14 / 15

CHAP.	VER	
28	16	nor by dreams: therefore I have called thee, that thou mayest make known unto me what I shall do. Then said Samuel, **Wherefore then dost thou ask of me, seeing the** LORD **is departed from thee, and is**
	7	**become thine enemy?**
29	3²	Then said the princes of the Philistines, **What** *do* **these Hebrews** *here?* And Achish said unto the princes of the Philistines, *Is* **not this David, the servant of Saul the king of Israel, which hath been with me these days, or these years, and I have found no fault in him since he fell** *unto me* **unto this day?** And the princes of the Philistines were wroth with him, and the princes of the Philistines said unto him, Make this fellow return, that he may go again to his place which thou hast appointed him, and let him not go down with us to battle, lest in the battle he be an
	4²	adversary to us: **for wherewith should he reconcile himself unto his master?** *should it* **not** *be* **with the**
	5	**heads of these men?** *Is* **not this David, of whom they sang one to another in dances, saying, Saul slew his thousands, and David his ten thousands?**
	8²	And David said unto Achish, **But what have I done? and what hast thou found in thy servant so long as I have been with thee unto this day,**
	7	**that I may not go fight against the enemies of my lord the king?**
30	8²	And David inquired at the LORD, saying, **Shall I pursue after this troop? shall I overtake them?** And He answered him, Pursue. for thou shalt surely overtake *them*, and without fail recover *all*
	13²	And David said unto him, **To whom** *belongest* **thou? and whence** *art* **thou?** And he said, I *am* a young man of Egypt, servant to an Amalekite; and my master left me, because three days agone I fell sick. We made an invasion *upon* the south of the Cherethites, and upon

	CHAP	VER.
the coast which *belongeth* to Judah, and upon the south of Caleb; and we burned Ziklag with fire. And David said to him, **Canst thou bring me down to this company?** And he said, Swear unto me by God, that thou wilt neither kill me, nor deliver me into the hands of my master, and I will bring thee down to this company.	30	15
For who will hearken unto you in this matter? but as his part *is* that goeth down to the battle, so *shall* his part *be* that tarrieth by the stuff: they shall part alike.		24
		6
	First Samuel 157	

SECOND SAMUEL.

	CHAP.	VER
AND David said unto him, **From whence comest thou?** And he said unto him, Out of the camp of Israel am I escaped. And David said unto him, **How went the matter?** I pray thee, tell me. And he answered, That the people are fled from the battle, and many of the people also are fallen and dead; and Saul and Jonathan his son are dead also. And David said unto the young man that told him, **How knowest thou that Saul and Jonathan his son be dead?** And the young man that told him said, As I happened by chance upon mount Gilboa, behold, Saul leaned upon his spear; and, lo, the chariots and horsemen followed hard after him. And when he looked behind him, he saw me, and called unto me. And I answered, Here *am* I. And he said unto me, **Who** *art* **thou?** And I answered him, I *am* an Amalekite.	1	3
		4
		5
		8
And David said unto the young man that told him, **Whence** *art* **thou?** And he answered, I *am* the son of a stranger, an Amalekite. And David said unto him,		13

CHAP	VER	
1	14	**How wast thou not afraid to stretch forth thine hand to destroy the** LORD's **anointed?**
	6	

2	1²	And it came to pass after this, that David inquired of the LORD, saying, **Shall I go up into any of the cities of Judah?** And the LORD said unto him, Go up. And David said, **Whither shall I go up?** And He said, Unto Hebron.
	20	Then Abner looked behind him, and said, *Art* **thou Asahel?** And he answered, I *am*.
	22·	And Abner said again to Asahel, Turn thee aside from following me: **wherefore should I smite thee to the ground? how then should I hold up my face to Joab thy brother?**
	26³	Then Abner called to Joab, and said, **Shall the sword devour for ever? knowest thou not that it will be bitterness in the latter end? how long shall it be then, ere thou bid the people return from following their brethren?**
	8	

3	7	And Saul had a concubine, whose name *was* Rizpah, the daughter of Aiah: and *Ish-bosheth* said to Abner, **Wherefore hast thou gone in unto my father's concubine?** Then was Abner very wroth for the words of Ish-bosheth, and said, *Am* **I a dog's head, which against Judah do shew kindness this day unto the house of Saul thy father, to his brethren, and to his friends, and have not delivered thee into the hand of David, that thou chargest me to day with a fault concerning this woman?**
	8	
	12	And Abner sent messengers to David on his behalf, saying, **Whose** *is* **the land?** saying *also*, Make thy league with me, and, behold, my hand *shall be* with thee, to bring about all Israel unto thee.

	CHAP	VER
Then Joab came to the king, and said, **What hast thou done?** behold, Abner came unto thee; **why** *is* **it** *that* **thou hast sent him away, and he is quite gone?**	3	24²
And the king lamented over Abner, and said, **Died Abner as a fool dieth?**		33
And the king said unto his servants, **Know ye not that there is a prince and a great man fallen this day in Israel?**		38
		7
When one told me, saying, Behold, Saul is dead, thinking to have brought good tidings, I took hold of him, and slew him in Ziklag, who *thought* that I would have given him a reward for his tidings: **how much more, when wicked men have slain a righteous person in his own house upon his bed? shall I not therefore now require his blood of your hand, and take you away from the earth?**	4	11²
		2
And David inquired of the LORD, saying, **Shall I go up to the Philistines? wilt Thou deliver them into mine hand?** And the LORD said unto David, Go up. for I will doubtless deliver the Philistines into thine hand.	5	19²
		2
And David was afraid of the LORD that day, and said, **How shall the ark of the LORD come to me?**	6	9
		1
Go and tell my servant David, Thus saith the LORD, **Shalt thou build Me an house for Me to dwell in?**	7	5
In all *the places* wherein I have walked with all the children of Israel spake I a word with any of the tribes of Israel, whom I commanded to feed My people Israel, saying, **Why build ye not Me an house of cedar?**		7
According to all these words, and according to all this		

CHAP.	VER	
7	18[2]	vision, so did Nathan speak unto David. Then went king David in, and sat before the LORD, and he said, **Who** *am* **I, O Lord** GOD? **and what** *is* **my house, that Thou hast brought me hitherto?** And this was yet a small thing in Thy sight, O Lord GOD; but Thou hast spoken also of Thy servant's house for a great
	19	while to come. **And** *is* **this the manner of man, O**
	20	**Lord** GOD? **And what can David say more unto Thee?** for Thou, Lord GOD, knowest Thy servant.
	23	**And what one nation in the earth** *is* **like Thy people,** *even* **like Israel, whom God went to redeem for a people to Himself, and to make Him a name, and to do for you great things and terrible, for**
	7	**Thy land, before Thy people, which Thou redeemedst to Thee from Egypt,** *from* **the nations and their gods?**
9	1	And David said, **Is there yet any that is left of the house of Saul, that I may shew him kindness for Jonathan's sake?** And *there was* of the house of Saul a servant whose name *was* Ziba. And when they
	2	had called him unto David, the king said unto him, *Art* **thou Ziba?** And he said, Thy servant *is he*. And the
	3	king said, *Is* **there not yet any of the house of Saul, that I may shew the kindness of God unto him?** And Ziba said unto the king, Jonathan hath yet a son, *which is* lame on *his* feet. And the king said unto him,
	4	**Where** *is* **he?** And Ziba said unto the king, Behold, he *is* in the house of Machir, the son of Ammiel, in Lodebar.
	8	And he bowed himself, and said, **What** *is* **thy servant, that thou shouldest look upon such a dead**
	5	**dog as I** *am*?
10	3[2]	And the princes of the children of Ammon said unto Hanun their lord, **Thinkest thou that David doth**
	2	**honour thy father, that he hath sent comforters**

	CHAP.	VER
unto thee? hath not David *rather* sent his servants unto thee, to search the city, and to spy it out, and to overthrow it?		
And David sent and inquired after the woman. And *one* said, *Is* **not this Bath-sheba, the daughter of Eliam, the wife of Uriah the Hittite?**	11	3
And when they had told David, saying, Uriah went not down unto his house, David said unto Uriah, **Camest thou not from** *thy* **journey? why** *then* **didst thou not go down unto thine house?** And Uriah said unto David, The ark, and Israel, and Judah, abide in tents; and my lord Joab, and the servants of my lord, are encamped in the open fields; **shall I then go into mine house, to eat and to drink, and to lie with my wife?** *as* thou livest, and *as* thy soul liveth, I will not do this thing		10² 11
And if so be that the king's wrath arise, and he say unto thee, **Wherefore approached ye so nigh unto the city when ye did fight? knew ye not that they would shoot from the wall? Who smote Abimelech the son of Jerubbesheth? did not a woman cast a piece of a millstone upon him from the wall, that he died in Thebez? why went ye nigh the wall?** then say thou, Thy servant Uriah the Hittite is dead also.		20² 21³ 9
Wherefore hast thou despised the commandment of the Lord, **to do evil in His sight?** thou hast killed Uriah the Hittite with the sword, and hast taken his wife *to be* thy wife, and hast slain him with the sword of the children of Ammon.	12	9
And it came to pass on the seventh day, that the child died. And the servants of David feared to tell him that the child was dead: for they said, Behold, while the child was yet alive, we spake unto him, and he would not		

CHAP	VER.	
12	18	hearken unto our voice **how will he then vex himself, if we tell him that the child is dead?** But when David saw that his servants whispered, David perceived that the child was dead: therefore David said
	19	unto his servants, **Is the child dead?** And they said, He is dead.
	21	Then said his servants unto him, **What thing** *is* **this that thou hast done?** thou didst fast and weep for the child, *while it was* alive; but when the child was dead, thou didst rise and eat bread. And he said, While the child was yet alive, I fasted and wept: for I said,
	22	**Who can tell** *whether* GOD **will be gracious to me,**
	23[2]	**that the child may live? But now he is dead, wherefore should I fast? can I bring him back**
	7	**again?** I shall go to him, but he shall not return to me.
13	4[2]	And he said unto him, **Why** *art* **thou,** *being* **the king's son, lean from day to day? wilt thou not tell me?** And Amnon said unto him, I love Tamar, my brother Absalom's sister.
	13	**And I, whither shall I cause my shame to go?** and as for thee, thou shalt be as one of the fools in Israel. Now therefore, I pray thee, speak unto the king, for he will not withhold me from thee.
	20	And Absalom her brother said unto her, **Hath Amnon thy brother been with thee?** but hold now thy peace, my sister: he *is* thy brother; regard not this thing. So Tamar remained desolate in her brother Absalom's house.
	26	Then said Absalom, If not, I pray thee, let my brother Amnon go with us. And the king said unto him, **Why should he go with thee?**
		Now Absalom had commanded his servants, saying,

Mark ye now when Amnon's heart is merry with wine, and when I say unto you, Smite Amnon ; then kill him, fear not : **have not I commanded you ?** be courageous, and be valiant. | **13** 28

| 6

And when the woman of Tekoah spake to the king, she fell on her face to the ground, and did obeisance, and said, Help, O king. And the king said unto her, **What aileth thee ?** And she answered, I *am* indeed a widow woman, and mine husband is dead. | **14** 5

And the woman said, **Wherefore then hast thou thought such a thing against the people of God ?** for the king doth speak this thing as one which is faulty, in that the king doth not fetch home again his banished. | 13

And the king said, *Is not* **the hand of Joab with thee in all this?** And the woman answered and said, *As* thy soul liveth, my lord the king, none can turn to the right hand or to the left from ought that my lord the king hath spoken : for thy servant Joab, he bade me, and he put all these words in the mouth of thine handmaid to fetch about this form of speech hath thy servant Joab done this thing : and my lord *is* wise, according to the wisdom of an angel of God, to know all *things* that *are* in the earth. | 19

Then Joab arose, and came to Absalom unto *his* house, and said unto him, **Wherefore have thy servants set my field on fire ?** And Absalom answered Joab, Behold, I sent unto thee, saying, Come hither, that I may send thee to the king, to say, **Wherefore am I come from Geshur ?** *it had been* good for me *to have been* there still : now therefore let me see the king's face ; and if there be *any* iniquity in me, let him kill me. | 31

| 32

| 5

And Absalom rose up early, and stood beside the way of the gate : and it was *so*, that when any man that had a controversy came to the king for judgment, then

CHAP.	VER.	
15	2	Absalom called unto him, and said, **Of what city** *art* **thou?** And he said, Thy servant *is* of one of the tribes of Israel.
	19	Then said the king to Ittai the Gittite, **Wherefore goest thou also with us?** return to thy place, and abide with the king: for thou *art* a stranger, and also an
	20	exile. **Whereas thou camest** *but* **yesterday, should I this day make thee go up and down with us?** seeing I go whither I may, return thou, and take back thy brethren: mercy and truth *be* with thee.
	27	The king said also unto Zadok the priest, *Art not* **thou a seer?** return into the city in peace, and your two sons with you, Ahimaaz thy son, and Jonathan the son of Abiathar.
	35	**And** *hast thou* **not there with thee Zadok and Abiathar the priests?** therefore it shall be, *that* what
	5	thing soever thou shalt hear out of the king's house, thou shalt tell *it* to Zadok and Abiathar the priests.
16	2	And the king said unto Ziba, **What meanest thou by these?** And Ziba said, The asses *be* for the king's household to ride on; and the bread and summer fruit for the young men to eat; and the wine, that such as be faint in the wilderness may drink. And the king said,
	3	**And where** *is* **thy master's son?** And Ziba said unto the king, Behold, he abideth at Jerusalem: for he said, To day shall the house of Israel restore me the kingdom of my father.
	9	Then said Abisnai the son of Zeruiah unto the ng, **Why should this dead dog curse my lord the king?** let me go over, I pray thee, and take off his
	10²	head. And the king said, **What have I to do with you, ye sons of Zeruiah?** so let him curse, because the LORD hath said unto him, Curse David. **Who shall then say, Wherefore hast thou done so?**

SECOND SAMUEL:—XVI.-XVIII.

	CHAP	VER

And David said to Abishai, and to all his servants, Behold, my son, which came forth of my bowels, seeketh my life: **how much more now** *may this* **Benjamite** *do it?* let him alone, and let him curse; for the LORD hath bidden him. — 16 11

And Absalom said to Hushai, *Is* **this thy kindness to thy friend? why wentest thou not with thy friend?** — 17²

And again, **whom should I serve?** *should I not serve* **in the presence of his son?** as I have served in thy father's presence, so will I be in thy presence. — 19² / 10

And when Hushai was come to Absalom, Absalom spake unto him, saying, Ahithophel hath spoken after this manner: **shall we do** *after* **his saying?** if not; speak thou. — 17 6

And when Absalom's servants came to the woman to the house, they said, **Where** *is* **Ahimaaz and Jonathan?** And the woman said unto them, They be gone over the brook of water. And when they had sought and could not find *them*, they returned to Jerusalem. — 20 / 2

And Joab said unto the man that told him, And, behold, thou sawest *him*, and **why didst thou not smite him there to the ground?** and I would have given thee ten *shekels* of silver, and a girdle. — 18 11

Then said Ahimaaz the son of Zadok yet again to Joab, But howsoever, let me, I pray thee, also run after Cushi. And Joab said, **Wherefore wilt thou run, my son, seeing that thou hast no tidings ready?** — 22

And Ahimaaz called, and said unto the king, All is well. And he fell down to the earth upon his face before the king, and said, Blessed *be* the LORD thy God, which hath delivered up the men that lifted up their hand

CHAP.	VER.	
18	29	against my lord the king. And the king said, **Is the young man Absalom safe?** And Ahimaaz answered, When Joab sent the king's servant, and *me* thy servant, I saw a great tumult, but I knew not what *it was*. And the king said *unto him*, Turn aside, *and* stand here. And he turned aside, and stood still. And, behold, Cushi came, and Cushi said, Tidings, my lord the king: for the LORD hath avenged thee this day of all them that rose up against thee. And the king said unto Cushi,
	32	*Is* **the young man Absalom safe?** And Cushi answered, The enemies of my lord the king, and all that
	4	rise against thee to do *thee* hurt, be as *that* young man *is*.

19	10	And Absalom, whom we anointed over us, is dead in battle **Now therefore why speak ye not a word of bringing the king back?** And king David sent to Zadok and to Abiathar the priests, saying, Speak unto
	11	the elders of Judah, saying, **Why are ye the last to bring the king back to his house?** seeing the speech of all Israel is come to the king, *even* to his house Ye
	12	*are* my brethren, ye *are* my bones and my flesh · **wherefore then are ye the last to bring back the king?**
	13	And say ye to Amasa, *Art* **thou not of my bone, and of my flesh?** God do so to me, and more also, if thou be not captain of the host before me continually in the room of Joab.

For thy servant doth know that I have sinned. therefore, behold, I am come the first this day of all the house of Joseph to go down to meet my lord the king. But

	21	Abishai the son of Zeruiah answered and said, **Shall not Shimei be put to death for this, because he cursed**
	22 3	**the** LORD's **anointed?** And David said, **What have I to do with you, ye sons of Zeruiah, that ye should this day be adversaries unto me? shall there any man be put to death this day in Israel? for do not I know that I** *am* **this day king over Israel?**

SECOND SAMUEL:—XIX. 75

| | CHAP. | VER. |

And Mephibosheth the son of Saul came down to meet the king, and had neither dressed his feet, nor trimmed his beard, nor washed his clothes, from the day the king departed until the day he came *again* in peace. And it came to pass, when he was come to Jerusalem to meet the king, that the king said unto him, **Wherefore wentest not thou with me, Mephibosheth ?** 19 25

For all *of* my father's house were but dead men before my lord the king: yet didst thou set thy servant among them that did eat at thine own table. **What right therefore have I yet to cry any more unto the king ?** 28
And the king said unto him, **Why speakest thou any more of thy matters ?** I have said, Thou and Ziba divide the land. 29

And the king said unto Barzillai, Come thou over with me, and I will feed thee with me in Jerusalem. And Barzillai said unto the king, **How long have I to live, that I should go up with the king unto Jerusalem ?** 34
I *am* this day fourscore years old: *and* **can I discern between good and evil ? can thy servant taste what I eat or what I drink ? can I hear any more the voice of singing men and singing women ? wherefore then should thy servant be yet a burden unto my lord the king ?** 35⁴
Thy servant will go a little way over Jordan with the king: **and why should the king recompense it me with such a reward ?** 36

And, behold, all the men of Israel came to the king, and said unto the king, **Why have our brethren the men of Judah stolen thee away, and have brought the king, and his household, and all David's men with him, over Jordan ?** 41
And all the men of Judah answered the men of Israel, Because the king *is* near of kin to us: **wherefore then be ye angry for this matter ? have we eaten at all of the king's** *cost ?* **or hath he given us any gift ?** 42³

CHAP.	VER.	
19	43	And the men of Israel answered the men of Judah, and said, We have ten parts in the king, and we have also more *right* in David than ye: **why then did ye despise us, that our advice should not be first had in bringing back our king?** And the words of the men of Judah were fiercer than the words of the men of Israel.
	22	
20	9	And Joab said to Amasa, *Art* **thou in health, my brother?** And Joab took Amasa by the beard with the right hand to kiss him.
	17	Then cried a wise woman out of the city, Hear, hear; say, I pray you, unto Joab, Come near hither, that I may speak with thee. And when he was come near unto her, the woman said, *Art* **thou Joab?** And he answered, I *am he*. Then she said unto him, Hear the words of thine handmaid. And he answered, I do hear. Then she spake, saying, They were wont to speak in old time, saying, They shall surely ask *counsel* at Abel: and so they ended *the matter.* I *am one of them that are* peaceable *and* faithful in Israel: thou seekest to destroy a city and a mother in Israel: **why wilt thou swallow up the inheritance of the** LORD?
	19	
	3	
21	3²	Wherefore David said unto the Gibeonites, **What shall I do for you? and wherewith shall I make the atonement, that ye may bless the inheritance of the** LORD?
	2	
22	32²	As *for* God, His way *is* perfect; the word of the LORD *is* tried: He *is* a buckler to all them that trust in Him. **For who** *is* **God, save the** LORD**? and who** *is* **a rock, save our God?** God *is* my strength *and* power: and He maketh my way perfect.
	2	

And David *was* then in an hold, and the garrison of the Philistines *was* then *in* Beth-lehem. And David longed, and said, Oh that one would give me drink of the water of the well of Beth-lehem, which *is* by the gate! And the three mighty men brake through the host of the Philistines, and drew water out of the well of Beth-lehem, that *was* by the gate, and took *it*, and brought *it* to David: nevertheless he would not drink thereof, but poured it out unto the LORD. And he said, Be it far from me, O LORD, that I should do this: *is not this* **the blood of the men that went in jeopardy of their lives?** therefore he would not drink it. These things did these three mighty men. And Abishai, the brother of Joab, the son of Zeruiah, was chief among three. And he lifted up his spear against three hundred, *and* slew *them*, and had the name among three. **Was he not most honourable of three?** therefore he was their captain: howbeit he attained not unto the *first* three.

23 17

19

2

And again the anger of the LORD was kindled against Israel, and he moved David against them to say, Go, number Israel and Judah. For the king said to Joab the captain of the host, which *was* with him, Go now through all the tribes of Israel, from Dan even to Beer-sheba, and number ye the people, that I may know the number of the people. And Joab said unto the king, Now the LORD thy God add unto the people, how many soever they be, an hundredfold, and that the eyes of my lord the king may see *it*: **but why doth my lord the king delight in this thing?**

24 3

So Gad came to David, and told him, and said unto him, **Shall seven years of famine come unto thee in thy land? or wilt thou flee three months before thine enemies, while they pursue thee? or that there be three days' pestilence in thy land?** now advise, and see what answer I shall return to him that sent me.

13³

And David spake unto the LORD when he saw the angel that smote the people, and said, Lo, I have sinned,

CHAP.	VER.	
24	17	and I have done wickedly: **but these sheep, what have they done?** let Thine hand, I pray Thee, be against me, and against my father's house.
	21	And Araunah said, **Wherefore is my lord the king come to his servant?** And David said, To buy the threshingfloor of thee, to build an altar unto the LORD,
	6	that the plague may be stayed from the people.

Second Samuel 125

FIRST KINGS.

CHAP.	VER.	
1	6	THEN Adonijah the son of Haggith exalted himself, saying, I will be king: and he prepared him chariots and horsemen, and fifty men to run before him. And his father had not displeased him at any time in saying, **Why hast thou done so?** and he also *was a* very goodly *man;* and *his mother* bare him after Absalom.
	11	Wherefore Nathan spake unto Bath-sheba the mother of Solomon, saying, **Hast thou not heard that Adonijah the son of Haggith doth reign, and David our lord knoweth** *it* **not?** Now therefore come, let me, I pray thee, give thee counsel, that thou mayest save thine own life, and the life of thy son Solomon. Go and
	13[2]	get thee in unto king David, and say unto him, **Didst not thou, my lord, O king, swear unto thine handmaid, saying, Assuredly Solomon thy son shall reign after me, and he shall sit upon my throne?** **why then doth Adonijah reign?** Behold, while thou yet talkest there with the king, I also will come in after thee, and confirm thy words. And Bath-sheba went in unto the king into the chamber: and the king was very old; and Abishag the Shunammite

	CHAP.	VER

ministered unto the king. And Bath-sheba bowed, and did obeisance unto the king. And the king said, **What wouldest thou?** — 1 16

And Nathan said, **My lord, O king, hast thou said, Adonijah shall reign after me, and he shall sit upon my throne?** For he is gone down this day, and hath slain oxen and fat cattle and sheep in abundance, and hath called all the king's sons, and the captains of the host, and Abiathar the priest; and, behold, they eat and drink before him, and say, God save king Adonijah. But me, *even* me thy servant, and Zadok the priest, and Benaiah the son of Jehoiada, and thy servant Solomon, hath he not called. **Is this thing done by my lord the king, and thou hast not shewed** *it* **unto thy servant, who should sit on the throne of my lord the king after him?** — 24 / 27

And Adonijah and all the guests that *were* with him heard *it* as they had made an end of eating. And when Joab heard the sound of the trumpet, he said, **Wherefore** *is this* **noise of the city being in an uproar?** — 41 / 8

And Adonijah the son of Haggith came to Bath-sheba the mother of Solomon. And she said, **Comest thou peaceably?** And he said, Peaceably. — 2 13

And king Solomon answered and said unto his mother, **And why dost thou ask Abishag the Shunammite for Adonijah?** ask for him the kingdom also, for he *is* mine elder brother; even for him, and for Abiathar the priest, and for Joab the son of Zeruiah. — 22

And the king sent and called for Shimei, and said unto him, **Did I not make thee to swear by the** LORD, **and protested unto thee, saying, Know for a certain, on the day thou goest out, and walkest abroad any whither, that thou shalt surely die?** and thou saidst unto me, The word *that* I have heard *is* — 42

CHAP.	VER
2	43
	4

good. **Why then hast thou not kept the oath of the** Lord, **and the commandment that I have charged thee with?**

| 3 | 9 |
| | 1 |

Give therefore Thy servant an understanding heart to judge Thy people, that I may discern between good and bad: for **who is able to judge this Thy so great a people?**

| 8 | 27[2] |
| | 2 |

But will God indeed dwell on the earth? behold, the heaven and heaven of heavens cannot contain Thee; **how much less this house that I have builded?**

| 9 | 8 |

But if ye shall at all turn from following Me, ye or your children, and will not keep My commandments *and* my statutes which I have set before you, but go and serve other gods, and worship them: then will I cut off Israel out of the land which I have given them; and this house, which I have hallowed for My name, will I cast out of My sight; and Israel shall be a proverb and a byword among all people: and at this house, *which* is high, every one that passeth by it shall be astonished, and shall hiss; and they shall say, **Why hath the** Lord **done thus unto this land, and to this house?** And they shall answer, Because they forsook the Lord their God, who brought forth their fathers out of the land of Egypt, and have taken hold upon other gods, and have worshipped them, and served them: therefore hath the Lord brought upon them all this evil.

| | 13 |
| | 2 |

And Hiram came out from Tyre to see the cities which Solomon had given him; and they pleased him not. And he said, **What cities** *are* **these which thou hast given me, my brother?** And he called them the land of Cabul unto this day.

And when Hadad heard in Egypt that David slept with his fathers, and that Joab the captain of the host was dead, Hadad said to Pharaoh, Let me depart, that I may go to mine own country. Then Pharaoh said unto him, **But what hast thou lacked with me, that, behold, thou seekest to go to thine own country?** And he answered, Nothing. howbeit let me go in any wise. | **11** 22

And the rest of the acts of Solomon, and all that he did, and his wisdom, *are* **they not written in the book of the acts of Solomon?** And the time that Solomon reigned in Jerusalem over all Israel *was* forty years. | 41

2

And king Rehoboam consulted with the old men, that stood before Solomon his father while he yet lived, and said, **How do ye advise that I may answer this people?** And they spake unto him, saying, If thou wilt be a servant unto this people this day, and wilt serve them, and answer them, and speak good words to them, then they will be thy servants for ever. But he forsook the counsel of the old men, which they had given him, and consulted with the young men that were grown up with him, *and* which stood before him: and he said unto them, **What counsel give ye that we may answer this people, who have spoken to me, saying, Make the yoke which thy father did put upon us lighter?** | **12** 6

9

So when all Israel saw that the king hearkened not unto them, the people answered the king, saying, **What portion have we in David?** neither *have we* inheritance in the son of Jesse: to your tents, O Israel: now see to thine own house, David. So Israel departed unto their tents. | 16

3

And their father said unto them, **What way went he?** For his sons had seen what way the man of God went, which came from Judah. And he said unto his sons, Saddle me the ass. So they saddled him the ass: and he rode thereon, and went after the man of God, | **13** 12

CHAP	VER	
13	14	and found him sitting under an oak: and he said unto him, *Art* **thou the man of God that camest from Judah?** And he said, I *am*. Then he said unto him, Come home with me, and eat bread.
	2	
14	6	And the LORD said unto Ahijah, Behold, the wife of Jeroboam cometh to ask a thing of thee for her son; for he *is* sick: thus and thus shalt thou say unto her: for it shall be, when she cometh in, that she shall feign herself *to be* another *woman*. And it was *so*, when Ahijah heard the sound of her feet, as she came in at the door, that he said, Come in, thou wife of Jeroboam; **why feignest thou thyself** *to be* **another?** for I *am* sent to thee *with* heavy *tidings*.
	14	Moreover the LORD shall raise Him up a king over Israel, who shall cut off the house of Jeroboam that day: **but what?** even now. For the LORD shall smite Israel, as a reed is shaken in the water, and He shall root up Israel out of this good land, which He gave to their fathers, and shall scatter them beyond the river, because they have made their groves, provoking the LORD to anger. And He shall give Israel up because of the sins of Jeroboam, who did sin, and who made Israel to sin.
	29	**Now the rest of the acts of Rehoboam, and all that he did,** *are* **they not written in the book of the chronicles of the kings of Judah?**
	3	
15	7	**Now the rest of the acts of Abijam, and all that he did,** *are* **they not written in the book of the chronicles of the kings of Judah?**
	23	**The rest of all the acts of Asa, and all his might, and all that he did, and the cities which he built,** *are* **they not written in the book of the chronicles of the kings of Judah?** Nevertheless in the time of his old age he was diseased in his feet.

	CHAP	VER
Now the rest of the acts of Nadab, and all that he did, *are* they not written in the book of the chronicles of the kings of Israel?	15	31
		3
Now the rest of the acts of Baasha, and what he did, and his might, *are* they not written in the book of the chronicles of the kings of Israel?	16	5
Now the rest of the acts of Elah, and all that he did, *are* they not written in the book of the chronicles of the kings of Israel?		14
Now the rest of the acts of Zimri, and his treason that he wrought, *are* they not written in the book of the chronicles of the kings of Israel?		20
Now the rest of the acts of Omri which he did, and his might that he shewed, *are* they not written in the book of the chronicles of the kings of Israel?		27
		4
And it came to pass after these things, *that* the son of the woman, the mistress of the house, fell sick; and his sickness was so sore, that there was no breath left in him. And she said unto Elijah, **What have I to do with thee, O thou man of God? art thou come unto me to call my sin to remembrance, and to slay my son?** And he said unto her, Give me thy son. And he took him out of her bosom, and carried him up into a loft, where he abode, and laid him upon his own bed. And he cried unto the Lord, and said, **O Lord my God, hast Thou also brought evil upon the widow with whom I sojourn, by slaying her son?** And he stretched himself upon the child three times, and cried unto the Lord, and said, O Lord my God, I pray Thee, let this child's soul come into him again. And the Lord heard the voice of Elijah; and the soul of the child came into him again, and he revived. And Elijah took the child, and brought him down out of the	17	18[2]
		20
		3

CHAP.	VER.	
18	7	chamber into the house, and delivered him unto his mother: and Elijah said, See, thy son liveth.

And as Obadiah was in the way, behold, Elijah met him: and he knew him, and fell on his face, and said, *Art* **thou that my lord Elijah?** And he answered him, I *am :* go, tell thy lord, Behold, Elijah *is here.* |
	9	And he said, **What have I sinned, that thou wouldest deliver thy servant into the hand of Ahab, to slay me?**
	13	**Was it not told my lord what I did when Jezebel slew the prophets of the** LORD, **how I hid an hundred men of the** LORD'S **prophets by fifty in a cave, and fed them with bread and water?**
	17	And it came to pass, when Ahab saw Elijah, that Ahab said unto him, *Art* **thou he that troubleth Israel?**
	21	And Elijah came unto all the people, and said, **How long halt ye between two opinions?** if the LORD
19	5	be God, follow Him: but if Baal, *then* follow him. And the people answered him not a word.
	9	And he came thither unto a cave, and lodged there; and, behold, the word of the LORD *came* to him, and he said unto him, **What doest thou here, Elijah?**

And, behold, the LORD passed by, and a great and strong wind rent the mountains, and brake in pieces the rocks before the LORD; *but* the LORD *was* not in the wind: and after the wind an earthquake; *but* the LORD *was* not in the earthquake. And after the earthquake a fire; *but* the LORD *was* not in the fire: and after the fire a still small voice. And it was *so,* when Elijah heard *it,* that he wrapped his face in his mantle, and went out, and stood in the entering in of the cave. And, behold, |

FIRST KINGS:—XIX.-XXI.   85

| | CHAP | VER. |

there came a voice unto him, and said, **What doest thou here, Elijah?** | 19 | 13

So he departed thence, and found Elisha the son of Shaphat, who *was* plowing *with* twelve yoke *of oxen* before him, and he with the twelfth: and Elijah passed by him, and cast his mantle upon him. And he left the oxen, and ran after Elijah, and said, Let me, I pray thee, kiss my father and my mother, and *then* I will follow thee. And he said unto him, Go back again: **for what have I done to thee?**

| | | 20 |
| | | 3 |

And, behold, there came a prophet unto Ahab king of Israel, saying, Thus saith the Lord, **Hast thou seen all this great multitude?** behold, I will deliver it into thine hand this day; and thou shalt know that I *am* the Lord. And Ahab said, **By whom?** And he said, Thus saith the Lord, *Even* by the young men of the princes of the provinces. Then he said, **Who shall order the battle?** And he answered, Thou.

| | 20 | 13 |
| | | 14² |

So they girded sackcloth on their loins, and *put* ropes on their heads, and came to the king of Israel, and said, Thy servant Ben-hadad saith, I pray thee, let me live. And he said, *Is* **he yet alive?** he *is* my brother.

| | | 32 |
| | | 4 |

But Jezebel his wife came to him, and said unto him, **Why is thy spirit so sad, that thou eatest no bread?** And he said unto her, Because I spake unto Naboth the Jezreelite, and said unto him, Give me thy vineyard for money; or else, if it please thee, I will give thee *another* vineyard for it: and he answered, I will not give thee my vineyard. And Jezebel his wife said unto him, **Dost thou now govern the kingdom of Israel?** arise, *and* eat bread, and let thine heart be merry: I will give thee the vineyard of Naboth the Jezreelite.

| | 21 | 5 |
| | | 7 |

And the word of the Lord came to Elijah the Tishbite,

CHAP.	VER.	
21	19	saying, Arise, go down to meet Ahab king of Israel, which *is* in Samaria: behold, *he is* in the vineyard of Naboth, whither he is gone down to possess it. And thou shalt speak unto him, saying, Thus saith the Lord, **Hast thou killed, and also taken possession?** And thou shalt speak unto him, saying, Thus saith the Lord, In the place where dogs licked the blood of Naboth shall dogs lick thy blood, even thine. And Ahab
	20	said to Elijah, **Hast thou found me, O mine enemy?** And he answered, I have found *thee* · because thou hast sold thyself to work evil in the sight of the Lord.
	29	And the word of the Lord came to Elijah the Tishbite, saying, **Seest thou how Ahab humbleth himself before Me?** because he humbleth himself before Me,
	5	I will not bring the evil in his days: *but* in his son's days will I bring the evil upon his house.
22	3	And the king of Israel said unto his servants, **Know ye that Ramoth in Gilead *is* ours, and we *be* still, *and* take it not out of the hand of the king of
	4	Syria?** And he said unto Jehoshaphat, **Wilt thou go with me to battle to Ramoth-gilead?** And Jehoshaphat said to the king of Israel, I *am* as thou *art*, my people as thy people, my horses as thy horses. And Jehoshaphat said unto the king of Israel, Inquire, I pray thee, at the word of the Lord to-day. Then the king of Israel gathered the prophets together, about four hundred
	6	men, and said unto them, **Shall I go against Ramoth-gilead to battle, or shall I forbear?** And they said, Go up; for the Lord shall deliver *it* into the hand of
	7	the king. And Jehoshaphat said, *Is there* **not here a prophet of the** Lord **besides, that we might inquire of him?**
	15	And Micaiah said, *As* the Lord liveth, what the Lord saith unto me, that will I speak. So he came to the king. And the king said unto him, **Micaiah, shall we go against Ramoth-gilead to battle, or shall we**

	CHAP. VER.
forbear? And he answered him, Go, and prosper for the LORD shall deliver *it* into the hand of the king. And the king said unto him, **How many times shall I adjure thee that thou tell me nothing but** *that which is* **true in the name of the** LORD? And he said, I saw all Israel scattered upon the hills, as sheep that have not a shepherd: and the LORD said, These have no master: let them return every man to his house in peace. And the king of Israel said unto Jehoshaphat, **Did I not tell thee that he would prophesy no good concerning me, but evil?** And he said, Hear thou therefore the word of the LORD: I saw the LORD sitting on His throne, and all the host of heaven standing by Him on His right hand and on His left. And the LORD said, **Who shall persuade Ahab, that he may go up and fall at Ramoth-gilead?** And one said on this manner, and another said on that manner. And there came forth a spirit, and stood before the LORD, and said, I will persuade him. And the LORD said unto him, **Wherewith?** And he said, I will go forth, and I will be a lying spirit in the mouth of all his prophets. And He said, Thou shalt persuade *him*, and prevail also: go forth, and do so. Now therefore, behold, the LORD hath put a lying spirit in the mouth of all these thy prophets, and the LORD hath spoken evil concerning thee. But Zedekiah the son of Chenaanah went near, and smote Micaiah on the cheek, and said, **Which way went the Spirit of the** LORD **from me to speak unto thee?** And Micaiah said, Behold, thou shalt see in that day, when thou shalt go into an inner chamber to hide thyself.	22 16 18 20 22 24
Now the rest of the acts of Ahab, and all that he did, and the ivory house which he made, and all the cities that he built, *are* **they not written in the book of the chronicles of the kings of Israel?**	39

And Jehoshaphat made peace with the king of Israel.

CHAP.	VER.	
22	45	Now the rest of the acts of Jehoshaphat, and his might that he shewed, and how he warred, *are* they not written in the book of the chronicles of the kings of Judah ?
	12	

First Kings 66

SECOND KINGS.

CHAP.	VER.	
1	3	BUT the angel of the LORD said to Elijah the Tishbite, Arise, go up to meet the messengers of the king of Samaria, and say unto them, *Is it* **not because** *there is* **not a God in Israel,** *that* **ye go to inquire of Baal-zebub the god of Ekron ?** Now therefore thus saith the LORD, Thou shalt not come down from that bed on which thou art gone up, but shalt surely die. And Elijah departed. And when the messengers turned back unto
	5	him, he said unto them, **Why are ye now turned back ?** And they said unto him, There came a man up to meet us, and said unto us, Go, turn again unto the king that sent you, and say unto him, Thus saith the
	6	LORD, *Is it* **not because** *there is* **not a God in Israel,** *that* **thou sendest to inquire of Baal-zebub the god of Ekron ?** therefore thou shalt not come down from that bed on which thou art gone up, but shalt surely die.
	7	And he said unto them, **What manner of man** *was he* **which came up to meet you, and told you these words ?**
	16	And he said unto him, Thus saith the LORD, Forasmuch as thou hast sent messengers to inquire of Baal-zebub the god of Ekron, *is it* **not because** *there is* **no God in Israel to inquire of his word ?** therefore thou shalt not come down off that bed on which thou art gone up, but shalt surely die. So he died according to

the word of the LORD which Elijah had spoken. And Jehoram reigned in his stead in the second year of Jehoram the son of Jehoshaphat king of Judah; because he had no son. **Now the rest of the acts of Ahaziah which he did,** *are* **they not written in the book of the chronicles of the kings of Israel?**

1 18

6

And the sons of the prophets that *were* at Beth-el came forth to Elisha, and said unto him, **Knowest thou that the** LORD **will take away thy master from thy head to day?** And he said, Yea, I know *it;* hold ye your peace.

2 3

And the sons of the prophets that *were* at Jericho came to Elisha, and said unto him, **Knowest thou that the** LORD **will take away thy master from thy head to day?** And he answered, Yea, I know *it;* hold ye your peace.

5

He took up also the mantle of Elijah that fell from him, and went back, and stood by the bank of Jordan; and he took the mantle of Elijah that fell from him, and smote the waters, and said, **Where** *is* **the** LORD **God of Elijah?** and when he also had smitten the waters, they parted hither and thither. and Elisha went over.

14

And they said unto him, Behold now, there be with thy servants fifty strong men; let them go, we pray thee, and seek thy master: lest peradventure the Spirit of the LORD hath taken him up, and cast him upon some mountain, or into some valley. And he said, Ye shall not send. And when they urged him till he was ashamed, he said, Send. They sent therefore fifty men; and they sought three days, but found him not. And when they came again to him, (for he tarried at Jericho,) he said unto them, **Did I not say unto you, Go not?**

18

4

And he went and sent to Jehoshaphat the king of Judah, saying, The king of Moab hath rebelled against

CHAP	VER	
3	7	me **wilt thou go with me against Moab to battle?** And he said, I will go up: I *am* as thou *art*, my people as thy people, *and* my horses as thy horses. And he
	8	said, **Which way shall we go up?** And he answered, The way through the wilderness of Edom.

And the king of Israel said, Alas! that the LORD hath called these three kings together, to deliver them into the
11 hand of Moab! But Jehoshaphat said, *Is there* **not here a prophet of the** LORD, **that we may inquire of the** LORD **by him?** And one of the king of Israel's servants answered and said, Here *is* Elisha the son of Shaphat, which poured water on the hands of Elijah.

13 And Elisha said unto the king of Israel, **What have I to do with thee?** get thee to the prophets of thy
4 father, and to the prophets of thy mother.

4 2² And Elisha said unto her, **What shall I do for thee? tell me, what hast thou in the house?** And she said, Thine handmaid hath not any thing in the house, save a pot of oil.

And he said unto him, Say now unto her, Behold,
13² thou hast been careful for us with all this care; **what** *is* **to be done for thee? wouldest thou be spoken for to the king, or to the captain of the host?** And she answered, I dwell among mine own people.
14 And he said, **What then** *is* **to be done for her?**

23 And he said, **Wherefore wilt thou go to him to day?** *it is* neither new moon, nor sabbath. And she said, *It shall be* well.

So she went and came unto the man of God to mount Carmel. And it came to pass, when the man of God saw her afar off, that he said to Gehazi his servant, Behold, *yonder is* that Shunammite run now, I pray
26³ thee, to meet her, and say unto her, *Is it* **well with**

	CHAP.	VER.

thee? *is it* **well with thy husband?** *is it* **well with the child?** And she answered, *It is* well

Then she said, **Did I desire a son of my lord?** did I not say, **Do not deceive me?**

4 | 28[2]

And his servitor said, **What, should I set this before an hundred men?** He said again, Give the people, that they may eat· for thus saith the LORD, They shall eat, and shall leave *thereof.*

43

12

And it came to pass, when the king of Israel had read the letter, that he rent his clothes, and said, *Am* **I God, to kill and to make alive, that this man doth send unto me to recover a man of his leprosy?** wherefore consider, I pray you, and see how he seeketh a quarrel against me. And it was *so,* when Elisha the man of God had heard that the king of Israel had rent his clothes, that he sent to the king, saying, **Wherefore hast thou rent thy clothes?** let him come now to me, and he shall know that there is a prophet in Israel

5 | 7

8

Are **not Abana and Pharpar, rivers of Damascus, better than all the waters of Israel? may I not wash in them, and be clean?** So he turned and went away in a rage. And his servants came near, and spake unto him, and said, **My father,** *if* **the prophet had bid thee** *do some* **great thing, wouldest thou not have done** *it?* **how much rather then, when he saith to thee, Wash, and be clean?**

12[2]

13[2]

And Naaman said, **Shall there not then, I pray thee, be given to thy servant two mules' burden of earth?** for thy servant will henceforth offer neither burnt offering nor sacrifice unto other gods, but unto the LORD.

17

So Gehazi followed after Naaman. And when Naaman

CHAP.	VER.	
5	21	saw *him* running after him, he lighted down from the chariot to meet him, and said, *Is* **all well?**
	25	But he went in, and stood before his master. And Elisha said unto him, **Whence** *comest thou*, **Gehazi?** And he said, Thy servant went no whither. And he
	26²	said unto him, **Went not mine heart** *with thee*, **when the man turned again from his chariot to meet thee?** *Is it* **a time to receive money, and to**
	11	**receive garments, and oliveyards, and vineyards, and sheep, and oxen, and menservants, and maidservants?**
6	6	And the man of God said, **Where fell it?** And he shewed him the place. And he cut down a stick, and cast *it* in thither; and the iron did swim.
	11	Therefore the heart of the king of Syria was sore troubled for this thing; and he called his servants, and said unto them, **Will ye not shew me which of us** *is* **for the king of Israel?**
	15	And when the servant of the man of God was risen early, and gone forth, behold, an host compassed the city both with horses and chariots. And his servant said unto him, **Alas, my master! how shall we do?**
	21²	And the king of Israel said unto Elisha, when he saw them, **My father, shall I smite** *them?* **shall I smite** *them?* And he answered, Thou shalt not smite *them:*
	22	**wouldest thou smite those whom thou hast taken captive with thy sword and with thy bow?** set bread and water before them, that they may eat and drink, and go to their master.
	27²	And he said, **If the** L<small>ORD</small> **do not help thee, whence shall I help thee?** **out of the barnfloor, or out of**
	28	**the winepress?** And the king said unto her, **What aileth thee?** And she answered, This woman said

unto me, Give thy son, that we may eat him to day, and we will eat my son to morrow.

But Elisha sat in his house, and the elders sat with him; and *the king* sent a man from before him: but ere the messenger came to him, he said to the elders, **See ye how this son of a murderer hath sent to take away mine head?** look, when the messenger cometh, shut the door, and hold him fast at the door: *is* **not the sound of his master's feet behind him?** And while he yet talked with them, behold, the messenger came down unto him: and he said, Behold, this evil *is* of the LORD; **what should I wait for the** LORD **any longer?** | 6 32[2]
| 33
| 12

Then a lord on whose hand the king leaned answered the man of God, and said, **Behold,** *if* **the** LORD **would make windows in heaven, might this thing be?** And he said, Behold, thou shalt see *it* with thine eyes, but shalt not eat thereof. And there were four leprous men at the entering in of the gate: and they said one to another, **Why sit we here until we die?** | 7 2
| 3

And it came to pass as the man of God had spoken to the king, saying, Two measures of barley for a shekel, and a measure of fine flour for a shekel, shall be to morrow about this time in the gate of Samaria · and that lord answered the man of God, and said, **Now, behold,** *if* **the** LORD **should make windows in heaven, might such a thing be?** And he said, Behold, thou shalt see it with thine eyes, but shalt not eat thereof. | 19
| 3

And Elisha came to Damascus; and Ben-hadad the king of Syria was sick; and it was told him, saying, The man of God is come hither. And the king said unto Hazael, Take a present in thine hand, and go, meet the man of God, and inquire of the LORD by him, saying, **Shall I recover of this disease?** So Hazael went to | 8 8

CHAP.	VER.	
8	9	meet him, and took a present with him, even of every good thing of Damascus, forty camels' burden, and came and stood before him, and said, Thy son Ben-hadad king of Syria hath sent me to thee, saying, **Shall I recover of this disease?** And Elisha said unto him, Go, say unto him, Thou mayest certainly recover: howbeit the LORD hath shewed me that he shall surely die. And he settled his countenance stedfastly, until he was ashamed:
	12	and the man of God wept. And Hazael said, **Why weepeth my lord?** And he answered, Because I know the evil that thou wilt do unto the children of Israel: their strong holds wilt thou set on fire, and their young men wilt thou slay with the sword, and wilt dash their children, and rip up their women with child. And
	13	Hazael said, **But what, is thy servant a dog, that he should do this great thing?** And Elisha answered, The LORD hath shewed me that thou *shalt be* king over Syria. So he departed from Elisha, and came to his
	14	master; who said to him, **What said Elisha to thee?** And he answered, He told me *that* thou shouldest surely recover.
	23	**And the rest of the acts of Joram, and all that he did,** *are* **they not written in the book of the**
	6	**chronicles of the kings of Judah?**
9	5	So the young man, *even* the young man the prophet, went to Ramoth-gilead. And when he came, behold, the captains of the host *were* sitting; and he said, I have an errand to thee, O captain. And Jehu said, **Unto which of all us?** And he said, To thee, O captain.
	11[2]	Then Jehu came forth to the servants of his lord: and *one* said unto him, *Is* **all well? wherefore came this mad** *fellow* **to thee?** And he said unto them, Ye know the man, and his communication. And they said, *It is* false; tell us now. And he said, Thus and thus spake he to me, saying, Thus saith the LORD, I have anointed thee king over Israel.

SECOND KINGS:—IX., X.

	CHAP	VER

And there stood a watchman on the tower in Jezreel, and he spied the company of Jehu as he came, and said, I see a company. And Joram said, Take an horseman, and send to meet them, and let him say, *Is it* **peace ?** So there went one on horseback to meet him, and said, Thus saith the king, *Is it* **peace ?** And Jehu said, **What hast thou to do with peace ?** turn thee behind me And the watchman told, saying, The messenger came to them, but he cometh not again. Then he sent out a second on horseback, which came to them, and said, Thus saith the king, *Is it* **peace ?** And Jehu answered, **What hast thou to do with peace ?** turn thee behind me

9 17

18²

19²

———

And it came to pass, when Joram saw Jehu, that he said, *Is it* **peace, Jehu ?** And he answered, **What peace, so long as the whoredoms of thy mother Jezebel and her witchcrafts** *are so* **many ?**

22²

———

And when Jehu was come to Jezreel, Jezebel heard *of it;* and she painted her face, and tired her head, and looked out at a window. And as Jehu entered in at the gate, she said, *Had* **Zimri peace, who slew his master ?** And he lifted up his face to the window, and said, **Who** *is* **on my side ? who ?** And there looked out to him two *or* three eunuchs.

31

32²

13

———

And Ahab had seventy sons in Samaria. And Jehu wrote letters, and sent to Samaria, unto the rulers of Jezreel, to the elders, and to them that brought up Ahab's *children,* saying, Now as soon as this letter cometh to you, seeing your master's sons *are* with you, and *there are* with you chariots and horses, a fenced city also, and armour; look even out the best and meetest of your master's sons, and set *him* on his father's throne, and fight for your master's house. But they were exceedingly afraid, and said, Behold, two kings stood not before him : **how then shall we stand ?**

10 4

CHAP.	VER.	
10	9	And there came a messenger, and told him, saying, They have brought the heads of the king's sons. And he said, Lay ye them in two heaps at the entering in of the gate until the morning. And it came to pass in the morning, that he went out, and stood, and said to all the people, Ye *be* righteous: behold, I conspired against my master, and slew him: **but who slew all these?**
	13	And he arose and departed, and came to Samaria. *And* as he *was* at the shearing house in the way, Jehu met with the brethren of Ahaziah king of Judah, and said, **Who** *are* **ye?** And they answered, We *are* the brethren of Ahaziah, and we go down to salute the children of the king and the children of the queen. And he said, Take them alive. And they took them alive, and slew them at the pit of the shearing house, *even* two and forty men; neither left he any of them. And when he was departed thence, he lighted on Jehonadab the son of Rechab *coming* to meet him: and he saluted him, and
	15	said to him, **Is thine heart right, as my heart** *is* **with thy heart?** And Jehonadab answered, It is. If it be, give *me* thine hand. And he gave *him* his hand; and he took him up to him into the chariot.
	34 5	**Now the rest of the acts of Jehu, and all that he did, and all his might,** *are* **they not written in the book of the chronicles of the kings of Israel?**
12	7	Then king Jehoash called for Jehoiada the priest, and the *other* priests, and said unto them, **Why repair ye not the breaches of the house?** now therefore receive no *more* money of your acquaintance, but deliver it for the breaches of the house.
	19 2	**And the rest of the acts of Joash, and all that he did,** *are* **they not written in the book of the chronicles of the kings of Judah?**
13	8	**Now the rest of the acts of Jehoahaz, and all**

	CHAP.	VER.
that he did, and his might, *are* they not written in the book of the chronicles of the kings of Israel?		
And the rest of the acts of Joash, and all that he did, and his might wherewith he fought against Amaziah king of Judah, *are* they not written in the book of the chronicles of the kings of Israel?	13	12
		2
Thou hast indeed smitten Edom, and thine heart hath lifted thee up: glory *of this*, and tarry at home: **for why shouldest thou meddle to** *thy* **hurt, that thou shouldest fall,** *even* **thou, and Judah with thee?**	14	10
Now the rest of the acts of Jehoash which he did, and his might, and how he fought with Amaziah king of Judah, *are* **they not written in the book of the chronicles of the kings of Israel?**		15
And the rest of the acts of Amaziah, *are* they not written in the book of the chronicles of the kings of Judah?		18
Now the rest of the acts of Jeroboam, and all that he did, and his might, how he warred, and how he recovered Damascus, and Hamath, *which belonged* **to Judah, for Israel,** *are* **they not written in the book of the chronicles of the kings of Israel?**		28
		4
And the rest of the acts of Azariah, and all that he did, *are* they not written in the book of the chronicles of the kings of Judah?	15	6
And the rest of the acts of Menahem, and all that he did, *are* they not written in the book of the chronicles of the kings of Israel?		21
Now the rest of the acts of Jotham, and all that he did, *are* they not written in the book of the chronicles of the kings of Judah?		36
		3

CHAP	VER	
16	19	Now the rest of the acts of Ahaz which he did, *are* they not written in the book of the chronicles of the kings of Judah?
	1	

18	19	And Rab-shakeh said unto them, Speak ye now to Hezekiah, Thus saith the great king, the king of Assyria, **What confidence** *is* **this wherein thou trustest?** Thou sayest, (but *they are but* vain words,) *I have* counsel
	20	and strength for the war. **Now on whom dost thou trust, that thou rebellest against me?** Now, behold, thou trustest upon the staff of this bruised reed, *even* upon Egypt, on which if a man lean, it will go into his hand, and pierce it: so *is* Pharaoh king of Egypt unto all that trust on him. But if ye say unto me, We trust in the LORD our God: *is* not that He, whose high places and whose altars Hezekiah hath taken away, and
	22	hath said to Judah and Jerusalem, **Ye shall worship before this altar in Jerusalem?** Now therefore, I pray thee, give pledges to my lord the king of Assyria, and I will deliver thee two thousand horses, if thou be
	24	able on thy part to set riders upon them. **How then wilt thou turn away the face of one captain of the least of my master's servants, and put thy trust on Egypt for chariots and for horsemen?**
	25	**Am I now come up without the** LORD **against this place to destroy it?** The LORD said to me, Go up against this land, and destroy it.
	27²	But Rab-shakeh said unto them, **Hath my master sent me to thy master, and to thee, to speak these words?** *hath he* not *sent me* to the men which sit on the wall, that they may eat their own dung, and drink their own piss with you?
	33	**Hath any of the gods of the nations delivered at all his land out of the hand of the king of**
	34³	**Assyria? Where** *are* **the gods of Hamath, and of Arpad? where** *are* **the gods of Sepharvaim, Hena, and Ivah? have they delivered Samaria**

out of mine hand? **Who** *are* **they among all the gods of the countries, that have delivered their country out of mine hand, that the** Lord **should deliver Jerusalem out of mine hand?**

CHAP	VER
18	35
	12

Thus shall ye speak to Hezekiah king of Judah, saying, Let not thy God in whom thou trustest deceive thee, saying, Jerusalem shall not be delivered into the hand of the king of Assyria. Behold, thou hast heard what the kings of Assyria have done to all lands, by destroying them utterly: **and shalt thou be delivered? Have the gods of the nations delivered them which my fathers have destroyed;** *as* **Gozan, and Haran, and Rezeph, and the children of Eden which** *were* **in Thelasar? Where** *is* **the king of Hamath, and the king of Arpad, and the king of the city of Sepharvaim, of Hena, and Ivah?**

19	11
	12
	13

Then Isaiah the son of Amoz sent to Hezekiah, saying, Thus saith the Lord God of Israel, *That* which thou hast prayed to me against Sennacherib king of Assyria I have heard. This *is* the word that the Lord hath spoken concerning him, The virgin the daughter of Zion hath despised thee, *and* laughed thee to scorn; the daughter of Jerusalem hath shaken her head at thee. **Whom hast thou reproached and blasphemed? and against whom hast thou exalted** *thy* **voice, and lifted up thine eyes on high?** *even* against the Holy *One* of Israel.

	22[2]

I have digged and drunk strange waters, and with the sole of my feet have I dried up all the rivers of besieged places. **Hast thou not heard long ago** *how* **I have done it,** *and* **of ancient times that I have formed it?** now have I brought it to pass, that thou shouldest be to lay waste fenced cities *into* ruinous heaps.

	25
	6

And Hezekiah said unto Isaiah, **What** *shall be* **the sign that the** Lord **will heal me, and that I shall**

20	8

CHAP.	VER	
20	9	go up into the house of the LORD the third day? And Isaiah said, This sign shalt thou have of the LORD, that the LORD will do the thing that He hath spoken: **shall the shadow go forward ten degrees, or go back ten degrees?**
	14[2]	Then came Isaiah the prophet unto king Hezekiah, and said unto him, **What said these men? and from whence came they unto thee?** And Hezekiah said, They are come from a far country, *even* from Babylon.
	15	And he said, **What have they seen in thine house?** And Hezekiah answered, All *the things* that *are* in mine house have they seen: there is nothing among my treasures that I have not shewed them.
	19 20 7	Then said Hezekiah unto Isaiah, Good *is* the word of the LORD which thou hast spoken. And he said, *Is it* not *good*, **if peace and truth be in my days?** And the rest of the acts of Hezekiah, and all his might, and how he made a pool, and a conduit, and brought water into the city, *are* they not written in the book of the chronicles of the kings of Judah?
21	17	Now the rest of the acts of Manasseh, and all that he did, and his sin that he sinned, *are* they not written in the book of the chronicles of the kings of Judah?
	25 2	Now the rest of the acts of Amon which he did, *are* they not written in the book of the chronicles of the kings of Judah?
23	17	And as Josiah turned himself, he spied the sepulchres that *were* there in the mount, and sent, and took the bones out of the sepulchres, and burned *them* upon the altar, and polluted it, according to the word of the LORD which the man of God proclaimed, who proclaimed these words. Then he said, **What title *is* that that I see?**

And the men of the city told him, *It is* the sepulchre of the man of God, which came from Judah, and proclaimed these things that thou hast done against the altar of Beth-el. And he said, Let him alone ; let no man move his bones. So they let his bones alone, with the bones of the prophet that came out of Samaria.

Now the rest of the acts of Josiah, and all that he did, *are* **they not written in the book of the chronicles of the kings of Judah ?**   23   28
    2

Now the rest of the acts of Jehoiakim, and all that he did, *are* **they not written in the book of the chronicles of the kings of Judah ?**   24   5
    1

Second Kings 118

FIRST CHRONICLES.

NOW three of the thirty captains went down to the rock to David, into the cave of Adullam ; and the host of the Philistines encamped in the valley of Rephaim. And David *was* then in the hold, and the Philistines' garrison *was* then at Beth-lehem. And David longed, and said, Oh that one would give me drink of the water of the well of Beth-lehem, that *is* at the gate ! And the three brake through the host of the Philistines, and drew water out of the well of Beth-lehem, that *was* by the gate, and took *it*, and brought *it* to David : but David would not drink *of* it, but poured it out to the LORD, and said, My God forbid it me, that I should do this thing : **shall I drink the blood of these men that have put their lives in jeopardy ?** for with *the jeopardy of* their lives they brought it. Therefore he would not drink it.   11   19
    1

CHAP.	VER.	
13	12	And David was afraid of God that day, saying, **How shall I bring the ark of God** *home* **to me?** So David brought not the ark *home* to himself to the city of David, but carried it aside into the house of Obed-edom the Gittite.
	1	
14	10²	And David inquired of God, saying, **Shall I go up against the Philistines? and wilt Thou deliver them into mine hand?** And the LORD said unto him, Go up; for I will deliver them into thine hand.
	2	
17	6	Wheresoever I have walked with all Israel, spake I a word to any of the judges of Israel, whom I commanded to feed My people, saying, **Why have ye not built Me an house of cedars?**
	16	And David the king came and sat before the LORD, and said, **Who** *am* **I, O** LORD **God, and what** *is* **mine house, that Thou hast brought me hitherto?**
	18	**What can David** *speak* **more to Thee for the honour of Thy servant?** for Thou knowest Thy servant.
	21	**And what one nation in the earth** *is* **like Thy people Israel, whom God went to redeem** *to be* **His own people, to make Thee a name of greatness and terribleness, by driving out nations from before Thy people, whom Thou hast redeemed out of Egypt?**
	4	
19	3²	But the princes of the children of Ammon said to Hanun, **Thinkest thou that David doth honour thy father, that he hath sent comforters unto thee? are not his servants come unto thee for to search, and to overthrow, and to spy out the land?**
	2	

And Satan stood up against Israel, and provoked David

FIRST CHRONICLES:—XXI.-XXIX.

	CHAP	VER.
to number Israel. And David said to Joab and to the rulers of the people, Go, number Israel from Beer-sheba even to Dan, and bring the number of them to me, that I may know *it*. And Joab answered, The LORD make his people an hundred times so many more as they *be* **but, my lord the king,** *are* **they not all my lord's servants? why then doth my lord require this thing? why will he be a cause of trespass to Israel?** | **21** | 3³

And David said unto God, *Is it* **not I** *that* **commanded the people to be numbered?** even I it is that have sinned and done evil indeed; **but** *as for* **these sheep, what have they done?** let Thine hand, I pray thee, O LORD my God, be on me, and on my father's house; but not on Thy people, that they should be plagued. | | 17²

| | | 5 |

David also commanded all the princes of Israel to help Solomon his son, *saying,* **Is not the** LORD **your God with you? and hath He** *not* **given you rest on every side?** for He hath given the inhabitants of the land into mine hand; and the land is subdued before the LORD, and before His people. Now set your heart and your soul to seek the LORD your God; arise therefore, and build ye the sanctuary of the LORD God. | **22** | 18²

| | | 2 |

Moreover, because I have set my affection to the house of my God, I have of mine own proper good, of gold and silver, *which* I have given to the house of my God, over and above all that I have prepared for the holy house, *even* three thousand talents of gold, of the gold of Ophir, and seven thousand talents of refined silver, to overlay the walls of the houses *withal*: the gold for *things* of gold, and the silver for *things* of silver, and for all manner of work *to be made* by the hands of artificers. **And who** *then* **is willing to consecrate his service this day unto the** LORD? | **29** | 5

Now, therefore, our God, we thank Thee, and praise

CHAP.	VER.	
29	14	Thy glorious name. **But who** *am* **I, and what** *is* **my people, that we should be able to offer so willingly after this sort?** for all things *come* of Thee, and of Thine own have we given Thee.
	2	

First Chronicles 19

SECOND CHRONICLES.

CHAP.	VER.	
1	10	NOW, O LORD God, let Thy promise unto David my father be established for Thou hast made me king over a people like the dust of the earth in multitude. Give me now wisdom and knowledge, that I may go out and come in before this people · **for who can judge this Thy people,** *that is so* **great?**
	1	
2	6²	And the house which I build *is* great : for great *is* our God above all gods. **But who is able to build Him an house, seeing the heaven and heaven of heavens cannot contain Him?** who *am* **I then, that I should build Him an house, save only to burn sacrifice before Him?**
	2	
6	18	**But will God in very deed dwell with men on the earth?** behold, heaven and the heaven of heavens cannot contain Thee; how much less this house which I have built!
	1	
7	21	And this house, which is high, shall be an astonishment to every one that passeth by it; so that he shall say, **Why hath the** LORD **done thus unto this land, and unto this house?**
	1	
9	29	Now the rest of the acts of Solomon, first and last, *are* they not written in the book of Nathan the prophet, and in the prophecy of Ahijah the
	1	

SECOND CHRONICLES —X.-XIII.

	CHAP.	VER.
Shilonite, and in the visions of Iddo the seer against Jeroboam the son of Nebat?		
And king Rehoboam took counsel with the old men that had stood before Solomon his father while he yet lived, saying, **What counsel give ye** *me* **to return answer to this people?**	10	6
And he said unto them, **What advice give ye that we may return answer to this people, which have spoken to me, saying, Ease somewhat the yoke that thy father did put upon us?**		9
And when all Israel *saw* that the king would not hearken unto them, the people answered the king, saying, **What portion have we in David?** and *we have* none inheritance in the son of Jesse: every man to your tents, O Israel: *and* now, David, see to thine own house. So all Israel went to their tents.		16
		3
Now the acts of Rehoboam, first and last, *are* **they not written in the book of Shemaiah the prophet, and of Iddo the seer concerning genealogies?** And *there were* wars between Rehoboam and Jeroboam continually.	12	15
		1
And Abijah stood up upon mount Zemaraim, which *is* in mount Ephraim, and said, Hear me, thou Jeroboam, and all Israel, **Ought ye not to know that the** LORD **God of Israel gave the kingdom over Israel to David for ever,** *even* **to him and to his sons by a covenant of salt?**	13	5
Have ye not cast out the priests of the LORD, **the sons of Aaron, and the Levites, and have made you priests after the manner of the nations of** *other* **lands?** so that whosoever cometh to consecrate himself with a young bullock and seven rams, *the same* may be a priest of *them that are* no gods.		9
		2

CHAP	VER	
16	8	**Were not the Ethiopians and the Lubims a huge host, with very many chariots and horse-**
	1	**men?** yet, because thou didst rely on the LORD, He delivered them into thine hand
18	3	And Ahab king of Israel said unto Jehoshaphat king of Judah, **Wilt thou go with me to Ramoth-gilead?** And he answered him, I *am* as thou *art*, and my people as thy people; and *we will be* with thee in the war.
	5	Therefore the king of Israel gathered together of prophets four hundred men, and said unto them, **Shall we go to Ramoth-gilead to battle, or shall I forbear?** And they said, Go up: for God will deliver *it* into the
	6	king's hand. But Jehoshaphat said, *Is there* **not here a prophet of the** LORD **besides, that we might inquire of him?**
	14	And Micaiah said, *As* the LORD liveth, even what my God saith, that will I speak. And when he was come to the king, the king said unto him, **Micaiah, shall we go to Ramoth-gilead to battle, or shall I forbear?** And he said, Go ye up, and prosper, and they shall be delivered into your hand. And the king said to him,
	15	**How many times shall I adjure thee that thou say nothing but the truth to me in the name of the** LORD? Then he said, I did see all Israel scattered upon the mountains, as sheep that have no shepherd. and the LORD said, These have no master; let them return *therefore* every man to his house in peace. And the king of
	17	Israel said to Jehoshaphat, **Did I not tell thee** *that* **he would not prophesy good unto me, but evil?** Again he said, Therefore hear the word of the LORD; I saw the LORD sitting upon His throne, and all the host of heaven standing on His right hand and *on* His left. And
	19	the LORD said, **Who shall entice Ahab king of Israel, that he may go up and fall at Ramoth-gilead?** And one spake saying after this manner, and another saying after that manner. Then there came out

SECOND CHRONICLES:—XVIII.-XXIV.

	CHAP	VER.
a spirit, and stood before the Lord, and said, I will entice him. And the Lord said unto him, **Wherewith?**	18	20
Then Zedekiah the son of Chenaanah came near, and smote Micaiah upon the cheek, and said, **Which way went the Spirit of the** Lord **from me to speak unto thee?**		23
		9
And Jehu the son of Hanani the seer went out to meet him, and said to king Jehoshaphat, **Shouldest thou help the ungodly, and love them that hate the** Lord? therefore *is* wrath upon thee from before the Lord.	19	2
		1
And Jehoshaphat stood in the congregation of Judah and Jerusalem, in the house of the Lord, before the new court, and said, **O** Lord **God of our fathers,** *art* not **Thou God in heaven?** **and rulest** *not* **Thou over all the kingdoms of the heathen? and in Thine hand** *is there not* **power and might, so that none is able to withstand Thee?** *Art* not **Thou our God,** *who* **didst drive out the inhabitants of this land before Thy people Israel, and gavest it to the seed of Abraham Thy friend for ever?**	20	6³
		7
O our God, wilt Thou not judge them? for we have no might against this great company that cometh against us; neither know we what to do: but our eyes *are* upon Thee.		12
		5
And it came to pass after this, *that* Joash was minded to repair the house of the Lord. And he gathered together the priests and the Levites, and said to them, Go out unto the cities of Judah, and gather of all Israel money to repair the house of your God from year to year, and see that ye hasten the matter. Howbeit the Levites hastened *it* not. And the king called for Jehoiada the chief, and said unto him, **Why hast thou not required of the Levites to bring in out of Judah and out of**	24	6

CHAP.	VER.	
		Jerusalem the collection, *according to the commandment* of Moses the servant of the LORD, and of the congregation of Israel, for the tabernacle of witness?
24	20	And the Spirit of God came upon Zechariah the son of Jehoiada the priest, which stood above the people, and said unto them, Thus saith God, **Why transgress ye the commandments of the** LORD, **that ye cannot**
	2	**prosper?** because ye have forsaken the LORD, He hath also forsaken you.
25	9	And Amaziah said to the man of God, **But what shall we do for the hundred talents which I have given to the army of Israel?** And the man of God answered, The LORD is able to give thee much more than this.
	15	Wherefore the anger of the LORD was kindled against Amaziah, and He sent unto him a prophet, which said unto him, **Why hast thou sought after the gods of the people, which could not deliver their own people out of thine hand?** And it came to pass, as he talked with him, that *the king* said unto him,
	16[2]	**Art thou made of the king's counsel?** forbear; **why shouldest thou be smitten?** Then the prophet forbare, and said, I know that God hath determined to destroy thee, because thou hast done this, and hast not hearkened unto my counsel.
	19	Thou sayest, Lo, thou hast smitten the Edomites; and thine heart lifteth thee up to boast: abide now at home; **why shouldest thou meddle to** *thine* **hurt, that thou shouldest fall,** *even* **thou, and Judah with thee?**
	26	**Now the rest of the acts of Amaziah, first and last, behold,** *are* **they not written in the book of**
	6	**the kings of Judah and Israel?**

	CHAP.	VER.
And now ye purpose to keep under the children of Judah and Jerusalem for bondmen and bondwomen unto you: *but are there* **not with you, even with you, sins against the** LORD **your God?**	28	10
		1
So there was gathered much people together, who stopped all the fountains, and the brook that ran through the midst of the land, saying, **Why should the kings of Assyria come, and find much water?**	32	4
Thus saith Sennacherib king of Assyria, **Whereon do ye trust, that ye abide in the siege in Jerusalem? Doth not Hezekiah persuade you to give over yourselves to die by famine and by thirst, saying, The** LORD **our God shall deliver us out of the hand of the king of Assyria?** Hath not the same Hezekiah taken away his high places and his altars, and commanded Judah and Jerusalem, saying, **Ye shall worship before one altar, and burn incense upon it? Know ye not what I and my fathers have done unto all the people of** *other* **lands? were the gods of the nations of those lands any ways able to deliver their lands out of mine hand? Who** *was there* **among all the gods of those nations that my fathers utterly destroyed, that could deliver his people out of mine hand, that your God should be able to deliver you out of mine hand?** Now therefore let not Hezekiah deceive you, nor persuade you on this manner, neither yet believe him: for no god of any nation or kingdom was able to deliver his people out of mine hand, and out of the hand of my fathers: **how much less shall your God deliver you out of mine hand?**		10
		11
		12
		13a
		14
		15
		8
After all this, when Josiah had prepared the temple, Necho king of Egypt came up to fight against Charchemish by Euphrates: and Josiah went out against him. But he sent ambassadors to him, saying, **What have I to do with thee, thou king of Judah?** *I*	35	21
		1

CHAP.	VER.	
		come not against thee this day, but against the house wherewith I have war: for God commanded me to make haste: forbear thee from *meddling with* God, who *is* with me, that He destroy thee not.
36	23	Thus saith Cyrus king of Persia, All the kingdoms of the earth hath the LORD God of heaven given me; and He hath charged me to build Him an house in Jerusalem, which *is* in Judah. **Who** *is there* **among you of all His people?** The LORD his God *be* with him, and let
	1	him go up.

Second Chronicles 47

EZRA.

CHAP	VER.	
1	3	**WHO** *is there* **among you of all His people?** his God be with him, and let him go up to Jerusalem,
	1	which *is* in Judah, and build the house of the LORD God of Israel, (He is the God,) which *is* in Jerusalem.
4	22	Give ye now commandment to cause these men to cease, and that this city be not builded, until *another* commandment shall be given from me. Take heed now that ye fail not to do this. **why should damage grow**
	1	**to the hurt of the kings?**
5	3	At the same time came to them Tatnai, governor on this side the river, and Shethar-boznai, and their companions, and said thus unto them, **Who hath commanded you to build this house, and to make up this wall?** Then said we unto them after this manner,
	4	**What are the names of the men that make this building?**

Then asked we those elders, *and* said unto them thus,

	CHAP.	VER.
Who commanded you to build this house, and to make up these walls?	5	9
		3
Whatsoever is commanded by the God of heaven, let it be diligently done for the house of the God of heaven: **for why should there be wrath against the realm of the king and his sons?**	7	23
		1
And now, O our God, **what shall we say after this?** for we have forsaken Thy commandments, which Thou hast commanded by Thy servants the prophets, saying, The land, unto which ye go to possess it, is an unclean land with the filthiness of the people of the lands, with their abominations, which have filled it from one end to another with their uncleanness.	9	10
And after all that is come upon us for our evil deeds, and for our great trespass, seeing that Thou our God hast punished us less than our iniquities *deserve*, and hast given us *such* deliverance as this; **should we again break Thy commandments, and join in affinity with the people of these abominations? wouldest not Thou be angry with us till Thou hadst consumed** *us,* **so that** *there should be* **no remnant nor escaping?** O LORD God of Israel, Thou *art* righteous for we remain yet escaped, as *it is* this day: behold, we *are* before Thee in our trespasses: for we cannot stand before Thee because of this.		14²
		3
	Ezra 9	

NEHEMIAH.

	CHAP.	VER.
WHEREFORE the king said unto me, **Why** *is* **thy countenance sad, seeing thou** *art* **not sick?** this *is* nothing *else* but sorrow of heart. Then I was very sore afraid, and said unto the king, Let the king	2	2

CHAP	VER	
2	3	live for ever. **why should not my countenance be sad, when the city, the place of my fathers' sepulchres,** *lieth* **waste, and the gates thereof are consumed with fire?** Then the king said unto me,
	4	**For what dost thou make request?** So I prayed to the God of heaven.
	6²	And the king said unto me, (the queen also sitting by him,) **For how long shall thy journey be? and when wilt thou return?** So it pleased the king to send me; and I set him a time.
	19²	But when Sanballat the Horonite, and Tobiah the servant, the Ammonite, and Geshem the Arabian, heard *it,* they laughed us to scorn, and despised us, and said, **What** *is* **this thing that ye do? will ye rebel
	7	against the king?**
4	2⁵	But it came to pass, that when Sanballat heard that we builded the wall, he was wroth, and took great indignation, and mocked the Jews. And he spake before his brethren and the army of Samaria, and said, **What do these feeble Jews? will they fortify themselves?**
	5	**will they sacrifice? will they make an end in a day? will they revive the stones out of the heaps of the rubbish which are burned?**
5	8²	And I said unto them, We after our ability have redeemed our brethren the Jews, which were sold unto the heathen, **and will ye even sell your brethren? or shall they be sold unto us?** Then held they their peace, and found nothing *to answer.* Also I said, It *is*
	9	not good that ye do: **ought ye not to walk in the fear of our God because of the reproach of the
	3	heathen our enemies?**

Sanballat and Geshem sent unto me, saying, Come, let us meet together in *some one of* the villages in the plain of Ono. But they thought to do me mischief. And I

NEHEMIAH :--VI., XIII.

	CHAP.	VER.
sent messengers unto them, saying, I *am* doing a great work, so that I cannot come down : **why should the work cease, whilst I leave it, and come down to you ?**	**6**	3
And I said, **Should such a man as I flee ? and who** *is there*, **that,** *being* **as I** *am*, **would go into the temple to save his life ?** I will not go in.		11² 3
Then contended I with the rulers, and said, **Why is the house of God forsaken ?** And I gathered them together, and set them in their place.	**13**	11
Then I contended with the nobles of Judah, and said unto them, **What evil thing** *is* **this that ye do, and profane the sabbath day ? Did not your fathers thus, and did not our God bring all this evil upon us, and upon this city ?** yet ye bring more wrath upon Israel by profaning the sabbath.		17 18
Then I testified against them, and said unto them, **Why lodge ye about the wall ?** if ye do *so* again, I will lay hands on you. From that time forth came they no *more* on the sabbath.		21
Did not Solomon king of Israel sin by these things ? yet among many nations was there no king like him, who was beloved of his God, and God made him king over all Israel : nevertheless even him did outlandish women cause to sin. **Shall we then hearken unto you to do all this great evil, to transgress against our God in marrying strange wives ?**		26 27 6

Nehemiah 24

ESTHER.

CHAP.	VER.	

1 15
—
1

THEN the king said to the wise men, which knew the times, (for so *was* the king's manner toward all that knew law and judgment: and the next unto him *was* Carshena, Shethar, Admatha, Tarshish, Meres, Marsena, *and* Memucan, the seven princes of Persia and Media, which saw the king's face, *and* which sat the first in the kingdom:) **What shall we do unto the queen Vashti according to law, because she hath not performed the commandment of the king Ahasuerus by the chamberlains?**

3 3
—
1

Then the king's servants, which *were* in the king's gate, said unto Mordecai, **Why transgressest thou the king's commandment?**

4 14
—
1

And they told to Mordecai Esther's words. Then Mordecai commanded to answer Esther, Think not with thyself that thou shalt escape in the king's house, more than all the Jews. For if thou altogether holdest thy peace at this time, *then* shall there enlargement and deliverance arise to the Jews from another place; but thou and thy father's house shall be destroyed: **and who knoweth whether thou art come to the kingdom for** *such* **a time as this?**

5 3²

Then said the king unto her, **What wilt thou, queen Esther? and what** *is* **thy request?** it shall be even given thee, to the half of the kingdom.

6²
—
4

And the king said unto Esther at the banquet of wine, **What** *is* **thy petition?** and it shall be granted thee: **and what** *is* **thy request?** even to the half of the kingdom it shall be performed.

And it was found written, that Mordecai had told of

Bıgthana and Teresh, two of the king's chamberlains, the keepers of the door, who sought to lay hand on the king Ahasuerus. And the king said, **What honour and dignity hath been done to Mordecai for this?** Then said the king's servants that ministered unto him, There is nothing done for him. And the king said, **Who is in the court?** Now Haman was come into the outward court of the king's house, to speak unto the king to hang Mordecai on the gallows that he had prepared for him. And the king's servants said unto him, Behold, Haman standeth in the court. And the king said, Let him come in. So Haman came in. And the king said unto him, **What shall be done unto the man whom the king delighteth to honour?** Now Haman thought in his heart, **To whom would the king delight to do honour more than to myself?**

CHAP.	VER.
6	3
	4
	6²
	4

So the king and Haman came to banquet with Esther the queen. And the king said again unto Esther on the second day at the banquet of wine, **What is thy petition, queen Esther?** and it shall be granted thee: and **what is thy request?** and it shall be performed, *even* to the half of the kingdom.

| 7 | 2² |

Then the king Ahasuerus answered and said unto Esther the queen, **Who is he, and where is he, that durst presume in his heart to do so?** And Esther said, The adversary and enemy *is* this wicked Haman. Then Haman was afraid before the king and the queen. and the king arising from the banquet of wine in his wrath *went* into the palace garden: and Haman stood up to make request for his life to Esther the queen; for he saw that there was evil determined against him by the king. Then the king returned out of the palace garden into the place of the banquet of wine; and Haman was fallen upon the bed whereon Esther *was.* Then said the king, **Will he force the queen also before me in the house?** As the word went out of the king's mouth, they covered Haman's face.

	5
8	
	4

CHAP.	VER.	
8	6²	Then the king held out the golden sceptre toward Esther. So Esther arose, and stood before the king, and said, If it please the king, and if I have found favour in his sight, and the thing *seem* right before the king, and I *be* pleasing in his eyes, let it be written to reverse the letters devised by Haman the son of Hammedatha the Agagite, which he wrote to destroy the Jews which *are* in all the king's provinces: **for how can I endure to see the evil that shall come unto my people?** or **how can I endure to see the destruction of my kindred?**
	2	
9	12³	And the king said unto Esther the queen, The Jews have slain and destroyed five hundred men in Shushan the palace, and the ten sons of Haman; **what have they done in the rest of the king's provinces? now what** *is* **thy petition?** and it shall be granted thee: or **what** *is* **thy request further?** and it shall be done.
	3	
10	2	And the king Ahasuerus laid a tribute upon the land, and *upon* the isles of the sea. **And all the acts of his power and of his might, and the declaration of the greatness of Mordecai, whereunto the king advanced him,** *are* **they not written in the book of the chronicles of the kings of Media and Persia?** For Mordecai the Jew *was* next unto king Ahasuerus, and great among the Jews, and accepted of the multitude of his brethren, seeking the wealth of his people, and speaking peace to all his seed.
	1	

Esther 21

JOB.

	CHAP.	VER.

NOW there was a day when the sons of God came to present themselves before the LORD, and Satan came also among them. And the LORD said unto Satan, **Whence comest thou?** Then Satan answered the LORD, and said, From going to and fro in the earth, and from walking up and down in it. And the LORD said unto Satan, **Hast thou considered My servant Job, that** *there is* **none like him in the earth, a perfect and an upright man, one that feareth God, and escheweth evil?** Then Satan answered the LORD, and said, **Doth Job fear God for nought? Hast not Thou made an hedge about him, and about his house, and about all that he hath on every side?** Thou hast blessed the work of his hands, and his substance is increased in the land. — 1 7, 8, 9, 10, 4

And the LORD said unto Satan, **From whence comest thou?** And Satan answered the LORD, and said, From going to and fro in the earth, and from walking up and down in it. And the LORD said unto Satan, **Hast thou considered My servant Job, that** *there is* **none like him in the earth, a perfect and an upright man, one that feareth God, and escheweth evil?** and still he holdeth fast his integrity, although thou movedst Me against him, to destroy him without cause. — 2 2, 3

Then said his wife unto him, **Dost thou still retain thine integrity?** curse God, and die. But he said unto her, Thou speakest as one of the foolish women speaketh. **What? shall we receive good at the hand of God, and shall we not receive evil?** In all this did not Job sin with his lips. — 9, 10ᶜ, 5

Why died I not from the womb? *why* **did I** *not* **give up the ghost when I came out of the belly?** — 3 11²

CHAP.	VER
3	12²

Why did the knees prevent me? or why the breasts that I should suck? For now should I have lain still and been quiet, I should have slept: then had I been at rest.

20   **Wherefore is light given to him that is in misery, and life unto the bitter** *in* **soul; which long for death, but it** *cometh* **not; and dig for it more than for hid treasures; which rejoice exceedingly,** *and*

23   **are glad, when they can find the grave?** *Why is*

6   *light given* **to a man whose way is hid, and whom God hath hedged in?**

4   2²   Then Eliphaz the Temanite answered and said, *If* **we assay to commune with thee, wilt thou be grieved? but who can withhold himself from speaking?**

6   *Is* **not** *this* **thy fear, thy confidence, thy hope,**

7²   **and the uprightness of thy ways? Remember, I pray thee, who** *ever* **perished, being innocent? or where were the righteous cut off?**

   Then a spirit passed before my face; the hair of my flesh stood up: it stood still, but I could not discern the form thereof: an image *was* before mine eyes, *there was*

17²   silence, and I heard a voice, *saying*, **Shall mortal man be more just than God? shall a man be more pure than his Maker?** Behold, He put no trust in

19   His servants; and His angels He charged with folly: **how much less** *in* **them that dwell in houses of clay, whose foundation** *is* **in the dust,** *which* **are crushed before the moth?** They are destroyed from morning to evening: they perish for ever without any regarding

21   *it*   **Doth not their excellency** *which is* **in them go**

9   **away?** they die, even without wisdom.

5   1   Call now, if there be any that will answer thee; and

1   **to which of the saints wilt thou turn?**

JOB:—VI., VII. 119

	CHAP.	VER
Doth the wild ass bray when he hath grass? or loweth the ox over his fodder? Can that which is unsavoury be eaten without salt? or is there *any* taste in the white of an egg?	6	5² 6²
What *is* my strength, that I should hope? and what *is* mine end, that I should prolong my life? Is my strength the strength of stones? or *is* my flesh of brass? *Is* not my help in me? and is wisdom driven quite from me?		11² 12² 13²
Did I say, Bring unto me? or, Give a reward for me of your substance? or, Deliver me from the enemy's hand? or, Redeem me from the hand of the mighty? Teach me, and I will hold my tongue: and cause me to understand wherein I have erred. How forcible are right words! but what doth your arguing reprove? Do ye imagine to reprove words, and the speeches of one that is desperate, *which are* as wind?		22² 23² 25 26
Is there iniquity in my tongue? cannot my taste discern perverse things?		30² 18
Is there not an appointed time to man upon earth? *are not* his days also like the days of an hireling?	7	1²
When I lie down, I say, When shall I arise, and the night be gone? and I am full of tossings to and fro unto the dawning of the day.		4
Am I a sea, or a whale, that Thou settest a watch over me?		12
What *is* man, that Thou shouldest magnify him? and that Thou shouldest set Thine heart upon him? And *that* Thou shouldest visit him every morning, *and* try him every moment? How long		17² 18 19

CHAP.	VER.	
7	20²	wilt Thou not depart from me, nor let me alone till I swallow down my spittle? I have sinned; what shall I do unto Thee, O Thou Preserver of men? why hast Thou set me as a mark against
	21	Thee, so that I am a burden to myself? And why dost Thou not pardon my transgression, and
	11	take away mine iniquity? for now shall I sleep in the dust; and Thou shalt seek me in the morning, but I *shall* not *be*.
8	2²	Then answered Bildad the Shuhite, and said, How long wilt thou speak these *things?* and *how long shall* the words of thy mouth *be like* a strong
	3²	wind? Doth God pervert judgment? or doth the Almighty pervert justice?
	10	Shall not they teach thee, *and* tell thee, and
	11²	utter words out of their heart? Can the rush
	7	grow up without mire? can the flag grow without water?
9	2	Then Job answered and said, I know *it is* so of a truth: but how should man be just with God? If He will contend with him, he cannot answer Him one of a thousand. *He is* wise in heart, and mighty in
	4	strength: who hath hardened *himself* against Him, and hath prospered?
	12²	Behold, He taketh away, who can hinder Him? who will say unto Him, What doest Thou? *If* God will not withdraw His anger, the proud helpers do
	14	stoop under Him. How much less shall I answer Him, *and* choose out my words *to reason* with Him?
	19	If *I speak* of strength, lo *He is* strong: and if of judgment, who shall set me a time *to plead?*
	24	The earth is given into the hand of the wicked: he covereth the faces of the judges thereof; if not, where, *and* who *is* He?

	CHAP	VER.
If **I be wicked, why then labour I in vain?**	9	29
		8
Is it **good unto Thee that Thou shouldest oppress, that Thou shouldest despise the work of Thine hands, and shine upon the counsel of the wicked? Hast Thou eyes of flesh? or seest Thou as man seeth?** *Are* **Thy days as the days of man?** *are* **Thy years as man's days, that Thou inquirest after mine iniquity, and searchest after my sin?**	10	3
		4^2
		5^2
Remember, I beseech Thee, that Thou hast made me as the clay; and **wilt Thou bring me into dust again? Hast Thou not poured me out as milk, and curdled me like cheese?**		9
		10
Wherefore then hast Thou brought me forth out of the womb? Oh that I had given up the ghost, and no eye had seen me! I should have been as though I had not been; I should have been carried from the womb to the grave. *Are* **not my days few?** cease *then, and* let me alone, that I may take comfort a little, before I go *whence* I shall not return, *even* to the land of darkness and the shadow of death; a land of darkness, as darkness *itself; and* of the shadow of death, without any order, and *where* the light *is* as darkness.		18
		20
		9
Then answered Zophar the Naamathite, and said, **Should not the multitude of words be answered? and should a man full of talk be justified? Should thy lies make men hold their peace?** and **when thou mockest, shall no man make thee ashamed?**	11	2^2
		3^2
Canst thou by searching find out God? canst thou find out the Almighty unto perfection? *It is* as high as heaven, **what canst thou do?** deeper than hell; **what canst thou know?** The measure thereof *is* longer than the earth, and broader than the		7^2
		8^2

CHAP.	VER.	
11	10	sea. **If He cut off, and shut up, or gather together, then who can hinder Him?** For He knoweth vain
	11	men: He seeth wickedness also; **will He not then**
	10	**consider** *it?*

And Job answered and said, No doubt but ye *are* the people. and wisdom shall die with you. But I have understanding as well as you; I *am* not inferior to you:
yea, who knoweth not such things as these?

12   3

9   **Who knoweth not in all these that the hand of the** LORD **hath wrought this?** in whose hand *is* the soul of every living thing, and the breath of all mankind   **Doth not the ear try words? and the mouth taste His meat?**

11²
4

13   7²   **Will ye speak wickedly for God? and talk deceitfully for Him? Will ye accept His person?**
8²
9²   **will ye contend for God? Is it good that He should search you out?** or as one man mocketh another, do ye *so* mock Him? He will surely reprove you, if ye do secretly accept persons   **Shall not His excellency make you afraid? and His dread fall upon you?**

11²

14   **Wherefore do I take my flesh in my teeth, and put my life in mine hand?** Though He slay me, yet will I trust in Him: but I will maintain mine own ways before Him.

19   **Who** *is* **he** *that* **will plead with me?** for now, if I hold my tongue, I shall give up the ghost.

23   **How many** *are* **mine iniquities and sins?** make
24   me to know my transgression and my sin. **Wherefore hidest Thou Thy face, and holdest me for Thine**
25²   **enemy? Wilt Thou break a leaf driven to and**
14   **fro? and wilt Thou pursue the dry stubble?**

JOB :—XIV., XV.

	CHAP.	VER
Man *that is* born of a woman *is* of few days, and full of trouble. He cometh forth like a flower, and is cut down: he fleeth also as a shadow, and continueth not. And **dost Thou open Thine eyes upon such an one, and bringest me into judgment with Thee? Who can bring a clean** *thing* **out of an unclean?** not one.	14	3 4
For there is hope of a tree, if it be cut down, that it will sprout again, and that the tender branch thereof will not cease. Though the root thereof wax old in the earth, and the stock thereof die in the ground; *yet* through the scent of water it will bud, and bring forth boughs like a plant. But man dieth, and wasteth away: yea, man giveth up the ghost, **and where** *is* **he?**		10
If a man die, shall he live *again?* all the days of my appointed time will I wait, till my change come.		14
For now Thou numberest my steps: **dost Thou not watch over my sin?**		16
		5
Should a wise man utter vain knowledge, and fill his belly with the east wind? Should he reason with unprofitable talk? or with speeches wherewith he can do no good?	15	2 3²
Art **thou the first man** *that* **was born? or wast thou made before the hills? Hast thou heard the secret of God? and dost thou restrain wisdom to thyself? What knowest thou, that we know not?** *what* **understandest thou, which** *is* **not in us?** With us *are* both the gray-headed and very aged men, much elder than thy father. *Are* **the consolations of God small with thee? is there any secret thing with thee? Why doth thine heart carry thee away?** **and what do thy eyes wink at, that thou turnest thy spirit against God, and lettest** *such* **words go out of thy mouth? What** *is* **man,**		7² 8² 9² 11² 12² 14²

CHAP	VER	
15	16	that he should be clean ? and *he which is* born of a woman, that he should be righteous ? Behold, He putteth no trust in His saints; yea, the heavens are not clean in His sight. How much more abominable and filthy *is* man, which drinketh iniquity like water ?
	23	He wandereth abroad for bread, *saying*, Where *is it ?* he knoweth that the day of darkness is ready at his hand.
	17	
16	3²	Then Job answered and said, I have heard many such things. miserable comforters *are* ye all Shall vain words have an end ? or what emboldeneth thee that thou answerest ?
	6	Though I speak, my grief is not asswaged . and *though* I forbear, what am I eased ?
17	3	
	2²	My breath is corrupt, my days are extinct, the graves *are ready* for me. *Are there* not mockers with me ? and doth not mine eye continue in their provocation ? Lay down now, put me in a surety with Thee; who *is* he *that* will strike hands with me ?
	3	
	15²	I have said to corruption, Thou *art* my father to the worm, *Thou art* my mother, and my sister. And where *is* now my hope ? as for my hope, who shall see it ? They shall go down to the bars of the pit, when *our* rest together *is* in the dust.
	5	
18	2	Then answered Bildad the Shuhite, and said, How long *will it be ere* ye make an end of words ? mark, and afterwards we will speak. Wherefore are we counted as beasts, *and* reputed vile in your sight ? He teareth himself in his anger. shall the earth be forsaken for thee ? and shall the rock be removed out of his place ? Yea, the light of the wicked shall be put out, and the spark of his fire shall not shine.
	3	
	4²	
	4	

	CHAP.	VER.

Then Job answered and said, **How long will ye vex my soul, and break me in pieces with words?** These ten times have ye reproached me: ye are not ashamed *that* ye make yourselves strange to me. — 19, 2

Have pity upon me, have pity upon me, O ye my friends; for the hand of God hath touched me. **Why do ye persecute me as God, and are not satisfied with my flesh?** — 22

But ye should say, **Why persecute we him, seeing the root of the matter is found in me?** — 28

— 3

Knowest thou *not* **this of old, since man was placed upon earth, that the triumphing of the wicked** *is* **short, and the joy of the hypocrite** *but* **for a moment?** Though his excellency mount up to the heavens, and his head reach unto the clouds; *yet* he shall perish for ever like his own dung: they which have seen him shall say, **Where** *is* **he?** He shall fly away as a dream, and shall not be found: yea, he shall be chased away as a vision of the night. — 20, 4

— 7

— 2

But Job answered and said, Hear diligently my speech, and let this be your consolations. Suffer me that I may speak; and after that I have spoken, mock on. As for me, *is* **my complaint to man?** and if *it were so*, **why should not my spirit be troubled?** Mark me, and be astonished, and lay *your* hand upon *your* mouth. Even when I remember, I am afraid, and trembling taketh hold on my flesh. **Wherefore do the wicked live, become old, yea, are mighty in power?** Their seed is established in their sight with them, and their offspring before their eyes. — 21, 4²

— 7

Therefore they say unto God, Depart from us; for we desire not the knowledge of Thy ways. **What** *is* **the Almighty, that we should serve Him? and what profit should we have, if we pray unto Him?** Lo, — 15²

CHAP.	VER.	
		their good *is* not in their hand: the counsel of the wicked is far from me.
21	21	God layeth up his iniquity for his children: He rewardeth him, and he shall know *it*. His eyes shall see his destruction, and he shall drink of the wrath of the Almighty. **For what pleasure** *hath* **he in his house after him, when the number of his months is cut off in the midst? Shall** *any* **teach God knowledge?** seeing He judgeth those that are high.
	22	
	28²	Behold, I know your thoughts, and the devices *which* ye wrongfully imagine against me. For ye say, **Where** *is* **the house of the prince?** and **where** *are* **the dwelling places of the wicked? Have ye not asked them that go by the way?** and **do ye not know their tokens, that the wicked is reserved to the day of destruction?** they shall be brought forth to the day of wrath. **Who shall declare his way to his face? and who shall repay him** *what* **he hath done?** Yet shall he be brought to the grave, and shall remain in the tomb. The clods of the valley shall be sweet unto him, and every man shall draw after him, as *there are* innumerable before him. **How then comfort ye me in vain, seeing in your answers there remaineth falsehood?**
	29²	
	31²	
	34	
	14	
22	2	Then Eliphaz the Temanite answered and said, **Can a man be profitable unto God, as he that is wise may be profitable unto himself?** *Is it* **any pleasure to the Almighty, that thou art righteous? or** *is it* **gain** *to Him*, **that thou makest thy ways perfect? Will He reprove thee for fear of thee? will He enter with thee into judgment?** *Is* **not thy wickedness great? and thine iniquities infinite?**
	3²	
	4²	
	5²	
	12	*Is* **not God in the height of heaven?** and behold the height of the stars, how high they are! And thou

JOB:—XXII.-XXV.

	CHAP.	VER
sayest, **How doth God know? can He judge through the dark cloud?** Thick clouds *are* a covering to Him, that He seeth not; and He walketh in the circuit of heaven. **Hast thou marked the old way which wicked men have trodden?** which were cut down out of time, whose foundation was overflown with a flood: which said unto God, Depart from us: and **what can the Almighty do for them?** Yet He filled their houses with good *things:* but the counsel of the wicked is far from me.

22 13[2]

15

17

12

Will He plead against me with *His* **great power?** No; but He would put *strength* in me.

23 6

Neither have I gone back from the commandment of His lips; I have esteemed the words of His mouth more than my necessary *food.* **But He** *is* **in one** *mind,* **and who can turn Him?** and *what* His soul desireth, even *that* He doeth. For He performeth *the thing that is* appointed for me: and many such *things are* with Him.

13

2

Why, seeing times are not hidden from the Almighty, **do they that know Him not see His days?** *Some* remove the landmarks; they violently take away flocks, and feed *thereof.*

24 1

He draweth also the mighty with his power: he riseth up, and no *man* is sure of life. *Though* it be given him *to be* in safety, whereon he resteth; yet His eyes *are* upon their ways. They are exalted for a little while, but are gone and brought low; they are taken out of the way as all *other,* and cut off as the tops of the ears of corn. **And if** *it be* **not** *so* **now, who will make me a liar, and make my speech nothing worth?**

25

2

Then answered Bildad the Shuhite, and said, Dominion and fear *are* with Him, He maketh peace in His high places. **Is there any number of His armies? and upon whom doth not His light arise? How then**

25 3[2]

4[2]

CHAP.	VER.	
25	6²	can man be justified with God? or how can he be clean *that is* born of a woman? Behold even to the moon, and it shineth not; yea, the stars are not pure in His sight. **How much less man,** *that is* **a worm?**
	6	and the son of man, *which is* a worm?
26	2²	But Job answered and said, **How hast thou helped** *him that is* **without power?** *how* **savest thou the**
	3²	**arm** *that hath* **no strength? How hast thou counselled** *him that hath* **no wisdom?** and *how* **hast thou**
	4²	**plentifully declared the thing as it is? To whom hast thou uttered words? and whose spirit came from thee?**
		He divideth the sea with His power, and by His understanding He smiteth through the proud. By His spirit He hath garnished the heavens; His hand hath formed the crooked serpent. Lo, these *are* parts of His ways:
	14²	**but how little a portion is heard of Him?** but the thunder of His power who can understand?
	8	
27	8	For what *is* the hope of the hypocrite, though he hath gained, when God taketh away his soul?
	9	Will God hear his cry when trouble cometh upon
	10²	him? Will he delight himself in the Almighty? will he always call upon God? I will teach you by the hand of God: *that* which *is* with the Almighty will I not conceal. Behold, all ye yourselves have seen *it;*
	12	**why then are ye thus altogether vain?**
	5	
28	12²	**But where shall wisdom be found? and where** *is* **the place of understanding?**
	20²	**Whence then cometh wisdom? and where** *is*
	4	**the place of understanding?**
30	2	But now *they that are* younger than I have me in derision, whose fathers I would have disdained to have set with the dogs of my flock. **Yea, whereto** *might* **the**

JOB —XXX.-XXXIV.

	CHAP.	VER.

strength of their hands *profit* me, in whom old age was perished?

Did not I weep for him that was in trouble? was *not* my soul grieved for the poor? — **30** 25[2], 3

I made a covenant with mine eyes; **why then should I think upon a maid? For what portion of God** *is there* **from above? and** *what* **inheritance of the Almighty from on high?** *Is* **not destruction to the wicked? and a strange** *punishment* **to the workers of iniquity? Doth not He see my ways, and count all my steps?** If I have walked with vanity, or if my foot hath hasted to deceit; let me be weighed in an even balance, that God may know mine integrity. — **31** 1, 2[2], 3[2], 4

If I did despise the cause of my manservant or of my maidservant, when they contended with me; **what then shall I do when God riseth up? and when He visiteth, what shall I answer Him? Did not He that made me in the womb make him? and did not one fashion us in the womb?** — 14[2], 15[2]

If I covered my transgressions as Adam, by hiding mine iniquity in my bosom: did I fear a great multitude, or did the contempt of families terrify me, that I kept silence, *and* **went not out of the door?** — 34, 11

Behold, *in* this thou art not just: I will answer thee, that God is greater than man. **Why dost thou strive against Him?** for He giveth not account of any of His matters. For God speaketh once, yea twice, *yet man* perceiveth it not. — **33** 13, 1

For Job hath said, I am righteous: and God hath taken away my judgment. **Should I lie against my right?** my wound *is* incurable without transgression. **What** — **34** 6, 7

9

CHAP.	VER.	
		man *is* **like Job,** *who* **drinketh up scorning like water?** Which goeth in company with the workers of iniquity, and walketh with wicked men.
34	13²	Yea, surely God will not do wickedly, neither will the Almighty pervert judgment. **Who hath given Him a charge over the earth?** or **who hath disposed the whole world?**
	17²	All flesh shall perish together, and man shall turn again unto dust. If now *thou hast* understanding, hear this: hearken to the voice of my words. **Shall even he that hateth right govern?** and **wilt thou condemn him
	18²	that is most just?** *Is it fit* **to say to a king,** *Thou
	19	art* **wicked?** *and* **to princes,** *Ye are* **ungodly?** *How much less to Him* **that accepteth not the persons of princes, nor regardeth the rich more than the poor?** for they all *are* the work of His hands.
	29²	**When He giveth quietness, who then can make trouble?** **and when He hideth** *His* **face, who then can behold Him?** whether *it be done* against a nation, or against a man only: that the hypocrite reign not, lest the people be ensnared. Surely it is meet to be said unto God, I have borne *chastisement*, I will not offend *any more*. *that which* I see not teach Thou me: if I have
	33	done iniquity, I will do no more. *Should it be* **according to thy mind?** He will recompense it, whether thou
	12	refuse, or whether thou choose; and not I: therefore speak what thou knowest.
35	2	Elihu spake moreover, and said, **Thinkest thou this to be right,** *that* **thou saidst, My righteousness** *is
	3²	more than God's?** For thou saidst, **What advantage will it be unto thee?** *and*, **What profit shall I have** *if I be cleansed* **from my sin?** I will answer thee, and thy companions with thee. Look unto the heavens, and see: and behold the clouds *which* are higher than thou.
	6²	**If thou sinnest, what doest thou against Him?** or

JOB:—XXXV.-XXXVII.

	CHAP.	VER
if thy transgressions be multiplied, what doest thou unto Him? If thou be righteous, what givest thou Him? or what receiveth He of thine hand?	35	7²
By reason of the multitude of oppressions they make *the oppressed* to cry: they cry out by reason of the arm of the mighty. But none saith, **Where** *is* **God my Maker, who giveth songs in the night; who teacheth us more than the beasts of the earth, and maketh us wiser than the fowls of heaven?** There they cry, but none giveth answer, because of the pride of evil men.		11 8
Because *there is* wrath, *beware* lest He take thee away with *His* stroke: then a great ransom cannot deliver thee. **Will He esteem thy riches?** *no*, not gold, nor all the forces of strength.	36	19
Behold, God exalteth by His power: **who teacheth like Him? Who hath enjoined Him His way? or who can say Thou hast wrought iniquity?**		22 23²
Also **can** *any* **understand the spreadings of the clouds,** *or* **the noise of His tabernacle?** Behold, He spreadeth His light upon it, and covereth the bottom of the sea.		29 5
Hearken unto this, O Job stand still, and consider the wondrous works of God. **Dost thou know when God disposed them, and caused the light of His cloud to shine? Dost thou know the balancings of the clouds, the wondrous works of Him which is perfect in knowledge?** ~ **How thy garments** *are* **warm, when He quieteth the earth by the south** *wind?* **Hast thou with Him spread out the sky,** *which is* **strong,** *and* **as a molten looking glass?** Teach us what we shall say unto Him; *for* we cannot	37	15 16 17 18

JOB —XXXVII., XXXVIII.

CHAP. 37 VER. 20 order *our speech* by reason of darkness. **Shall it be told Him that I speak?** if a man speak, surely he shall be swallowed up

5

---

38 2 Then the LORD answered Job out of the whirlwind, and said, **Who** *is* **this that darkeneth counsel by words without knowledge?** Gird up now thy loins like a man; for I will demand of thee, and answer thou Me. **4 Where wast thou when I laid the foundations of the earth?** declare, if thou hast understanding. **5² Who hath laid the measures thereof, if thou knowest?** or **who hath stretched the line upon it? 6² Whereupon are the foundations thereof fastened?** or **who laid the corner stone thereof; when the morning stars sang together, and all the sons of God shouted for joy?** or *who* **8 shut up the sea with doors, when it brake forth,** *as if* **it had issued out of the womb?** When I made the cloud the garment thereof, and thick darkness a swaddlingband for it, and brake up for it My decreed *place*, and set bars and doors, and said, Hitherto shalt thou **11** come, but no further and **here shall thy proud 12 waves be stayed? Hast thou commanded the morning since thy days;** *and* **caused the dayspring to know his place; that it might take hold of the ends of the earth, that the wicked might be shaken out of it?** It is turned as clay to the seal; and they stand as a garment. And from the wicked their light is withholden, and the high arm shall **16²** be broken. **Hast thou entered into the springs of the sea?** or **hast thou walked in the search of the 17² depth? Have the gates of death been opened unto thee?** or **hast thou seen the doors of the 18 shadow of death? Hast thou perceived the breadth of the earth?** declare if thou knowest it all. **19² Where** *is* **the way** *where* **light dwelleth?** and *as for* darkness, **where** *is* **the place thereof, that thou shouldest take it to the bound thereof, and that thou shouldest know the paths** *to* **the house**

JOB.—XXXVIII.

	CHAP.	VER
thereof? Knowest thou *it*, because thou wast then born? or *because* the number of thy days *is* great? Hast thou entered into the treasures of the snow? or hast thou seen the treasures of the hail, which I have reserved against the time of trouble, against the day of battle and war? By what way is the light parted, *which* scattereth the east wind upon the earth? Who hath divided a watercourse for the overflowing of waters, or a way for the lightning of thunder; to cause it to rain on the earth, *where* no man *is;* on the wilderness, wherein *there is* no man; to satisfy the desolate and waste *ground;* and to cause the bud of the tender herb to spring forth? Hath the rain a father? or who hath begotten the drops of dew? Out of whose womb came the ice? and the hoary frost of heaven, who hath gendered it? The waters are hid as *with* a stone, and the face of the deep is frozen. Canst thou bind the sweet influences of Pleiades, or loose the bands of Orion? Canst thou bring forth Mazzaroth in his season? or canst thou guide Arcturus with his sons? Knowest thou the ordinances of heaven? canst thou set the dominion thereof in the earth? Canst thou lift up thy voice to the clouds, that abundance of waters may cover thee? Canst thou send lightnings, that they may go, and say unto thee, Here we *are?* Who hath put wisdom in the inward parts? or who hath given understanding to the heart? Who can number the clouds in wisdom? or who can stay the bottles of heaven, when the dust groweth into hardness, and the clods cleave fast together? Wilt thou hunt the prey for the lion? or fill the appetite of the young lions, when they couch in *their* dens, *and* abide in the covert to lie in wait? Who provideth for the raven his food? when his young ones cry unto God, they wander for lack of meat.	38	21² 22² 24 25 28² 29² 31 32² 33² 34 35 36² 37² 39² 41 40

CHAP	VER.	
39	1²	**Knowest thou the time when the wild goats of the rock bring forth?** *or* **canst thou mark**
	2²	**when the hinds do calve? Canst thou number the months** *that* **they fulfil? or knowest thou the time when they bring forth?** They bow themselves, they bring forth their young ones, they cast out their sorrows. Their young ones are in good liking, they grow up with corn; they go forth, and return not unto
	5²	them. **Who hath sent out the wild ass free? or who hath loosed the bands of the wild ass?** whose house I have made the wilderness, and the barren land his dwellings. He scorneth the multitude of the city, neither regardeth he the crying of the driver. The range of the mountains *is* his pasture, and he
	9	searcheth after every green thing. **Will the unicorn be willing to serve thee, or abide by thy crib?**
	10²	**Canst thou bind the unicorn with his band in the furrow?** or **will he harrow the valleys after**
	11²	**thee? Wilt thou trust him, because his strength** *is* **great? or wilt thou leave thy labour to him?**
	12	**Wilt thou believe him, that he will bring home**
	13²	**thy seed, and gather** *it into* **thy barn?** *Gavest thou* **the goodly wings unto the peacocks? or wings and feathers unto the ostrich?** which leaveth her eggs in the earth, and warmeth them in dust, and forgetteth that the foot may crush them, or that the wild beast may break them. She is hardened against her young ones, as though *they were* not hers: her labour is in vain without fear; because God hath deprived her of wisdom, neither hath He imparted to her understanding
	19²	**Hast thou given the horse strength? hast**
	20	**thou clothed his neck with thunder? Canst thou make him afraid as a grasshopper?** the glory of his nostrils *is* terrible.
	26	**Doth the hawk fly by thy wisdom,** *and* **stretch**
	27	**her wings toward the south? Doth the eagle**
	19	**mount up at thy command, and make her nest**

JOB.—XL., XLI.

on high? She dwelleth and abideth on the rock, upon the crag of the rock, and the strong place. From thence she seeketh the prey, *and* her eyes behold afar off. Her young ones also suck up blood : and where the slain *are*, there *is* she.

Moreover the LORD answered Job, and said, **Shall he that contendeth with the Almighty instruct** *Him?* he that reproveth God, let him answer it. Then Job answered the LORD, and said, Behold, I am vile; **what shall I answer Thee?** I will lay mine hand upon my mouth. Once have I spoken; but I will not answer: yea, twice; but I will proceed no further.

Then answered the LORD unto Job out of the whirlwind, and said, Gird up thy loins now like a man : I will demand of thee, and declare thou unto Me. **Wilt thou also disannul My judgment? wilt thou condemn Me, that thou mayest be righteous? Hast thou an arm like God?** or **canst thou thunder with a voice like Him?**

Canst thou draw out leviathan with an hook? or his tongue with a cord *which* thou lettest down? **Canst thou put an hook into his nose?** or bore his jaw through with a thorn? **Will he make many supplications unto thee? will he speak soft** *words* **unto thee? Will he make a covenant with thee? wilt thou take him for a servant for ever? Wilt thou play with him as** *with* **a bird? or wilt thou bind him for thy maidens? Shall the companions make a banquet of him? shall they part him among the merchants? Canst thou fill his skin with barbed irons? or his head with fish spears?** Lay thine hand upon him, remember the battle, do no more. Behold, the hope of him is in vain : **shall not** *one* **be cast down even at the sight of him?** None *is so* fierce that dare stir him up: **who then is able to stand before Me? Who hath**

CHAP.	VER.
40	2
	4
	8²
	9²
	6
41	1²
	2²
	3²
	4²
	5²
	6²
	7²
	9
	10
	11

CHAP.	VER	
41	13²	prevented **Me, that I should repay** *him?* *whatsoever* *is* under the whole heaven is Mine. I will not conceal his parts, nor his power, nor his comely proportion. **Who can discover the face of his garment?** *or* **who can come** *to him* **with his double bridle? Who can open the doors of his face?** his teeth *are* terrible round about.
	14	
	20	
42	3	Then Job answered the LORD, and said, I know that Thou canst do every *thing,* and *that* no thought can be withholden from Thee. **Who** *is* **he that hideth counsel without knowledge?** therefore have I uttered that I understood not; things too wonderful for me, which I knew not.
	1	
Job 329		

PSALMS.

CHAP.	VER	
2	1	**WHY do the heathen rage, and the people imagine a vain thing?**
	1	
4	2²	O ye sons of men, **how long** *will ye turn* **my glory into shame?** *how long* **will ye love vanity,** *and* **seek after leasing?**
	6	*There be* many that say, **Who will shew us** *any* **good?** LORD, lift Thou up the light of Thy countenance upon us.
	3	
6	3	Have mercy upon me, O LORD; for I *am* weak: O LORD, heal me; for my bones are vexed My soul is also sore vexed: **but Thou, O** LORD, **how long?** Return, O LORD, deliver my soul: oh save me for Thy mercies' sake. For in death *there is* no remembrance of Thee: **in the grave who shall give Thee thanks?**
	5	
	2	When I consider Thy heavens, the work of Thy fingers,

	CHAP	VER.
the moon and the stars, which Thou hast ordained; **what is man, that Thou art mindful of him? and the son of man, that Thou visitest him?**	8	4²
		2
Why standest Thou afar off, O Lord? *why* **hidest Thou** *Thyself* **in times of trouble?**	10	1²
Wherefore doth the wicked contemn God? he hath said in his heart, Thou wilt not require *it*.		13
		3
In the Lord put I my trust: **how say ye to my soul, Flee** *as* **a bird to your mountain?** For, lo, the wicked bend *their* bow, they make ready their arrow upon the string, that they may privily shoot at the upright in heart. **If the foundations be destroyed, what can the righteous do?**	11	1
		3
		2
The Lord shall cut off all flattering lips, *and* the tongue that speaketh proud things: who have said, With our tongue will we prevail; our lips *are* our own **who** *is* **lord over us?**	12	4
		1
How long wilt Thou forget me, O Lord? **for ever? how long wilt Thou hide Thy face from me? How long shall I take counsel in my soul,** *having* **sorrow in my heart daily? how long shall mine enemy be exalted over me?**	13	1³
		2²
		5
They are all gone aside, they are *all* together become filthy: *there is* none that doeth good, no, not one. **Have all the workers of iniquity no knowledge?** who eat up My people *as* they eat bread, and call not upon the Lord.	14	4
		1
Lord, **who shall abide in Thy tabernacle? who shall dwell in Thy holy hill?**	15	1²
		2
For **who** *is* **God save the** Lord? **or who** *is* **a rock save our God?**	18	31²
		2

CHAP.	VER.	
19	12	**Who can understand** *his* **errors?** cleanse Thou me
	1	from secret *faults*.

| 22 | 1² | My God, my God, **why hast Thou forsaken me?** *why art Thou so* **far from helping me,** *and from* **the** |
| | 2 | **words of my roaring?** |

24	3²	**Who shall ascend into the hill of the** LORD? **or who shall stand in His holy place?** He that hath clean hands, and a pure heart; who hath not lifted up his soul unto vanity, nor sworn deceitfully.
	8	Lift up your heads, O ye gates; and be ye lift up, ye everlasting doors; and the King of glory shall come in. **Who** *is* **this King of glory?** The LORD strong and mighty, the LORD mighty in battle. Lift up your heads, O ye gates; even lift *them* up, ye everlasting doors; and
	10	the King of glory shall come in. **Who is this King of**
	4	**glory?** The LORD of hosts, He *is* the King of glory.

| 25 | 12 | **What man** *is* **he that feareth the** LORD? him shall |
| | 1 | He teach in the way *that* He shall choose. |

| 27 | 1² | The LORD *is* my light and my salvation; **whom shall I fear?** the LORD *is* the strength of my life; **of whom** |
| | 2 | **shall I be afraid?** |

| 30 | 9³ | **What profit** *is there* **in my blood, when I go down** |
| | 3 | **to the pit? Shall the dust praise Thee? shall it declare Thy truth?** |

| 34 | 12 | **What man** *is he that* **desireth life,** *and* **loveth** *many* |
| | 1 | **days, that he may see good?** |

| 35 | 10 | All my bones shall say, LORD, **who** *is* **like unto Thee, which deliverest the poor from him that is too strong for him, yea, the poor and the needy from him that spoileth him?** |

	CHAP	VER.
Lord, how long wilt Thou look on? rescue my soul from their destructions, my darling from the lions.	35	17
		2
And now, Lord, **what wait I for?** my hope *is* in Thee	39	7
		1
Mine enemies speak evil of me, **When shall he die, and his name perish?**	41	5
		1
As the hart panteth after the water brooks, so panteth my soul after Thee, O God. My soul thirsteth for God, for the living God: **when shall I come and appear before God?** My tears have been my meat day and night, while they continually say unto me, **Where** *is* **thy God?** When I remember these *things*, I pour out my soul in me: for I had gone with the multitude, I went with them to the house of God, with the voice of joy and praise, with a multitude that kept holyday. **Why art thou cast down, O my soul?** and *why* **art thou disquieted in me?** hope thou in God: for I shall yet praise Him *for* the help of His countenance	42	2
		3
		5²
I will say unto God my rock, **Why hast Thou forgotten me? why go I mourning because of the oppression of the enemy?** *As* with a sword in my bones, mine enemies reproach me; while they say daily unto me, **Where** *is* **thy God? Why art thou cast down, O my soul?** and **why art thou disquieted within me?** hope thou in God · for I shall yet praise Him *who is* the health of my countenance, and my God		9²
		10
		11²
		9
Judge me, O God, and plead my cause against an ungodly nation: O deliver me from the deceitful and unjust man. For Thou *art* the God of my strength: **why dost Thou cast me off? why go I mourning because of the oppression of the enemy?**	43	2²

CHAP	VER	
43	5²	**Why art thou cast down, O my soul?** and **why art thou disquieted within me?** hope in God : for I shall yet praise Him, *who is* the health of my countenance, and my God.
	4	

44	21	If we have forgotten the name of our God, or stretched out our hands to a strange god; **shall not God search this out?** for He knoweth the secrets of the heart. Yea, for Thy sake are we killed all the day long; we are counted as sheep for the slaughter. Awake, **why sleepest Thou, O Lord?** arise, cast *us* not off for ever. **Wherefore hidest Thou Thy face,** *and* **forgettest our affliction and our oppression?** For our soul is bowed down to the dust. our belly cleaveth unto the earth. Arise for our help, and redeem us for Thy mercies' sake.
	23	
	24	
	3	

49	5	**Wherefore should I fear in the days of evil,** *when* **the iniquity of my heels shall compass me about?**
	1	

50	13	If I were hungry, I would not tell thee : for the world *is* Mine, and the fulness thereof. **Will I eat the flesh of bulls, or drink the blood of goats?** Offer unto God thanksgiving; and pay thy vows unto the most High : and call upon Me in the day of trouble : I will deliver thee, and thou shalt glorify Me. But unto the wicked God saith, **What hast thou to do to declare My statutes, or** *that* **thou shouldest take My covenant in thy mouth?**
	16	
	2	

52	1	**Why boastest thou thyself in mischief, O mighty man?** the goodness of God *endureth* continually.
	1	

53	4	**Have the workers of iniquity no knowledge?** who eat up My people *as* they eat bread : they have not called upon God.
	1	

Every day they wrest my words : all their thoughts

PSALMS —LVI.-LXIV.

	CHAP.	VER.

are against me for evil. They gather themselves together, they hide themselves, they mark my steps, when they wait for my soul. **Shall they escape by iniquity?** | **56** | 7
in *Thine* anger cast down the people, O God. Thou tellest my wanderings . put Thou my tears into Thy bottle : *are they* **not in Thy book?** | | 8

Thy vows *are* upon me, O God I will render praises unto Thee For Thou hast delivered my soul from death . *wilt* **not** *Thou deliver* **my feet from falling, that I may walk before God in the light of the living?** | | 13
| | | 3

Do ye indeed speak righteousness, O congregation? do ye judge uprightly, O ye sons of men? | **58** | 1²
Yea, in heart ye work wickedness ; ye weigh the violence of your hands in the earth. | | 2

They return at evening : they make a noise like a dog, and go round about the city. Behold, they belch out with their mouth : swords *are* in their lips : for **who** *say* **they doth hear?** | **59** | 7
| | | 1

Who will bring me *into* **the strong city? who will lead me into Edom?** *Wilt* **not Thou, O God,** *which* **hadst cast us off? and** *Thou,* **O God,** *which* **didst not go out with our armies?** Give us help from trouble for vain *is* the help of man. | **60** | 9²
| | | 10²
| | | 4

How long will ye imagine mischief against a man? ye shall be slain all of you . as a bowing wall *shall ye be, and as* a tottering fence. | **62** | 3
| | | 1

They encourage themselves *in* an evil matter they commune of laying snares privily , they say, **Who shall see them?** They search out iniquities ; they accomplish a diligent search : both the inward *thought* of every one *of them,* and the heart, *is* deep. | **64** | 5
| | | 1

The hill of God *is as* the hill of Bashan ; an high hill

CHAP	VER.	
68	16	*as* the hill of Bashan. **Why leap ye, ye high hills?** *this is* the hill *which* God desireth to dwell in; yea, the LORD will dwell *in it* for ever.
	1	
73	11²	Therefore His people return hither: and waters of a full *cup* are wrung out to them. And they say, **How doth God know? and is there knowledge in the most High?** Behold, these *are* the ungodly, who prosper in the world; they increase *in* riches.
	25	**Whom have I in heaven** *but Thee?* and *there is* none upon earth *that* I desire beside Thee.
	3	
74	1²	O God, **why hast Thou cast** *us* **off for ever?** *why* **doth Thine anger smoke against the sheep of Thy pasture?**
	10²	O God, **how long shall the adversary reproach? shall the enemy blaspheme Thy name for ever? Why withdrawest Thou Thy hand, even Thy right hand?** pluck *it* out of Thy bosom
	11	
	5	
76	7	At Thy rebuke, O God of Jacob, both the chariot and horse are cast into a dead sleep. Thou, *even* Thou, *art* to be feared: and **who may stand in Thy sight when once Thou art angry?**
	1	
77	7²	**Will the Lord cast off for ever?** and **will He be favourable no more? Is His mercy clean gone for ever? doth** *His* **promise fail for evermore? Hath God forgotten to be gracious? hath He in anger shut up His tender mercies?** Selah. And I said, This *is* my infirmity: *but I will remember* the years of the right hand of the most High. I will remember the works of the LORD: surely I will remember Thy wonders of old.
	8²	
	9²	
	13	Thy way, O God, *is* in the sanctuary. **who** *is so* **great a God as** *our* **God?**
	7	

PSALMS:—LXXVIII.-LXXX.

	CHAP.	VER.

And they sinned yet more against Him by provoking the most High in the wilderness. And they tempted God in their heart by asking meat for their lust. Yea, they spake against God; they said, **Can God furnish a table in the wilderness?** Behold, He smote the rock, that the waters gushed out, and the streams overflowed; **can He give bread also? can He provide flesh for His people?** Therefore the LORD heard *this*, and was wroth: so a fire was kindled against Jacob, and anger also came up against Israel; because they believed not in God, and trusted not in His salvation: though He had commanded the clouds from above, and opened the doors of heaven, and had rained down manna upon them to eat, and had given them of the corn of heaven. | 78 | 19

20[2]

3

How long, LORD? **wilt Thou be angry for ever? shall Thy jealousy burn like fire?** Pour out Thy wrath upon the heathen that have not known Thee, and upon the kingdoms that have not called upon Thy name. For they have devoured Jacob, and laid waste his dwelling place. | 79 | 5[3]

Wherefore should the heathen say, **Where** *is* **their God?** let Him be known among the heathen in our sight *by* the revenging of the blood of Thy servants *which is* shed.

10

4

Turn us again, O God, and cause Thy face to shine; and we shall be saved. O LORD God of hosts, **how long wilt Thou be angry against the prayer of Thy people?** Thou feedest them with the bread of tears, and givest them tears to drink in great measure. | 80 | 4

Thou hast brought a vine out of Egypt: Thou hast cast out the heathen, and planted it. Thou preparedst *room* before it, and didst cause it to take deep root, and it filled the land. The hills were covered with the shadow of it, and the boughs thereof *were like* the goodly cedars. She sent out her boughs unto the sea, and her

CHAP.	VER.	
80	12	branches unto the river. **Why hast Thou** *then* **broken down her hedges, so that all they which pass by the way do pluck her?**
	2	

| 82 | 2 | God standeth in the congregation of the mighty; He judgeth among the gods. **How long will ye judge unjustly, and accept the persons of the wicked?** |
| | 1 | |

85	5²	Turn us, O God of our salvation, and cause Thine anger toward us to cease. **Wilt Thou be angry with us for ever? wilt Thou draw out Thine anger to all generations? Wilt Thou not revive us again: that Thy people may rejoice in Thee?** Shew us Thy mercy, O Lord, and grant us Thy salvation.
	6	
	3	

88	10²	Mine eye mourneth by reason of affliction: Lord, I have called daily upon Thee, I have stretched out my hands unto Thee. **Wilt Thou shew wonders to the dead? shall the dead arise** *and* **praise Thee? Shall Thy lovingkindness be declared in the grave?** *or* **Thy faithfulness in destruction? Shall Thy wonders be known in the dark? and Thy righteousness in the land of forgetfulness?** But unto Thee have I cried, O Lord; and in the morning shall my prayer prevent Thee. Lord, **why castest Thou off my soul?** *why* **hidest Thou Thy face from me?** I *am* afflicted and ready to die from *my* youth up: *while* I suffer Thy terrors I am distracted. Thy fierce wrath goeth over me; Thy terrors have cut me off
	11²	
	12²	
	14²	
	8	

| 89 | 6² | And the heavens shall praise Thy wonders, O Lord: Thy faithfulness also in the congregation of the saints. For **who in the heaven can be compared unto the** Lord? *who* **among the sons of the mighty can be likened unto the** Lord? God is greatly to be feared in the assembly of the saints, and to be had in reverence of all *them that are* about Him. O Lord God of hosts, **who** *is* **a strong** Lord **like unto Thee? or to Thy** |
| | 8² | |

faithfulness round about Thee? Thou rulest the raging of the sea: when the waves thereof arise, Thou stillest them.

How long, Lord? wilt Thou hide Thyself for ever? shall Thy wrath burn like fire? Remember how short my time is: wherefore hast Thou made all men in vain? What man *is he that* liveth, and shall not see death? shall he deliver his soul from the hand of the grave? Lord, where *are* Thy former lovingkindnesses, *which* Thou swarest unto David in Thy truth? Remember, Lord, the reproach of Thy servants; *how* I do bear in my bosom *the reproach of* all the mighty people; wherewith Thine enemies have reproached, O Lord; wherewith they have reproached the footsteps of Thine anointed.

For all our days are passed away in Thy wrath: we spend our years as a tale *that is told.* The days of our years *are* threescore years and ten; and if by reason of strength *they be* fourscore years, yet *is* their strength labour and sorrow; for it is soon cut off, and we fly away. Who knoweth the power of Thine anger? even according to Thy fear, so *is* Thy wrath. So teach *us* to number our days, that we may apply *our* hearts unto wisdom. Return, O Lord, how long? and let it repent Thee concerning Thy servants. O satisfy us early with Thy mercy; that we may rejoice and be glad all our days

Lord, how long shall the wicked, how long shall the wicked triumph? *How long* shall they utter *and* speak hard things? *and* all the workers of iniquity boast themselves? They break in pieces Thy people, O Lord, and afflict Thine heritage. They slay the widow and the stranger, and murder the fatherless. Yet they say, The Lord shall not see, neither shall the God of Jacob regard *it.* Understand, ye brutish among the people: and *ye* fools, when will

CHAP.	VER.
89	46³
	47
	48²
	49
	11
90	11
	13
	2
94	3
	4²
	8

CHAP.	VER.	
94	9²	**ye be wise?** He that planted the ear, **shall He not hear?** He that formed the eye, **shall He not see?**
	10²	He that chastiseth the heathen, **shall not He correct?** He that teacheth man knowledge, *shall not He know?* The LORD knoweth the thoughts of man, that they *are* vanity.
	16²	**Who will rise up for me against the evildoers?** *or* **who will stand up for me against the workers of iniquity?** Unless the LORD *had been* my help, my soul had almost dwelt in silence. When I said, My foot slippeth, Thy mercy, O LORD, held me up. In the multitude of my thoughts within me Thy comforts delight my soul **Shall the throne of iniquity have fellowship with Thee, which frameth mischief by a law?** They gather themselves together against the soul of the righteous, and condemn the innocent blood. But the LORD is my defence; and my God *is* the rock of my refuge.
	20	
	11	
101	2	I will sing of mercy and judgment: unto Thee, O LORD, will I sing. I will behave myself wisely in a perfect way. **O when wilt Thou come unto me?** I will walk within my house with a perfect heart.
	1	
106	2²	**Who can utter the mighty acts of the** LORD? *who* **can shew forth all His praise?**
	2	
108	10²	**Who will bring me into the strong city? who will lead me into Edom?** *Wilt* not *Thou,* **O God,** *who* **hast cast us off? and wilt not Thou, O God, go forth with our hosts?** Give us help from trouble: for vain *is* the help of man. Through God we shall do valiantly; for He *it is that* shall tread down our enemies.
	11²	
	4	

When Israel went out of Egypt, the house of Jacob from a people of strange language; Judah was His sanctuary, *and* Israel His dominion. The sea saw *it,* and fled: Jordan was driven back. The mountains

skipped like rams, *and* the little hills like lambs. **What** | 114 5²
ailed thee, O thou sea, that thou fleddest? thou
Jordan, *that* **thou wast driven back? ye moun-** | 6
tains, *that* **ye skipped like rams;** *and* **ye little hills,**
like lambs? Tremble, thou earth, at the presence of
the Lord, at the presence of the God of Jacob; which | 3
turned the rock *into* a standing water, the flint into a
fountain of waters.

Not unto us, O LORD, not unto us, but unto Thy
name give glory, for Thy mercy, *and* for Thy truth's
sake. Wherefore should the heathen say, **Where** *is* | 115 2
now their God? But our God *is* in the heavens: He | 1
hath done whatsoever He hath pleased.

What shall I render unto the LORD *for* **all His** | 116 12
benefits toward me? I will take the cup of salvation, and call upon the name of the LORD. I will pay
my vows unto the LORD now in the presence of all His | 1
people.

I called upon the LORD in distress: the LORD answered me, *and set me* in a large place. The LORD *is* on
my side; I will not fear: **what can man do unto me?** | 118 6
The LORD taketh my part with them that help me:
therefore shall I see *my desire* upon them that hate | 1
me.

Wherewithal shall a young man cleanse his | 119 9
way? by taking heed *thereto* according to Thy word.

Mine eyes fail for Thy word, saying, **When wilt** | 82
Thou comfort me? For I am become like a bottle
in the smoke; *yet* do I not forget Thy statutes. **How** | 84²
many *are* **the days of Thy servant? when wilt**
Thou execute judgment on them that persecute | 4
me?

Deliver my soul, O LORD, from lying lips, *and* from

CHAP	VER.	
120	3²	a deceitful tongue. **What shall be given unto thee? or what shall be done unto thee, thou false tongue?**
	2	

| 130 | 3 | Out of the depths have I cried unto Thee, O Lord. Lord, hear my voice: let Thine ears be attentive to the voice of my supplications. **If Thou, Lord, shouldest mark iniquities, O Lord, who shall stand?** But *there is* forgiveness with Thee, that Thou mayest be feared. |
| | 1 | |

| 137 | 4 | By the rivers of Babylon, there we sat down, yea, we wept, when we remembered Zion. We hanged our harps upon the willows in the midst thereof. For there they that carried us away captive required of us a song; and they that wasted us *required of us* mirth, *saying*, Sing us *one* of the songs of Zion. **How shall we sing the Lord's song in a strange land?** |
| | 1 | |

139	7²	**Whither shall I go from Thy Spirit? or whither shall I flee from Thy presence?** If I ascend up into heaven, Thou *art* there; if I make my bed in hell, behold, Thou *art there*.
	21²	Surely Thou wilt slay the wicked, O God: depart from me therefore, ye bloody men. For they speak against Thee wickedly, *and* Thine enemies take *Thy name* in vain. **Do not I hate them, O Lord, that hate Thee? and am not I grieved with those that rise up against Thee?** I hate them with perfect hatred: I count them mine enemies.
	4	

| 147 | 17 | He giveth snow like wool. He scattereth the hoarfrost like ashes. He casteth forth His ice like morsels. **who can stand before His cold?** |
| | 1 | |

Psalms 163

THE PROVERBS.

WISDOM crieth without; she uttereth her voice in the streets: she crieth in the chief place of concourse, in the openings of the gates: in the city she uttereth her words, *saying*, **How long, ye simple ones, will ye love simplicity? and the scorners delight in their scorning? and fools hate knowledge?** Turn you at my reproof: behold, I will pour out my spirit unto you, I will make known my words unto you.

Drink waters out of thine own cistern, and running waters out of thine own well. Let thy fountains be dispersed abroad, *and* rivers of waters in the streets Let them be only thine own, and not strangers' with thee. Let thy fountain be blessed: and rejoice with the wife of thy youth. *Let her be as* the loving hind and pleasant roe; let her breasts satisfy thee at all times, and be thou ravished always with her love. **And why wilt thou, my son, be ravished with a strange woman, and embrace the bosom of a stranger?** For the ways of man *are* before the eyes of the Lord, and He pondereth all his goings.

Go to the ant, thou sluggard, consider her ways, and be wise: which having no guide, overseer, or ruler, provideth her meat in the summer, *and* gathereth her food in the harvest. **How long wilt thou sleep, O sluggard? when wilt thou arise out of thy sleep?** *Yet* a little sleep, a little slumber, a little folding of the hands to sleep: so shall thy poverty come as one that travelleth, and thy want as an armed man.

Can a man take fire in his bosom, and his clothes not be burned? Can one go upon hot coals, and his feet not be burned? So he that goeth in to his neighbour's wife, whosoever toucheth her shall not be innocent.

CHAP.	VER.
1	22³
	3
5	20
	1
6	9²
	27
	28
	4

CHAP	VER	
8	1²	**Doth not wisdom cry? and understanding put forth her voice?** She standeth in the top of high places, by the way in the places of the paths. She crieth
	2	at the gates, at the entry of the city, at the coming in at the doors.
14	22	**Do they not err that devise evil?** but mercy and
	1	truth *shall be* to them that devise good.
15	11	Hell and destruction *are* before the Lord: **how much more then the hearts of the children of men?** A scorner loveth not one that reproveth him: neither will
	1	he go unto the wise.
17	16	**Wherefore** *is there* **a price in the hand of a fool**
	1	**to get wisdom, seeing** *he hath* **no heart** *to it?*
18	14	The spirit of a man will sustain his infirmity; but **a**
	1	**wounded spirit who can bear?**
19	7	All the brethren of the poor do hate him: **how much more do his friends go far from him?** he pursueth
	1	*them with* words, *yet* they *are* wanting *to him.*
20	6	Most men will proclaim every one his own goodness: but **a faithful man who can find?**
	9	**Who can say, I have made my heart clean, I am pure from my sin?**
	24	Man's goings *are* of the Lord; **how can a man then**
	3	**understand his own way?**
21	27	The sacrifice of the wicked *is* abomination: **how**
	1	**much more,** *when* **he bringeth it with a wicked mind?**
22	21	**Have not I written to thee excellent things in counsels and knowledge, that I might make thee know the certainty of the words of truth; that**

PROVERBS :—XXII.-XXIV.

	CHAP.	VER.
thou mightest answer the words of truth to them that send unto thee?		
Be not thou *one* of them that strike hands, *or* of them that are sureties for debts. **If thou hast nothing to pay, why should he take away thy bed from under thee?**	**22**	27
Seest thou a man diligent in his business? he shall stand before kings; he shall not stand before mean *men*.		29
		3
Labour not to be rich: cease from thine own wisdom. **Wilt thou set thine eyes upon that which is not?** for *riches* certainly make themselves wings; they fly away as an eagle toward heaven.	**23**	5
Who hath woe? who hath sorrow? who hath contentions? who hath babbling? who hath wounds without cause? who hath redness of eyes? They that tarry long at the wine; they that go to seek mixed wine.		29[6]
They have stricken me, *shalt thou say, and* I was not sick; they have beaten me, *and* I felt *it* not. **When shall I awake?** I will seek it yet again.		35
		8
If thou forbear to deliver *them that are* drawn unto death, and *those that are* ready to be slain; if thou sayest, Behold, we knew it not; **doth not He that pondereth the heart consider** *it?* **and He that keepeth thy soul, doth** *not* **He know** *it?* and **shall** *not* **He render to** *every* **man according to his works?**	**24**	12[3]
My son, fear thou the LORD and the king: *and* meddle not with them that are given to change: for their calamity shall rise suddenly; and **who knoweth the ruin of them both?**		22
		4

CHAP.	VER.	
25	16	**Hast thou found honey?** eat so much as is sufficient for thee, lest thou be filled therewith, and vomit it. Withdraw thy foot from thy neighbour's house; lest he be weary of thee, and *so* hate thee.
	1	
26	12	**Seest thou a man wise in his own conceit?** *there is* more hope of a fool than of him.
	19	As a mad *man* who casteth firebrands, arrows, and death, so *is* the man *that* deceiveth his neighbour, and saith, **Am not I in sport?**
	2	
27	4	Wrath *is* cruel, and anger *is* outrageous; but **who** *is* **able to stand before envy?**
	24	Be thou diligent to know the state of thy flocks, *and* look well to thy herds. For riches *are* not for ever; and **doth the crown** *endure* **to every generation?**
	2	
29	20	**Seest thou a man** *that is* **hasty in his words?** *there is* more hope of a fool than of him.
	1	
30	4 5	**Who hath ascended up into heaven, or descended? who hath gathered the wind in his fists? who hath bound the waters in a garment? who hath established all the ends of the earth? what** *is* **his name, and what** *is* **his son's name, if thou canst tell?**
	9	Two *things* have I required of Thee; deny me *them* not before I die: remove far from me vanity and lies: give me neither poverty nor riches; feed me with food convenient for me: lest I be full, and deny *Thee*, and say, **Who** *is* **the** Lord? or lest I be poor, and steal, and take the name of my God *in vain*.
	6	
31	2 3	**What, my son?** and **what, the son of my womb?** and **what, the son of my vows?** Give

	CHAP.	VER

not thy strength unto women, nor thy ways to that which destroyeth kings.

Who can find a virtuous woman? for her price *is* far above rubies. | **31** | 10 |
| | | 4 |
| Proverbs | 50 |

ECCLESIASTES.

	CHAP.	VER.
WHAT profit hath a man of all his labour which he taketh under the sun?	**1**	3
Is there *any* **thing whereof it may be said, See, this** *is* **new?** it hath been already of old time, which was before us.		10
		2
I said of laughter, *It* is mad: and of mirth, **What doeth it?**	**2**	2
And I turned myself to behold wisdom, and madness, and folly: for **what** *can* **the man** *do* **that cometh after the king?** *even* that which hath been already done.		12
Then said I in my heart, As it happeneth to the fool, so it happeneth even to me; and **why was I then more wise?** Then I said in my heart, that this also *is* vanity. For *there is* no remembrance of the wise more than of the fool for ever; seeing that which now *is* in the days to come shall all be forgotten. And **how dieth the wise** *man?* as the fool. Therefore I hated life; because the work that is wrought under the sun *is* grievous unto me: for all *is* vanity and vexation of spirit. Yea, I hated all my labour which I had taken under the sun: because I should leave it unto the man that shall		15
		16

CHAP.	VER.	
2	19	be after me. And **who knoweth whether he shall be a wise** *man* **or a fool?** yet shall he have rule over all my labour wherein I have laboured, and wherein I have shewed myself wise under the sun. This *is* also vanity.
	22	**For what hath man of all his labour, and of the vexation of his heart, wherein he hath laboured under the sun?** For all his days *are* sorrows, and his travail grief; yea, his heart taketh not rest in the night. This is also vanity. *There is* nothing better for a man, *than* that he should eat and drink, and *that* he should make his soul enjoy good in his labour.
	25	This also I saw, that it *was* from the hand of God. **For who can eat, or who else can hasten** *hereunto*, **more than I?**
	7	
3	9	**What profit hath he that worketh in that wherein he laboureth?**
	21	**Who knoweth the spirit of man that goeth upward, and the spirit of the beast that goeth downward to the earth?** Wherefore I perceive that *there is* nothing better, than that a man should rejoice in his own works; for that *is* his portion: for **who shall bring him to see what shall be after him?**
	22	
	3	
4	8	There is one *alone*, and *there is* not a second; yea, he hath neither child nor brother: yet *is there* no end of all his labour; neither is his eye satisfied with riches; neither *saith he*, **For whom do I labour, and bereave my soul of good?** This *is* also vanity, yea, it *is* a sore travail.
	11	Again, if two lie together, then they have heat: but **how can one be warm** *alone?*
	2	
5	6	Suffer not thy mouth to cause thy flesh to sin; neither say thou before the angel, that it *was* an error: **where-**

ECCLESIASTES:—V.-VII.

	CHAP.	VER.

fore should God be angry at thy voice, and destroy the work of thine hands?

When goods increase, they are increased that eat them: and **what good** *is there* **to the owners thereof, saving the beholding** *of them* **with their eyes?**   5   11

As he came forth of his mother's womb, naked shall he return to go as he came, and shall take nothing of his labour, which he may carry away in his hand. And this also *is* a sore evil, *that* in all points as he came, so shall he go: and **what profit hath he that hath laboured for the wind?**   16 / 3

Yea, though he live a thousand years twice *told*, yet hath he seen no good: **do not all go to one place?**   6   6
All the labour of man *is* for his mouth, and yet the appetite is not filled   **For what hath the wise more than the fool? what hath the poor, that knoweth to walk before the living?**   8[2]

Seeing there be many things that increase vanity, **what** *is* **man the better? For who knoweth what** *is* **good for man in** *this* **life, all the days of his vain life which he spendeth as a shadow? for who can tell a man what shall be after him under the sun?**   11 / 12[2] / 6

Say not thou, **What is** *the cause* **that the former days were better than these?** for thou dost not inquire wisely concerning this.   7   10

Consider the work of God: for **who can make** *that* **straight, which He hath made crooked?**   13

Be not righteous over much; neither make thyself over wise: **why shouldest thou destroy thyself?** Be not over much wicked, neither be thou foolish: **why shouldest thou die before thy time?**   16 / 17

CHAP	VER.	
7	24	That which is far off, and exceeding deep, who can find it out?
	5	
8	1²	**Who** *is* **as the wise** *man?* and **who knoweth the interpretation of a thing?** a man's wisdom maketh his face to shine, and the boldness of his face shall be changed.
	4	Where the word of a king *is*, *there is* power: and **who may say unto him, What doest thou?**
	7	Because to every purpose there is time and judgment, therefore the misery of man *is* great upon him For he knoweth not that which shall be: for **who can tell him when it shall be?**
	4	
10	14	A fool also is full of words: a man cannot tell what shall be; and **what shall be after him, who can tell him?**
	1	

Ecclesiastes 33

SONG OF SOLOMON.

CHAP.	VER	
1	7	TELL me, O thou whom my soul loveth, where thou feedest, where thou makest *thy flock* to rest at noon: for **why should I be as one that turneth aside by the flocks of thy companions?**
	1	
3	3	The watchmen that go about the city found me: *to whom I said*, **Saw ye him whom my soul loveth?**
	6	**Who** *is* **this that cometh out of the wilderness like pillars of smoke, perfumed with myrrh and frankincense, with all powders of the merchant?**
	2	

	CHAP. VER.

Behold his bed, which *is* Solomon's; threescore valiant men *are* about it, of the valiant of Israel

I have put off my coat; **how shall I put it on?** I have washed my feet; **how shall I defile them?** — **5** 3²

What *is* **thy beloved more than** *another* **beloved, O thou fairest among women?** what *is* thy beloved more than *another* **beloved, that thou dost so charge us?** — 9²

— 4

Whither is thy beloved gone, O thou fairest among women? whither is thy beloved turned aside? that we may seek him with thee. — **6** 1²

Who *is* **she** *that* **looketh forth as the morning, fair as the moon, clear as the sun,** *and* **terrible as** *an army* **with banners?** — 10

Return, return, O Shulamite; return, return, that we may look upon thee. **What will ye see in the Shulamite?** As it were the company of two armies. — 13

— 4

Who *is* **this that cometh up from the wilderness, leaning upon her beloved?** I raised thee up under the apple tree: there thy mother brought thee forth: there she brought thee forth *that* bare thee. — **8** 5

We have a little sister, and she hath no breasts: **what shall we do for our sister in the day when she shall be spoken for?** — 8

— 2

Song of Solomon 13

ISAIAH.

CHAP.	VER.	
1	5	**WHY should ye be stricken any more?** ye will revolt more and more: the whole head is sick, and the whole heart faint.
		Hear the word of the LORD, ye rulers of Sodom; give ear unto the law of our God, ye people of Gomorrah.
	11	**To what purpose** is **the multitude of your sacrifices unto Me?** saith the LORD. I am full of the burnt offerings of rams, and the fat of fed beasts; and I delight not in the blood of bullocks, or of lambs, or of he goats.
	12	**When ye come to appear before Me, who hath required this at your hand, to tread My courts?** Bring no more vain oblations; incense is an abomination
	3	unto Me; the new moons and sabbaths, the calling of assemblies, I cannot away with; it is iniquity, even the solemn meeting.
2	22	Cease ye from man, whose breath is in his nostrils:
	1	for **wherein is he to be accounted of?**
3	15	**What mean ye** that **ye beat My people to pieces,**
	1	**and grind the faces of the poor?** saith the Lord GOD of hosts.
5	4²	**What could have been done more to My vineyard, that I have not done in it?** wherefore,
	2	when I looked that it should bring forth grapes, brought it forth wild grapes?
6	8	Also I heard the voice of the Lord, saying, **Whom shall I send, and who will go for Us?** Then said I, Here am I; send me.
	11	Then said I, **Lord, how long?** And He answered,
	2	Until the cities be wasted without inhabitant, and the

houses without man, and the land be utterly desolate, and the LORD have removed men far away, and *there be* a great forsaking in the midst of the land.

And he said, Hear ye now, O house of David; *Is it* **a small thing for you to weary men, but will ye weary my God also?**

CHAP.	VER.
7	13
	1

And when they shall say unto you, Seek unto them that have familiar spirits, and unto wizards that peep and that mutter: **should not a people seek unto their God? for the living to the dead?**

8	19²
	2

Woe unto them that decree unrighteous decrees, and that write grievousness *which* they have prescribed; to turn aside the needy from judgment, and to take away the right from the poor of My people, that widows may be their prey, and *that* they may rob the fatherless ! And **what will ye do in the day of visitation, and in the desolation** *which* **shall come from far? to whom will ye flee for help?** and **where will ye leave your glory?**

| 10 | 3³ |

For he saith, *Are* **not my princes altogether kings?** *Is* **not Calno as Carchemish?** *is* **not Hamath as Arpad?** *is* **not Samaria as Damascus?** As my hand hath found the kingdoms of the idols, and whose graven images did excel them of Jerusalem and of Samaria, **shall I not, as I have done unto Samaria and her idols, so do to Jerusalem and her idols?**

	8
	9³
	11

Shall the axe boast itself against him that heweth therewith? *or* **shall the saw magnify itself against him that shaketh it?** as if the rod should shake *itself* against them that lift it up, *or* as if the staff should lift up *itself, as if it were* no wood.

	15²
	10

Hell from beneath is moved for thee to meet *thee* at thy coming: it stirreth up the dead for thee, *even* all the

CHAP.	VER.	
14	10²	chief ones of the earth; it hath raised up from their thrones all the kings of the nations. All they shall speak and say unto thee, **Art thou also become weak as we? art thou become like unto us?**
	17	They that see thee shall narrowly look upon thee, *and* consider thee, *saying*, *Is* **this the man that made the earth to tremble, that did shake kingdoms;** *that* **made the world as a wilderness, and destroyed the cities thereof;** *that* **opened not the house of his prisoners?**
	27²	For the LORD of hosts hath purposed, and **who shall disannul** *it?* and His hand *is* stretched out, and **who shall turn it back?**
	32	**What shall** *one* **then answer the messengers of the nation?** That the LORD hath founded Zion, and the poor of His people shall trust in it.
	6	
19	11	Surely the princes of Zoan *are* fools, the counsel of the wise counsellors of Pharaoh is become brutish: **how say ye unto Pharaoh, I** *am* **the son of the wise,**
	12²	**the son of ancient kings? Where** *are* **they? where** *are* **thy wise** *men?* and let them tell thee now, and let them know what the LORD of hosts hath purposed
	3	upon Egypt.
20	6	And the inhabitant of this isle shall say in that day, Behold, such *is* our expectation, whither we flee for help, to be delivered from the king of Assyria: and **how shall we escape?**
	1	
21	11²	The burden of Dumah. He calleth to me out of Seir, **Watchman, what of the night? Watchman, what of the night?** The watchman said, The morning cometh, and also the night: if ye will inquire, inquire ye. return, come.
	2	

ISAIAH:—XXII.-XXVIII.

| | CHAP. | VER. |

The burden of the valley of vision. **What aileth thee now, that thou art wholly gone up to the housetops?** Thou that art full of stirs, a tumultuous city, a joyous city: thy slain *men are* not slain with the sword, nor dead in battle. — **22** **1**

Thus saith the Lord God of hosts, Go, get thee unto this treasurer, *even* unto Shebna, which *is* over the house, *and say*, **What hast thou here?** **and whom hast thou here, that thou hast hewed thee out a sepulchre here,** *as* **he that heweth him out a sepulchre on high,** *and* **that graveth an habitation for himself in a rock?** — 16[2] — 3

Is **this your joyous** *city*, **whose antiquity** *is* **of ancient days?** her own feet shall carry her afar off to sojourn. **Who hath taken this counsel against Tyre, the crowning** *city*, **whose merchants** *are* **princes, whose traffickers** *are* **the honourable of the earth?** The Lord of hosts hath purposed it, to stain the pride of all glory, *and* to bring into contempt all the honourable of the earth. — **23** 7 — 8 — 2

I the Lord do keep it; I will water it every moment: lest *any* hurt it, I will keep it night and day. Fury *is* not in Me: **who would set the briers** *and* **thorns against Me in battle?** I would go through them, I would burn them together. — **27** 4

Hath He smitten him, as he smote those that smote him? *or* **is he slain according to the slaughter of them that are slain by him?** — 7[2] — 3

Whom shall he teach knowledge? and **whom shall he make to understand doctrine?** *them that are* weaned from the milk, *and* drawn from the breasts. For precept *must be* upon precept, precept upon precept; line upon line, line upon line; here a little, *and* there a — **28** 9[2]

11

CHAP.	VER.	
		little: for with stammering lips and another tongue will he speak to this people.
28	24²	**Doth the plowman plow all day to sow? doth he open and break the clods of his ground?**
	25	**When he hath made plain the face thereof, doth he not cast abroad the fitches, and scatter the cummin, and cast in the principal wheat and the appointed barley and the rie in their place?** For
	5	his God doth instruct him to discretion, *and* doth teach him.
		Woe unto them that seek deep to hide their counsel from the LORD, and their works are in the dark, and
29	15²	they say, **Who seeth us? and who knoweth us?** Surely your turning of things upside down shall be
	16²	esteemed as the potter's clay: for **shall the work say of him that made it, He made me not? or shall the thing framed say of him that framed it, He**
	17	**had no understanding?** *Is* it not yet a very little while, and Lebanon shall be turned into a fruit-
	5	ful field, and the fruitful field shall be esteemed as a forest?
	.	Hear, ye *that are* far off, what I have done; and, ye *that are* near, acknowledge My might. The sinners in Zion are afraid; fearfulness hath surprised the hypo-
33	14²	crites. **Who among us shall dwell with the devouring fire? who among us shall dwell with everlasting burnings?** He that walketh righteously, and speaketh uprightly; he that despiseth the gain of oppressions, that shaketh his hands from holding of bribes, that stoppeth his ears from hearing of blood, and shutteth his eyes from seeing evil; he shall dwell on high: his place of defence *shall be* the munitions of rocks: bread shall be given him: his waters *shall be* sure. Thine eyes shall see the king in his beauty: they shall behold the land that is very far off. Thine heart

shall meditate terror. **Where** is **the scribe? where** is **the receiver? where** is **he that counted the towers?**

33 18[3]

And Rabshakeh said unto them, Say ye now to Hezekiah, Thus saith the great king, the king of Assyria, **What confidence** is **this wherein thou trustest?** I say, *sayest thou,* (but *they are but* vain words) *I have* counsel and strength for war · now **on whom dost thou trust, that thou rebellest against me?** Lo, thou trustest in the staff of this broken reed, on Egypt; whereon if a man lean, it will go into his hand, and pierce it: so is Pharaoh king of Egypt to all that trust in him. But if thou say to me, We trust in the LORD our God: is it **not He, whose high places and whose altars Hezekiah hath taken away, and said to Judah and to Jerusalem, Ye shall worship before this altar?** Now therefore give pledges, I pray thee, to my master the king of Assyria, and I will give thee two thousand horses, if thou be able on thy part to set riders upon them. **How then wilt thou turn away the face of one captain of the least of my master's servants, and put thy trust on Egypt for chariots and for horsemen? And am I now come up without the** LORD **against this land to destroy it?** the LORD said unto me, Go up against this land, and destroy it. Then said Eliakim and Shebna and Joah unto Rabshakeh, Speak, I pray thee, unto thy servants in the Syrian language; for we understand *it*: and speak not to us in the Jews' language, in the ears of the people that *are* on the wall. But Rabshakeh said, **Hath my master sent me to thy master and to thee to speak these words?** *hath he* **not** *sent me* **to the men that sit upon the wall, that they may eat their own dung, and drink their own piss with you?** Then Rabshakeh stood, and cried with a loud voice in the Jews' language, and said, Hear ye the words of the great king, the king of Assyria.

36 4

5

7

9

10

12[2]

CHAP.	VER.	
36	18	*Beware* lest Hezekiah persuade you, saying, The LORD will deliver us. **Hath any of the gods of the nations delivered his land out of the hand of the king of**
	19³	**Assyria ? Where** *are* **the gods of Hamath and Arphad ?** where *are* **the gods of Sepharvaim ?** and have they delivered Samaria out of my hand ?
	20	**Who** *are they* **among all the gods of these lands, that have delivered their land out of my hand, that the** LORD **should deliver Jerusalem out of my hand ?** But they held their peace, and answered him
	12	not a word : for the king's commandment was, saying, Answer him not.

37	11	Behold, thou hast heard what the kings of Assyria have done to all lands by destroying them utterly ; **and**
	12	**shalt thou be delivered ? Have the gods of the nations delivered them which my fathers have destroyed,** *as* **Gozan, and Haran, and Rezeph, and the children of Eden which** *were* **in Telassar ?**
	13	**Where** *is* **the king of Hamath, and the king of Arphad, and the king of the city of Sepharvaim, Hena, and Ivah ?**

This *is* the word which the LORD hath spoken concerning him ; The virgin, the daughter of Zion, hath despised thee, *and* laughed thee to scorn ; the daughter of Jerusa-

| | 23² | lem hath shaken her head at thee. **Whom hast thou reproached and blasphemed ? and against whom hast thou exalted** *thy* **voice, and lifted up thine eyes on high ?** *even* against the Holy One of Israel. |

I have digged, and drunk water ; and with the sole of my feet have I dried up all the rivers of the besieged

| | 26 | places. **Hast thou not heard long ago,** *how* **I have done it ;** *and* **of ancient times, that I have formed** |
| | 6 | **it ?** now have I brought it to pass, that thou shouldest be to lay waste defenced cities *into* ruinous heaps. |

Like a crane *or* a swallow, so did I chatter : I did

ISAIAH:—XXXVIII.-XL.

	CHAP.	VER

mourn as a dove : mine eyes fail *with looking* upward : O Lord, I am oppressed ; undertake for me. **What shall I say?** He hath both spoken unto me, and Himself hath done *it* : I shall go softly all my years in the bitterness of my soul. O Lord, by these *things men* live, and in all these *things is* the life of my spirit : so wilt Thou recover me, and make me to live. | 38 | 15

Hezekiah also had said, **What** *is* **the sign that I shall go up to the house of the** Lord ? | | 22

| | | 2

Then came Isaiah the prophet unto king Hezekiah, and said unto him, **What said these men?** and **from whence came they unto thee?** And Hezekiah said, They are come from a far country unto me, *even* from Babylon. Then said he, **What have they seen in thine house?** And Hezekiah answered, All that *is* in mine house have they seen : there is nothing among my treasures that I have not shewed them. | 39 | 3²

| | | 4

| | | 3

The voice said, Cry. And he said, **What shall I cry?** All flesh *is* grass, and all the goodliness thereof *is* as the flower of the field : the grass withereth, the flower fadeth : because the spirit of the Lord bloweth upon it : surely the people *is* grass. The grass withereth, the flower fadeth : but the word of our God shall stand for ever. | 40 | 6

Who hath measured the waters in the hollow of his hand, and meted out heaven with the span, and comprehended the dust of the earth in a measure, and weighed the mountains in scales, and the hills in a balance? Who hath directed the Spirit of the Lord, **or** *being* **His counsellor hath taught Him? With whom took He counsel, and** *who* **instructed Him, and taught Him in the path of judgment, and taught Him knowledge, and shewed to Him the way of** | | 12

| | | 13

| | | 14

CHAP.	VER.	
		understanding? Behold, the nations *are* as a drop of a bucket, and are counted as the small dust of the balance: behold, He taketh up the isles as a very little thing.
40	18²	**To whom then will ye liken God?** or **what likeness will ye compare unto Him?**
	21⁴	**Have ye not known? have ye not heard? hath it not been told you from the beginning? have ye not understood from the foundations of the earth?** *It is* He that sitteth upon the circle of the earth, and the inhabitants thereof *are* as grasshoppers; that stretcheth out the heavens as a curtain, and spreadeth them out as a tent to dwell in: that bringeth the princes to nothing; He maketh the judges of the earth as vanity.
	25	**To whom then will ye liken Me, or shall I be equal?** saith the Holy One. Lift up your eyes on high, and behold who hath created these *things*, that bringeth out their host by number: He calleth them all by names by the greatness of His might, for that *He is* strong in power; not one faileth. **Why sayest thou, O Jacob,**
	27	**and speakest, O Israel, My way is hid from the** LORD, **and my judgment is passed over from my**
	28²	**God? Hast thou not known? hast thou not heard,** *that* **the everlasting God, the** LORD, **the Creator of the ends of the earth, fainteth not,**
	14	**neither is weary?** *there is* no searching of His understanding.
41	2	**Who raised up the righteous** *man* **from the east, called him to His foot, gave the nations before him, and made** *him* **rule over kings?** He gave *them* as the dust to his sword, *and* as driven stubble to his bow.
	4	**Who hath wrought and done** *it*, **calling the**

	CHAP.	VER.
generations from the beginning? I the LORD, the first, and with the last, I *am* He.		
Who hath declared from the beginning, that we may know? and beforetime, that we may say, *He is* **righteous?** yea, *there is* none that sheweth, yea, *there is* none that declareth, yea, *there is* none that heareth your words.	**41**	26[2]
		4
Hear, ye deaf; and look, ye blind, that ye may see. **Who** *is* **blind, but My servant? or deaf, as My messenger** *that* **I sent? who** *is* **blind as** *he that is* **perfect, and blind as the** LORD'S **servant?** Seeing many things, but thou observest not, opening the ears, but he heareth not.	**42**	19[3]
Who among you will give ear to this? *who* **will hearken and hear for the time to come? Who gave Jacob for a spoil, and Israel to the robbers? did not the** LORD, **He against whom we have sinned?** for they would not walk in His ways, neither were they obedient unto His law.		23[2]
		24[2]
		7
Let all the nations be gathered together, and let the people be assembled. **who among them can declare this, and shew us former things?** let them bring forth their witnesses, that they may be justified. or let them hear, and say, *It is* truth.	**43**	9
Yea, before the day *was* I *am* He; and *there is* none that can deliver out of My hand: **I will work, and who shall let it?**		13
Remember ye not the former things, neither consider the things of old. Behold, I will do a new thing; now it shall spring forth; **shall ye not know it?** I will even make a way in the wilderness, *and* rivers in the desert.		19
		3

CHAP.	VER.	
44	7	Thus saith the LORD the King of Israel, and His redeemer the LORD of hosts; I *am* the first, and I *am* the last; and beside Me *there is* no God. **And who, as I, shall call, and shall declare it, and set it in order for Me, since I appointed the ancient people?** and the things that are coming, and shall come, let them shew unto them. Fear ye not, neither
	8²	be afraid: **have not I told thee from that time, and have declared** *it?* ye *are* even My witnesses. **Is there a God beside Me?** yea, *there is* no God; I know not *any*. They that make a graven image *are* all of them vanity; and their delectable things shall not profit; and they *are* their own witnesses; they see not,
	10	nor know; that they may be ashamed. **Who hath formed a god, or molten a graven image** *that* **is profitable for nothing?**
		And none considereth in his heart, neither *is there* knowledge nor understanding to say, I have burned part of it in the fire; yea, also I have baked bread upon the coals thereof; I have roasted flesh, and eaten *it*: and
	19²	**shall I make the residue thereof an abomination? shall I fall down to the stock of a tree?** He feedeth on ashes: a deceived heart hath turned him
	20	aside, that he cannot deliver his soul, nor say, *Is there* **not a lie in my right hand?** Remember these, O Jacob and Israel; for thou *art* My servant: I have formed
	7	thee; thou *art* My servant: O Israel, thou shalt not be forgotten of Me.
		Woe unto him that striveth with his Maker! *Let* the potsherd *strive* with the potsherds of the earth.
45	9²	**Shall the clay say to him that fashioneth it, What makest thou? or thy work, He hath no hands?** Woe unto him that saith unto *his* father,
	10²	**What begettest thou?** or to the woman, **What hast thou brought forth?**
		Assemble yourselves and come; draw near together, ye

ISAIAH:—XLV.-XLIX.

| | CHAP. | VER. |

that are escaped of the nations: they have no knowledge that set up the wood of their graven image, and pray unto a god *that* cannot save. Tell ye, and bring *them* near; yea, let them take counsel together: **who hath declared this from ancient time?** *who* **hath told it from that time?** *have* **not I the** Lord? and *there is* no God else beside Me; a just God and a Saviour; *there is* none beside Me.   45   21₃

                      7

To whom will ye liken Me, and make Me equal, and compare Me, that we may be like?   46   5

                      1

Thou hast heard, see all this; and **will not ye declare** *it?* I have shewed thee new things from this time, even hidden things, and thou didst not know them.   48   6

Behold, I have refined thee, but not with silver; I have chosen thee in the furnace of affliction. For Mine own sake, *even* for Mine own sake, will I do *it:* **for how should** *My name* **be polluted?** and I will not give My glory unto another. Hearken unto Me, O Jacob and Israel, My called; I *am* He; I *am* the first, I also *am* the last. Mine hand also hath laid the foundation of the earth, and My right hand hath spanned the heavens: *when* I call unto them, they stand up together. All ye, assemble yourselves, and hear; **which among them hath declared these** *things?* The Lord hath loved him: he will do his pleasure on Babylon, and his arm *shall be on* the Chaldeans.   11

                      14

                      3

Can a woman forget her sucking child, that she should not have compassion on the son of her womb? yea, they may forget, yet will I not forget thee   49   15

The children which thou shalt have, after thou hast lost the other, shall say again in thine ears, The place *is* too strait for me: give place to me that I may dwell. Then shalt thou say in thine heart, **Who hath begotten me these, seeing I have lost my children, and am**   21₃

CHAP	VER	
		desolate, a captive, and removing to and fro? and who hath brought up these? Behold, I was left alone; **these, where** had **they** been?
49	24	**Shall the prey be taken from the mighty, or the lawful captive delivered?**
	5	
50	1²	Thus saith the LORD, **Where** is **the bill of your mother's divorcement, whom I have put away?** or **which of My creditors** is it **to whom I have sold you?** Behold, for your iniquities have ye sold yourselves, and for your transgressions is your mother put away. **Wherefore, when I came,** was there **no man? when I called,** was there **none to answer? Is My hand shortened at all, that it cannot redeem?** or **have I no power to deliver?** behold, at My rebuke I dry up the sea, I make the rivers a wilderness: their fish stinketh, because there is no water, and dieth for thirst.
	2⁴	
	8²	For the Lord GOD will help me; therefore shall I not be confounded: therefore have I set my face like a flint, and I know that I shall not be ashamed. He is near that justifieth me; **who will contend with me?** let us stand together: **who** is **mine adversary?** let him come near to me. Behold, the Lord GOD will help me; **who** is **he** that **shall condemn me?** lo, they all shall wax old as a garment; the moth shall eat them up. **Who** is **among you that feareth the** LORD, **that obeyeth the voice of His servant, that walketh** in **darkness, and hath no light?** let him trust in the name of the LORD, and stay upon his God.
	9	
	10	
	10	
51	9	Awake, awake, put on strength, O arm of the LORD; awake, as in the ancient days, in the generations of old. Art **thou not it that hath cut Rahab,** and **wounded the dragon?** Art **thou not it which hath dried the sea, the waters of the great deep; that hath made the depths of the sea a way for the ransomed to pass over?** Therefore the redeemed of the LORD shall
	10	

| | CHAP. | VER. |

return, and come with singing unto Zion; and everlasting joy *shall be* upon their head. they shall obtain gladness and joy; *and* sorrow and mourning shall flee away. I, *even* I, *am* he that comforteth you: **who** *art* **thou, that thou shouldest be afraid of a man** *that* **shall die, and of the son of man** *which* **shall be made** *as* **grass; and forgettest the** Lord **thy maker, that hath stretched forth the heavens, and laid the foundations of the earth; and hast feared continually every day because of the fury of the oppressor, as if he were ready to destroy?** and where *is* the fury of the oppressor?   51   13²

These two *things* are come unto thee; **who shall be sorry for thee?** desolation, and destruction, and the famine, and the sword: **by whom shall I comfort thee?**

19²
6

Now therefore, what have I here, saith the Lord, **that My people is taken away for nought?** they that rule over them make them to howl, saith the Lord; and My name continually every day *is* blasphemed. Therefore My people shall know My name: therefore *they shall know* in that day that I *am* He that doth speak: behold, *it is* I.   52   5

1

Who hath believed our report? and **to whom is the arm of the** Lord **revealed?**   53   1²

He was taken from prison and from judgment: and **who shall declare His generation?** for He was cut off out of the land of the living: for the transgression of my people was He stricken.

8
3

Ho, every one that thirsteth, come ye to the waters, and he that hath no money; come ye, buy, and eat; yea, come, buy wine and milk without money and without price. **Wherefore do ye spend money for** *that which* *is* **not bread?** **and your labour for** *that which*   55   2²

2

CHAP	VER	
		satisfieth not? hearken diligently unto Me, and eat ye *that which is* good, and let your soul delight itself in fatness.
57	4²	But draw near hither, ye sons of the sorceress, the seed of the adulterer and the whore. **Against whom do ye sport yourselves? against whom make ye a wide mouth,** *and* **draw out the tongue?**
	5	*are* **ye not children of transgression, a seed of falsehood, enflaming yourselves with idols under every green tree, slaying the children in the valleys under the clifts of the rocks?** Among the smooth *stones* of the stream *is* thy portion; they, they *are* thy lot: even to them hast thou poured a drink offering, thou hast offered a meat offering. **Should I receive comfort in these?**
	6	
	11²	Thou art wearied in the greatness of thy way; *yet* saidst thou not, There is no hope: thou hast found the life of thine hand; therefore thou wast not grieved. **And of whom hast thou been afraid or feared, that thou hast lied, and hast not remembered Me, nor laid** *it* **to thy heart? have not I held My peace even of old, and thou fearest Me not?**
	6	
58	3²	**Wherefore have we fasted,** *say they,* **and Thou seest not?** *wherefore* **have we afflicted our soul, and Thou takest no knowledge?** Behold, in the day of your fast ye find pleasure, and exact all your labours. Behold, ye fast for strife and debate, and to smite with the fist of wickedness: ye shall not fast as *ye do this* day, to make your voice to be heard on high. **Is it such a fast that I have chosen? a day for a man to afflict his soul?** *is it* **to bow down his head as a bulrush, and to spread sackcloth and ashes** *under him?* **wilt thou call this a fast, and an acceptable day to the** LORD? *Is* **not this the fast that I have chosen? to loose the bands of wickedness, to undo the heavy burdens, and to let the oppressed**
	5⁴	
	6²	

	CHAP.	VER.

go free, and that ye break every yoke? *Is it* not to deal thy bread to the hungry, and that thou bring the poor that are cast out to thy house? when thou seest the naked, that thou cover him; and that thou hide not thyself from thine own flesh?   **58**   7[2]

  10

All the flocks of Kedar shall be gathered together unto thee, the rams of Nebaioth shall minister unto thee: they shall come up with acceptance on Mine altar, and I will glorify the house of My glory. **Who** *are* **these** *that* **fly as a cloud, and as the doves to their windows?** Surely the isles shall wait for Me, and the ships of Tarshish first, to bring thy sons from far, their silver and their gold with them, unto the name of the LORD thy God, and to the Holy One of Israel, because He hath glorified thee.   **60**   8

  1

Who *is* **this that cometh from Edom, with dyed garments from Bozrah?** this *that is* **glorious in his apparel, travelling in the greatness of his strength?** I that speak in righteousness, mighty to save. **Wherefore** *art thou* **red in thine apparel, and thy garments like him that treadeth in the winefat?**   **63**   1[2]

  2

But they rebelled, and vexed His holy Spirit: therefore He was turned to be their enemy, *and* He fought against them. Then He remembered the days of old, Moses, *and* his people, *saying*, **Where** *is* **He that brought them up out of the sea with the shepherd of His flock?** where *is* **He that put His holy Spirit within him?** **That led** *them* **by the right hand of Moses with His glorious arm, dividing the water before them, to make Himself an everlasting name?** **That led them through the deep, as an horse in the wilderness,** *that* **they should not stumble?** As a beast goeth down into the valley, the Spirit of the LORD caused him   11[2]

  12

  13

CHAP.	VER.	

63 15² to rest: so didst Thou lead Thy people, to make Thyself a glorious name. Look down from heaven, and behold from the habitation of Thy holiness and of Thy glory: **where** *is* **Thy zeal and Thy strength, the sounding of Thy bowels and of Thy mercies toward me? are they restrained?** Doubtless Thou *art* our father, though Abraham be ignorant of us, and Israel acknowledge us not: Thou, O LORD, *art* our father, our

17 redeemer; Thy name *is* from everlasting. **O** LORD, **why hast Thou made us to err from Thy ways,** *and* **hardened our heart from Thy fear?** Return for Thy servants' sake, the tribes of Thine inheritance. The people of Thy holiness have possessed *it* but a little while: our adversaries have trodden down Thy sanctuary.

10 We are *Thine*: Thou never barest rule over them; they were not called by Thy name.

Be not wroth very sore, O LORD, neither remember iniquity for ever: behold, see, we beseech Thee, we *are* all Thy people. Thy holy cities are a wilderness, Zion is a wilderness, Jerusalem a desolation. Our holy and our beautiful house, where our fathers praised Thee, is burned up with fire: and all our pleasant things are laid waste.

64 12² **Wilt Thou refrain Thyself for these** *things*, **O** LORD?

2 **wilt Thou hold Thy peace, and afflict us very sore?**

66 1² Thus saith the LORD, The heaven *is* My throne, and the earth *is* My footstool: **where** *is* **the house that ye build unto Me? and where** *is* **the place of My rest?** For all those *things* hath Mine hand made, and all those *things* have been, saith the LORD: but to this *man* will I look, *even* to *him that is* poor and of a contrite spirit, and trembleth at My word.

A voice of noise from the city, a voice from the temple, a voice of the LORD that rendereth recompence to His enemies. Before she travailed, she brought forth; before

8⁴ her pain came, she was delivered of a man child. **Who**

	CHAP.	VER.
hath heard such a thing? who hath seen such things? Shall the earth be made to bring forth in one day? *or* shall a nation be born at once? for as soon as Zion travailed, she brought forth her children. **Shall I bring to the birth, and not cause to bring forth?** saith the Lord: **shall I cause to bring forth, and shut** *the womb*? saith thy God.	66	9²
		8

Isaiah 190

JEREMIAH.

	CHAP.	VER.
MOREOVER the word of the Lord came unto me, saying, **Jeremiah, what seest thou?** And I said, I see a rod of an almond tree. Then said the Lord unto me, Thou hast well seen: for I will hasten My word to perform it. And the word of the Lord came	1	11
unto me the second time, saying, **What seest thou?**		13
And I said, I see a seething pot; and the face thereof *is* toward the north.		2
Thus saith the Lord, **What iniquity have your fathers found in Me, that they are gone far from Me, and have walked after vanity, and are become vain?** Neither said they, **Where** *is* **the** Lord **that**	2	5
brought us up out of the land of Egypt, that led us through the wilderness, through a land of deserts and of pits, through a land of drought, and of the shadow of death, through a land that no man passed through, and where no man dwelt? And I brought you into a plentiful country, to eat the fruit thereof and the goodness thereof; but when ye entered, ye defiled My land, and made Mine heritage an		6
abomination. The priests said not, **Where** *is* **the** Lord? and they that handle the law knew Me not: the pastors		8

CHAP.	VER.	

2 11

14 3

17

18 2

21

23

24

also transgressed against Me, and the prophets prophesied by Baal, and walked after *things that* do not profit.

Hath a nation changed *their* **gods, which** *are* **yet no gods?** but My people have changed their glory for *that which* doth not profit.

Is **Israel a servant?** *is* **he a homeborn** *slave?* **why is he spoiled?** The young lions roared upon him, *and* yelled, and they made his land waste: his cities are burned without inhabitant. Also the children of Noph and Tahapanes have broken the crown of thy head. **Hast thou not procured this unto thyself, in that thou hast forsaken the** LORD **thy God, when He led thee by the way?** **And now what hast thou to do in the way of Egypt, to drink the waters of Sihor? or what hast thou to do in the way of Assyria, to drink the waters of the river?** Thine own wickedness shall correct thee, and thy backslidings shall reprove thee: know therefore and see that *it is* an evil *thing* and bitter, that thou hast forsaken the LORD thy God, and that My fear *is* not in thee, saith the Lord GOD of hosts. For of old time I have broken thy yoke, *and* burst thy bands; and thou saidst, I will not transgress; when upon every high hill and under every green tree thou wanderest, playing the harlot. Yet I had planted thee a noble vine, wholly a right seed: **how then art thou turned into the degenerate plant of a strange vine unto Me?** For though thou wash thee with nitre, and take thee much soap, *yet* thine iniquity is marked before Me, saith the Lord GOD. **How canst thou say, I am not polluted, I have not gone after Baalim?** see thy way in the valley, know what thou hast done: *thou art* a swift dromedary traversing her ways; a wild ass used to the wilderness, *that* snuffeth up the wind at her pleasure; **in her occasion who can turn her away?** all they that seek her will not weary themselves; in her month they shall find her.

JEREMIAH:—II., III.

	CHAP.	VER.

As the thief is ashamed when he is found, so is the house of Israel ashamed; they, their kings, their princes, and their priests, and their prophets, saying to a stock, Thou *art* my father; and to a stone, Thou hast brought me forth : for they have turned *their* back unto Me, and not *their* face : but in the time of their trouble they will say, Arise, and save us. **But where** *are* **thy gods that thou hast made thee?** let them arise, if they can save thee in the time of thy trouble: for *according to* the number of thy cities are thy gods, O Judah. **Wherefore will ye plead with Me?** ye all have transgressed against Me, saith the LORD. In vain have I smitten your children; they received no correction : your own sword hath devoured your prophets, like a destroying lion. O generation, see ye the word of the LORD. **Have I been a wilderness unto Israel? a land of darkness? wherefore say My people, We are lords; we will come no more unto Thee? Can a maid forget her ornaments,** *or* **a bride her attire?** yet My people have forgotten Me days without number. **Why trimmest thou thy way to seek love?** therefore hast thou also taught the wicked ones thy ways. Also in thy skirts is found the blood of the souls of the poor innocents : I have not found it by secret search, but upon all these. Yet thou sayest, Because I am innocent, surely His anger shall turn from me. Behold, I will plead with thee, because thou sayest, I have not sinned. **Why gaddest thou about so much to change thy way?** thou also shalt be ashamed of Egypt, as thou wast ashamed of Assyria. Yea, thou shalt go forth from him, and thine hands upon thine head : for the LORD hath rejected thy confidences, and thou shalt not prosper in them.

2 28
29
31 3
32
33
36
21

They say, **If a man put away his wife, and she go from him, and become another man's, shall he return unto her again? shall not that land be greatly polluted?** but thou hast played the harlot with many lovers; yet return again to Me, saith the LORD.

3 1 2

CHAP.	VER.	
3	4	**Wilt thou not from this time cry unto Me, My father,** Thou *art* **the guide of my youth? Will He reserve** *His anger* **for ever? will He keep** *it* **to the end?** Behold, thou hast spoken and done evil things as thou couldest.
	6	The LORD said also unto me in the days of Josiah the king, **Hast thou seen** *that* **which backsliding Israel hath done?** she is gone up upon every high mountain and under every green tree, and there hath played the harlot.
	19	In those days the house of Judah shall walk with the house of Israel, and they shall come together out of the land of the north to the land that I have given for an inheritance unto your fathers. But I said, **How shall I put thee among the children, and give thee a pleasant land, a goodly heritage of the hosts of nations?** and I said, Thou shalt call Me, My father; and shalt not turn away from Me.
	7	
4	14	O Jerusalem, wash thine heart from wickedness, that thou mayest be saved. **How long shall thy vain thoughts lodge within thee?**
	21	Destruction upon destruction is cried; for the whole land is spoiled: suddenly are my tents spoiled, *and* my curtains in a moment. **How long shall I see the standard,** *and* **hear the sound of the trumpet?** For my people *is* foolish, they have not known me; they *are* sottish children, and they have none understanding: they *are* wise to do evil, but to do good they have no knowledge.
	30	The whole city shall flee for the noise of the horsemen and bowmen; they shall go into thickets, and climb up upon the rocks: every city *shall be* forsaken, and not a man dwell therein. **And** *when* **thou** *art* **spoiled, what wilt thou do?** Though thou clothest thyself with
	3	

JEREMIAH:—V.

crimson, though thou deckest thee with ornaments of gold, though thou rentest thy face with painting, in vain shalt thou make thyself fair; *thy* lovers will despise thee, they will seek thy life.

O Lord, *are* **not Thine eyes upon the truth?** Thou hast stricken them, but they have not grieved; Thou hast consumed them, *but* they have refused to receive correction: they have made their faces harder than a rock; they have refused to return.   5   3

How shall I pardon thee for this? thy children have forsaken Me, and sworn by *them that are* no gods: when I had fed them to the full, they then committed adultery, and assembled themselves by troops in the harlots' houses. They were *as* fed horses in the morning: every one neighed after his neighbour's wife. **Shall I not visit for these** *things?* saith the Lord: **and shall not My soul be avenged on such a nation as this?**   7

   9²

And it shall come to pass, when ye shall say, **Wherefore doeth the** Lord **our God all these** *things* **unto us?** then shalt thou answer them, Like as ye have forsaken Me, and served strange gods in your land, so shall ye serve strangers in a land *that is* not yours. Declare this in the house of Jacob, and publish it in Judah, saying, Hear now this, O foolish people, and without understanding; which have eyes, and see not; which have ears, and hear not: **Fear ye not Me?** saith the Lord: **will ye not tremble at My presence, which have placed the sand** *for* **the bound of the sea by a perpetual decree, that it cannot pass it: and though the waves thereof toss themselves, yet can they not prevail; though they roar, yet can they not pass over it?** But this people hath a revolting and a rebellious heart; they are revolted and gone.   19

   22²

For among My people are found wicked *men:* they lay

CHAP.	VER.	
5	29[2]	wait, as he that setteth snares; they set a trap, they catch men. As a cage is full of birds, so *are* their houses full of deceit: therefore they are become great, and waxen rich. They are waxen fat, they shine: yea, they overpass the deeds of the wicked: they judge not the cause, the cause of the fatherless, yet they prosper; and the right of the needy do they not judge. **Shall I not visit for these** *things* **?** saith the Lord: **shall not My soul be avenged on such a nation as this?** A wonderful and horrible thing is committed in the land; the prophets prophesy falsely, and the priests bear rule by their means; and My people love *to have it* so: and
	31	**what will ye do in the end thereof?**
	10	
6	10	Thus saith the Lord of hosts, They shall throughly glean the remnant of Israel as a vine: turn back thine hand as a grapegatherer into the baskets. **To whom shall I speak, and give warning, that they may hear?** behold, their ear *is* uncircumcised, and they cannot hearken: behold, the word of the Lord is unto them a reproach: they have no delight in it.
	15	**Were they ashamed when they had committed abomination?** nay, they were not at all ashamed, neither could they blush: therefore they shall fall among them that fall: at the time *that* I visit them they shall be cast down, saith the Lord.
	20	**To what purpose cometh there to Me incense from Sheba, and the sweet cane from a far country?** your burnt offerings *are* not acceptable, nor your sacrifices sweet unto Me.
	3	
7	8	Behold, ye trust in lying words, that cannot profit. **Will ye steal, murder, and commit adultery, and swear falsely, and burn incense unto Baal, and walk after other gods whom ye know not; and come and stand before Me in this house, which is called by My name, and say, We are delivered to**

JEREMIAH :—VII., VIII.

	CHAP.	VER.
do all these abominations? **Is this house, which is called by My name, become a den of robbers in your eyes?** Behold, even I have seen *it*, saith the LORD. | **7** | 11

Seest thou not what they do in the cities of Judah and in the streets of Jerusalem? The children gather wood, and the fathers kindle the fire, and the women knead *their* dough, to make cakes to the queen of heaven, and to pour out drink offerings unto other gods, that they may provoke Me to anger. **Do they provoke Me to anger?** saith the LORD: *do they* not *provoke* **themselves to the confusion of their own faces?** | | 17

| | | 19[2] |
| | | 5 |

Moreover thou shalt say unto them, Thus saith the LORD; **Shall they fall, and not arise? shall he turn away, and not return?** Why *then* **is this people of Jerusalem slidden back by a perpetual backsliding?** they hold fast deceit, they refuse to return. I hearkened and heard, *but* they spake not aright: no man repented him of his wickedness, saying, **What have I done?** every one turned to his course, as the horse rusheth into the battle. Yea, the stork in the heaven knoweth her appointed times; and the turtle and the crane and the swallow observe the time of their coming; but My people know not the judgment of the LORD. **How do ye say, We** *are* **wise, and the law of the** LORD *is* **with us?** Lo, certainly in vain made He *it;* the pen of the scribes *is* in vain. The wise *men* are ashamed, they are dismayed and taken: lo, they have rejected the word of the LORD; and **what wisdom** *is* **in them?** | **8** | 4[2] |
		5
		6
		8
		9

Were they ashamed when they had committed abomination? nay, they were not at all ashamed, neither could they blush: therefore shall they fall among them that fall: in the time of their visitation they shall be cast down, saith the LORD. I will surely consume them, saith the LORD: *there shall be* no grapes on the | | 12

JEREMIAH.—VIII., IX

CHAP.	VER
8	14

vine, nor figs on the fig tree, and the leaf shall fade; and *the things that* I have given them shall pass away from them. **Why do we sit still?** assemble yourselves, and let us enter into the defenced cities, and let us be silent there: for the Lord our God hath put us to silence, and given us water of gall to drink, because we have sinned against the Lord. We looked for peace, but no good came; *and* for a time of health, and behold trouble!

19³ *When* I would comfort myself against sorrow, my heart *is* faint in me. Behold the voice of the cry of the daughter of My people because of them that dwell in a far country: *Is* **not the** Lord **in Zion?** *is* **not her king in her? Why have they provoked me to anger with their graven images,** *and* **with strange vanities?** The harvest is past, the summer is ended, and we are not saved. For the hurt of the daughter of my people am I hurt; I am black; astonishment hath taken hold on me.

22² *Is there* **no balm in Gilead;** *is there* **no physician**
13 **there? why then is not the health of the daughter of my people recovered?**

---

9 7 Thine habitation *is* in the midst of deceit; through deceit they refuse to know Me, saith the Lord. Therefore thus saith the Lord of hosts, Behold, I will melt them, and try them; **for how shall I do for the daughter of My people?** Their tongue *is as* an arrow shot out; it speaketh deceit; *one* speaketh peaceably to his neighbour with his mouth, but in heart he layeth his wait.

9² **Shall I not visit them for these** *things?* saith the Lord: **shall not My soul be avenged on such a nation as this?**

12² **Who** *is* **the wise man, that may understand this?** and *who is he* **to whom the mouth of the** Lord **hath spoken, that he may declare it, for what the**
5 **land perisheth** *and* **is burned up like a wilderness, that none passeth through?**

JEREMIAH:—X.-XIII.

| | CHAP. | VER. |

Who would not fear Thee, O King of nations? for to Thee doth it appertain: forasmuch as among all the wise *men* of the nations, and in all their kingdoms, *there is* none like unto Thee. — 10 7; 1

What hath My beloved to do in Mine house, *seeing* **she hath wrought lewdness with many, and the holy flesh is passed from thee?** when thou doest evil, then thou rejoicest. — 11 15; 1

Righteous *art* Thou, O LORD, when I plead with Thee: yet let me talk with Thee of *Thy* judgments: **Wherefore doth the way of the wicked prosper?** *wherefore* **are all they happy that deal very treacherously?** Thou hast planted them, yea, they have taken root: they grow, yea, they bring forth fruit: Thou *art* near in their mouth, and far from their reins. But Thou, O LORD, knowest me: Thou hast seen me, and tried mine heart toward Thee: pull them out like sheep for the slaughter, and prepare them for the day of slaughter. **How long shall the land mourn, and the herbs of every field wither, for the wickedness of them that dwell therein?** the beasts are consumed, and the birds; because they said, He shall not see our last end. **If thou hast run with the footmen, and they have wearied thee, then how canst thou contend with horses?** and *if* **in the land of peace,** *wherein* **thou trustedst,** *they wearied thee,* **then how wilt thou do in the swelling of Jordan?** — 12 1²; 4; 5²; 5

Therefore thou shalt speak unto them this word; Thus saith the LORD God of Israel, Every bottle shall be filled with wine: and they shall say unto thee, **Do we not certainly know that every bottle shall be filled with wine?** Then shalt thou say unto them, Thus saith the LORD, Behold, I will fill all the inhabitants of this land, even the kings that sit upon David's throne, and the priests, and the prophets, and all the inhabitants of Jerusalem, with drunkenness. And I will dash them one — 13 12

JEREMIAH:—XIII., XIV.

CHAP.	VER.	
		against another, even the fathers and the sons together, saith the LORD: I will not pity, nor spare, nor have mercy, but destroy them.
13	20	Lift up your eyes, and behold them that come from the north: **where** *is* **the flock** *that* **was given thee,**
	21²	**thy beautiful flock? What wilt thou say when He shall punish thee?** for thou hast taught them *to be* captains, *and* as chief over thee: **shall not sorrows take thee, as a woman in travail?** And
	22	if thou say in thine heart, **Wherefore come these things upon me?** For the greatness of thine iniquity are
	23	thy skirts discovered, *and* thy heels made bare. **Can the Ethiopian change his skin, or the leopard his spots?** *then* may ye also do good, that are accustomed to do evil.
		I have seen thine adulteries, and thy neighings, the lewdness of thy whoredom, *and* thine abominations on the hills in the fields. Woe unto thee, O Jerusalem!
	27²	**wilt thou not be made clean?** when *shall it* once
	8	be?
		O LORD, though our iniquities testify against us, do Thou *it* for Thy name's sake. for our backslidings are many; we have sinned against Thee. O the hope of Israel,
14	8	the saviour thereof in time of trouble, **why shouldest Thou be as a stranger in the land, and as a wayfaring man** *that* **turneth aside to tarry for a night?**
	9	**Why shouldest Thou be as a man astonied, as a mighty man** *that* **cannot save?** yet Thou, O LORD, *art* in the midst of us, and we are called by Thy name; leave us not.
	19³	**Hast Thou utterly rejected Judah? hath Thy soul lothed Zion? why hast Thou smitten us, and** *there is* **no healing for us?** we looked for peace, and *there is* no good; and for the time of healing, and behold

trouble! We acknowledge, O LORD, our wickedness, *and* the iniquity of our fathers: for we have sinned against Thee. Do not abhor us, for Thy name's sake, do not disgrace the throne of Thy glory: remember, break not Thy covenant with us. **Are there** *any* **among the vanities of the Gentiles that can cause rain?** or **can the heavens give showers?** *art* **not Thou He, O** LORD **our God?** therefore we will wait upon Thee: for Thou hast made all these *things*. | 14 | 22[3]
| | 8

Then said the LORD unto me, Though Moses and Samuel stood before Me, *yet* My mind *could* not *be* toward this people: cast *them* out of My sight, and let them go forth. And it shall come to pass, if they say unto thee, **Whither shall we go forth?** then thou shalt tell them, Thus saith the LORD; Such as *are* for death, to death; and such as *are* for the sword, to the sword; and such as *are* for the famine, to the famine; and such as *are* for the captivity, to the captivity. | 15 | 2

And I will cause them to be removed into all kingdoms of the earth, because of Manasseh the son of Hezekiah king of Judah, for *that* which he did in Jerusalem. **For who shall have pity upon thee, O Jerusalem?** or **who shall bemoan thee?** or **who shall go aside to ask how thou doest?** Thou hast forsaken Me, saith the LORD, thou art gone backward: therefore will I stretch out My hand against thee, and destroy thee; I am weary with repenting. | | 5[3]

Shall iron break the northern iron and the steel? | | 12

O LORD, Thou knowest: remember me, and visit me, and revenge me of my persecutors; take me not away in Thy longsuffering: know that for Thy sake I have suffered rebuke. Thy words were found, and I did eat them; and Thy word was unto me the joy and rejoicing of mine heart: for I am called by Thy name, O LORD God of

CHAP	VER	
15	18²	hosts. I sat not in the assembly of the mockers, nor rejoiced; I sat alone because of Thy hand: for Thou hast filled me with indignation. **Why is my pain perpetual, and my wound incurable,** *which* **refuseth to be healed? wilt Thou be altogether unto me as a liar,** *and as* **waters** *that* **fail?**
	7	
16	10³	And it shall come to pass, when thou shalt shew this people all these words, and they shall say unto thee, **Wherefore hath the** Lord **pronounced all this great evil against us?** or **what** *is* **our iniquity?** or **what** *is* **our sin that we have committed against the** Lord **our God?** Then shalt thou say unto them, Because your fathers have forsaken Me, saith the Lord, and have walked after other gods, and have served them, and have worshipped them, and have forsaken Me, and have not kept My law; and ye have done worse than your fathers; for, behold, ye walk every one after the imagination of his evil heart, that they may not hearken unto Me: therefore will I cast you out of this land into a land that ye know not, *neither* ye nor your fathers; and there shall ye serve other gods day and night; where I will not shew you favour.
	20	**Shall a man make gods unto himself, and they** *are* **no gods?** Therefore, behold, I will this once cause them to know, I will cause them to know Mine hand and My might; and they shall know that My name *is* The Lord.
	4	
17	9	The heart *is* deceitful above all *things*, and desperately wicked: **who can know it?** I the Lord search the heart, *I* try the reins, even to give every man according to his ways, *and* according to the fruit of his doings.
	15	Behold, they say unto me, **Where** *is* **the word of the** Lord? let it come now.
	2	
18	6	Then the word of the Lord came to me, saying, O

house of Israel, cannot I do with you as this potter? saith the LORD Behold, as the clay *is* in the potter's hand, so *are* ye in Mine hand, O house of Israel.

Will *a man* **leave the snow of Lebanon** *which cometh* **from the rock of the field?** *or* **shall the cold flowing waters that come from another place be forsaken?** | 18 | 14²

Give heed to me, O LORD, and hearken to the voice of them that contend with me **Shall evil be recompensed for good?** for they have digged a pit for my soul Remember that I stood before Thee to speak good for them, *and* to turn away Thy wrath from them. | | 20

| | 4

Wherefore came I forth out of the womb to see labour and sorrow, that my days should be consumed with shame? | 19 | 18

| | 1

Behold, I *am* against thee, O inhabitant of the valley, *and* rock of the plain, saith the LORD; which say, **Who shall come down against us?** or **who shall enter into our habitations?** But I will punish you according to the fruit of your doings, saith the LORD: and I will kindle a fire in the forest thereof, and it shall devour all things round about it. | 21 | 13²

| | 2

For thus saith the LORD unto the king's house of Judah; **Thou** *art* **Gilead unto Me,** *and* **the head of Lebanon:** *yet* surely I will make thee a wilderness, *and* cities *which* are not inhabited. And I will prepare destroyers against thee, every one with his weapons: and they shall cut down thy choice cedars, and cast *them* into the fire And many nations shall pass by this city, and they shall say every man to his neighbour, **Wherefore hath the** LORD **done thus unto this great city?** | 22 | 8

Woe unto him that buildeth his house by unrighteous-

Chap.	Ver.	
22	15²	ness, and his chambers by wrong; *that* useth his neighbour's service without wages, and giveth him not for his work; that saith, I will build me a wide house and large chambers, and cutteth him out windows; and *it is* cieled with cedar, and painted with vermilion. **Shalt thou reign, because thou closest** *thyself* **in cedar? did not thy father eat and drink, and do judgment and justice,** *and* **then** *it was* **well with him?** He judged the cause of the poor and needy; then *it was* well
	16	*with him: was* **not this to know Me?** saith the Lord.
	28³	*Is* **this man Coniah a despised broken idol?** *is he* **a vessel wherein** *is* **no pleasure? wherefore are they cast out, he and his seed, and are cast into a land which they know not?**
	7	
23	18²	**For who hath stood in the counsel of the** Lord, **and hath perceived and heard His word?** **who hath marked His word, and heard** *it?*
	23	*Am* **I a God at hand,** saith the Lord. **and not a God afar off? Can any hide himself in secret places that I shall not see him?** saith the Lord. **Do not I fill heaven and earth?** saith the Lord. I have heard what the prophets said, that prophesy lies in My name, saying, I have dreamed, I have dreamed.
	24²	
	26	**How long shall** *this* **be in the heart of the prophets that prophesy lies?** yea, *they are* prophets of the deceit of their own heart; which think to cause My people to forget My name by their dreams which they tell every man to his neighbour, as their fathers have forgotten My name for Baal. The prophet that hath a dream, let him tell a dream; and he that hath My word, let him speak My word faithfully. **What** *is* **the chaff to the wheat?** saith the Lord. *Is* **not My word like as a fire?** saith the Lord; **and like a hammer** *that* **breaketh the rock in pieces?**
	28	
	29²	

And when this people, or the prophet, or a priest,

	CHAP	VER.
shall ask thee, saying, **What** *is* **the burden of the** Lord? thou shalt then say unto them, **What burden?** I will even forsake you, saith the Lord. And *as for* the prophet, and the priest, and the people, that shall say, The burden of the Lord, I will even punish that man and his house. Thus shall ye say every one to his neighbour, and every one to his brother, **What hath the** Lord **answered?** and, **What hath the** Lord **spoken?** And the burden of the Lord shall ye mention no more: for every man's word shall be his burden; for ye have perverted the words of the living God, of the Lord of hosts our God. Thus shalt thou say to the prophet, **What hath the** Lord **answered thee?** and, **What hath the** Lord **spoken?** But since ye say, The burden of the Lord; therefore thus saith the Lord; Because ye say this word, The burden of the Lord, and I have sent unto you, saying, Ye shall not say, The burden of the Lord; therefore, behold, I, even I, will utterly forget you, and I will forsake you, and the city that I gave you and your fathers, *and cast you* out of My presence. and I will bring an everlasting reproach upon you, and a perpetual shame, which shall not be forgotten.	**23** .	33[2] 35[2] 37[2] 15
Then said the Lord unto me, **What seest thou, Jeremiah?** And I said, Figs; the good figs, very good; and the evil, very evil, that cannot be eaten, they are so evil.	**24**	3 1
For, lo, I begin to bring evil on the city which is called by My name, and **should ye be utterly unpunished?** Ye shall not be unpunished: for I will call for a sword upon all the inhabitants of the earth, saith the Lord of hosts.	**25**	29 1

Now it came to pass, when Jeremiah had made an end of speaking all that the Lord had commanded *him* to speak unto all the people, that the priests and the prophets and all the people took him, saying, Thou shalt

Chap. Ver.	
26 9	surely die. **Why hast thou prophesied in the name of the** Lord, **saying, This house shall be like Shiloh, and this city shall be desolate without an inhabitant?** And all the people were gathered against Jeremiah in the house of the Lord.
	Then said the princes and all the people unto the priests and to the prophets; This man *is* not worthy to die: for he hath spoken to us in the name of the Lord our God. Then rose up certain of the elders of the land, and spake to all the assembly of the people, saying, Micah the Morasthite prophesied in the days of Hezekiah king of Judah, and spake to all the people of Judah, saying, Thus saith the Lord of hosts; Zion shall be plowed *like* a field, and Jerusalem shall become heaps, and the mountain of the house as the high places of a
19²	forest. **Did Hezekiah king of Judah and all Judah put him at all to death? did he not fear the** Lord, **and besought the** Lord, **and the** Lord **repented**
3	**Him of the evil which He had pronounced against them?** Thus might we procure great evil against our souls.
27 13	I spake also to Zedekiah king of Judah according to all these words, saying, Bring your necks under the yoke of the king of Babylon, and serve him and his people, and live. **Why will ye die, thou and thy people, by the sword, by the famine, and by the pestilence, as the** Lord **hath spoken against the nation that will not serve the king of Babylon?** Therefore hearken not unto the words of the prophets that speak unto you, saying, Ye shall not serve the king of Babylon: for they prophesy a lie unto you.
	Also I spake to the priests and to all this people, saying, Thus saith the Lord; Hearken not to the words of your prophets that prophesy unto you, saying, Behold, the vessels of the Lord's house shall now shortly be

JEREMIAH :—XXVII.-XXX. 191

| | CHAP. | VER |

brought again from Babylon : for they prophesy a lie unto you. Hearken not unto them ; serve the king of Babylon, and live: **wherefore should this city be laid waste?** — **27** 17

— 2

Thus shalt thou also speak to Shemaiah the Nehelamite, saying, Thus speaketh the LORD of hosts, the God of Israel, saying, Because thou hast sent letters in thy name unto all the people that *are* at Jerusalem, and to Zephaniah the son of Maaseiah the priest, and to all the priests, saying, The LORD hath made thee priest in the stead of Jehoiada the priest, that ye should be officers in the house of the LORD, for every man *that is* mad, and maketh himself a prophet, that thou shouldest put him in prison, and in the stocks. **Now therefore why hast thou not reproved Jeremiah of Anathoth, which maketh himself a prophet to you?** — **29** 27

— 1

And these *are* the words that the LORD spake concerning Israel and concerning Judah. For thus saith the LORD ; We have heard a voice of trembling, of fear, and not of peace. **Ask ye now, and see whether a man doth travail with child? wherefore do I see every man with his hands on his loins, as a woman in travail, and all faces are turned into paleness?** — **30** 6²

All thy lovers have forgotten thee : they seek thee not ; for I have wounded thee with the wound of an enemy, with the chastisement of a cruel one, for the multitude of thine iniquity; *because* thy sins were increased. **Why criest thou for thine affliction?** thy sorrow *is* incurable for the multitude of thine iniquity : *because* thy sins were increased, I have done these things unto thee. — 15

And their nobles shall be of themselves, and their governor shall proceed from the midst of them ; and I will cause him to draw near, and he shall approach unto

CHAP.	VER.	
30	21	Me: **for who** *is* **this that engaged his heart to approach unto Me?** saith the LORD. And ye shall
	4	be My people, and I will be your God.

31	20²	*Is* **Ephraim My dear son?** *is he* **a pleasant child?** for since I spake against him, I do earnestly remember him still: therefore My bowels are troubled for him; I will surely have mercy upon him, saith the LORD. Set thee up waymarks, make thee high heaps: set thine heart toward the highway, *even* the way *which* thou wentest: turn again, O virgin of Israel, turn again to
	22	these thy cities. **How long wilt thou go about, O thou backsliding daughter?** for the LORD hath
	3	created a new thing in the earth, A woman shall compass a man.

| 32 | 5 | For Zedekiah king of Judah had shut him up, saying, **Wherefore dost thou prophesy, and say, Thus saith the** LORD, **Behold, I will give this city into the hand of the king of Babylon, and he shall take it; and Zedekiah king of Judah shall not escape out of the hand of the Chaldeans, but shall surely be delivered into the hand of the king of Babylon, and shall speak with him mouth to mouth, and his eyes shall behold his eyes;** and he shall lead Zedekiah to Babylon, and there shall he be until I visit him, saith the LORD: **though ye fight with the Chaldeans, ye shall not prosper?** |

| | 27 | Then came the word of the LORD unto Jeremiah, saying, Behold, I *am* the LORD, the God of all flesh: **is |
| | 2 | there any thing too hard for Me?** |

| 33 | 24 | Moreover the word of the LORD came to Jeremiah, saying, **Considerest thou not what this people have spoken, saying, The two families which the** LORD **hath chosen, He hath even cast them off?** thus |
| | 1 | they have despised My people, that they should be no more a nation before them. |

	CHAP. VER.

Then came the word of the LORD unto Jeremiah, saying, Thus saith the LORD of hosts, the God of Israel; Go and tell the men of Judah and the inhabitants of Jerusalem, **Will ye not receive instruction to hearken to My words?** saith the LORD.

35 13

1

Now it came to pass, when they had heard all the words, they were afraid both one and other, and said unto Baruch, We will surely tell the king of all these words. And they asked Baruch, saying, **Tell us now, How didst thou write all these words at his mouth?** Then Baruch answered them, He pronounced all these words unto me with his mouth, and I wrote *them* with ink in the book.

36 17

And thou shalt say to Jehoiakim king of Judah, Thus saith the LORD; Thou hast burned this roll, saying, **Why hast thou written therein, saying, The king of Babylon shall certainly come and destroy this land, and shall cause to cease from thence man and beast?**

29

2

When Jeremiah was entered into the dungeon, and into the cabins, and Jeremiah had remained there many days; then Zedekiah the king sent, and took him out: and the king asked him secretly in his house, and said, **Is there** *any* **word from the** LORD? And Jeremiah said, There is: for, said he, thou shalt be delivered into the hand of the king of Babylon. Moreover Jeremiah said unto king Zedekiah, **What have I offended against thee, or against thy servants, or against this people, that ye have put me in prison? Where** *are* **now your prophets which prophesied unto you, saying, The king of Babylon shall not come against you, nor against this land?**

37 17

18

19

3

Then Zedekiah the king sent, and took Jeremiah the prophet unto him into the third entry that *is* in the house of the LORD: and the king said unto Jeremiah, I will ask

CHAP.	VER.	
38	15²	thee a thing; hide nothing from me. Then Jeremiah said unto Zedekiah, **If I declare** *it* **unto thee, wilt thou not surely put me to death?** and **if I give thee counsel, wilt thou not hearken unto me?**
	2	
40	14	Moreover Johanan the son of Kareah, and all the captains of the forces that *were* in the fields, came to Gedaliah to Mizpah, and said unto him, **Dost thou certainly know that Baalis the king of the Ammonites hath sent Ishmael the son of Nethaniah to slay thee?** But Gedaliah the son of Ahikam believed them not. Then Johanan the son of Kareah spake to Gedaliah in Mizpah secretly, saying, Let me go, I pray thee, and I will slay Ishmael the son
	15	of Nethaniah, and no man shall know *it*: **wherefore should he slay thee, that all the Jews which are gathered unto thee should be scattered, and the remnant in Judah perish?** But Gedaliah the son of
	2·	Ahikam said unto Johanan the son of Kareah, Thou shalt not do this thing; for thou speakest falsely of Ishmael.
44	8	Therefore now thus saith the LORD, the God of hosts, the God of Israel; **Wherefore commit ye** *this* **great evil against your souls, to cut off from you man and woman, child and suckling, out of Judah, to leave you none to remain; in that ye provoke Me unto wrath with the works of your hands, burning incense unto other gods in the land of Egypt, whither ye be gone to dwell, that ye might cut yourselves off, and that ye might be a curse and a reproach among all the nations of the earth?**
	9	**Have ye forgotten the wickedness of your fathers, and the wickedness of the kings of Judah, and the wickedness of their wives, and your own wickedness, and the wickedness of your wives, which they have committed in the land of Judah, and in the streets of Jerusalem?** They are not humbled *even* unto this day, neither have they feared, nor walked

in My law, nor in My statutes, that I set before you and before your fathers.

And **when we burned incense to the queen of heaven, and poured out drink offerings unto her, did we make her cakes to worship her, and pour out drink offerings unto her, without our men?** Then Jeremiah said unto all the people, to the men, and to the women, and to all the people which had given him *that* answer, saying, **The incense that ye burned in the cities of Judah, and in the streets of Jerusalem, ye, and your fathers, your kings, and your princes, and the people of the land, did not the** Lord **remember them, and came it** *not* **into His mind?** So that the Lord could no longer bear, because of the evil of your doings, *and* because of the abominations which ye have committed; therefore is your land a desolation, and an astonishment, and a curse, without an inhabitant, as at this day.

Thus shalt thou say unto him, The Lord saith thus; Behold, *that* which I have built will I break down, and that which I have planted I will pluck up, even this whole land. And **seekest thou great things for thyself?** seek *them* not: for, behold, I will bring evil upon all flesh, saith the Lord: but thy life will I give unto thee for a prey in all places whither thou goest.

The word of the Lord which came to Jeremiah the prophet against the Gentiles; against Egypt, against the army of Pharaoh-necho king of Egypt, which was by the river Euphrates in Carchemish, which Nebuchadrezzar king of Babylon smote in the fourth year of Jehoiakim the son of Josiah king of Judah. Order ye the buckler and shield, and draw near to battle. Harness the horses; and get up, ye horsemen, and stand forth with *your* helmets; furbish the spears, *and* put on the brigandines. **Wherefore have I seen them dismayed** *and* **turned away back?** and their mighty

CHAP.	VER.
44	19
	21
	4
45	5
	1
46	5

CHAP.	VER.	
46	7	ones are beaten down, and are fled apace, and look not back : *for* fear *was* round about, saith the LORD. Let not the swift flee away, nor the mighty man escape ; they shall stumble and fall toward the north by the river Euphrates. **Who** *is* **this** *that* **cometh up as a flood, whose waters are moved as the rivers?** Egypt riseth up like a flood, and *his* waters are moved like the rivers ; and he saith, I will go up, *and* will cover the earth ; I will destroy the city and the inhabitants thereof.
	15	The word that the LORD spake to Jeremiah the prophet, how Nebuchadrezzar king of Babylon should come *and* smite the land of Egypt. Declare ye in Egypt, and publish in Migdol, and publish in Noph and in Tahpanhes : say ye, Stand fast, and prepare thee ; for the sword shall devour round about thee. **Why are thy valiant** *men* **swept away?** they stood not, because the LORD did drive them.
	3	
47	5	Baldness is come upon Gaza ; Ashkelon is cut off *with* the remnant of their valley : **how long wilt thou cut thyself? O thou sword of the** LORD, **how long** *will it be* **ere thou be quiet?** put up thyself into thy scabbard, rest, and be still. **How can it be quiet, seeing the** LORD **hath given it a charge against Ashkelon, and against the sea shore?** there hath He appointed it.
	6	
	7	
	3	
48	14	**How say ye, We** *are* **mighty and strong men for the war?**
	19	O inhabitant of Aroer, stand by the way, and espy ; ask him that fleeth, and her that escapeth, *and* say, **What is done?**

Make ye him drunken : for he magnified *himself* against the LORD : Moab also shall wallow in his vomit, and he

JEREMIAH:—XLVIII., XLIX.   197

| | CHAP. | VER. |

also shall be in derision. For **was not Israel a derision unto thee? was he found among thieves?** for since thou spakest of him, thou skippedst for joy. | **48** | 27²

Concerning the Ammonites, thus saith the LORD; **Hath Israel no sons? hath he no heir? why** *then* **doth their king inherit Gad, and his people dwell in his cities?** | **49** | 1³

Wherefore gloriest thou in the valleys, thy flowing valley, O backsliding daughter? that trusted in her treasures, *saying*, **Who shall come unto me?** | | 4²

Concerning Edom, thus saith the LORD of hosts; *Is* **wisdom no more in Teman? is counsel perished from the prudent? is their wisdom vanished?** Flee ye, turn back, dwell deep, O inhabitants of Dedan; for I will bring the calamity of Esau upon him, the time *that* I will visit him. **If grapegatherers come to thee, would they not leave** *some* **gleaning grapes?** if thieves by night, they will destroy till they have enough. | | 7³

| | | 9

For thus saith the LORD; Behold, they whose judgment *was* not to drink of the cup have assuredly drunken; and *art* **thou he** *that* **shall altogether go unpunished?** thou shalt not go unpunished, but thou shalt surely drink *of it*. For I have sworn by Myself, saith the LORD, that Bozrah shall become a desolation, a reproach, a waste, and a curse; and all the cities thereof shall be perpetual wastes. | | 12

Also Edom shall be a desolation: every one that goeth by it shall be astonished, and shall hiss at all the plagues thereof. As in the overthrow of Sodom and Gomorrah and the neighbour *cities* thereof, saith the LORD, no man shall abide there, neither shall a son of man dwell in it. Behold, he shall come up like a lion from the swelling of Jordan against the habitation of the strong: but I will

CHAP.	VER.	
49	19*	suddenly make him run away from her: and **who** *is* **a chosen** *man, that* **I may appoint over her?** for who *is* **like Me?** and **who will appoint Me the time?** and **who** *is* **that shepherd that will stand before Me?**
50	44*	The king of Babylon hath heard the report of them, and his hands waxed feeble: anguish took hold of him, *and* pangs as of a woman in travail. Behold, he shall come up like a lion from the swelling of Jordan unto the habitation of the strong: but I will make them suddenly run away from her. and **who** *is* **a chosen** *man, that* **I may appoint over her?** for **who** *is* **like Me?** and **who will appoint Me the time?** and **who** *is* **that shepherd that will stand before Me?**
	4	

Jeremiah 195

LAMENTATIONS.

CHAP.	VER.	
1	12	*I*S *it* **nothing to you, all ye that pass by?** behold, and see if there be any sorrow like unto my sorrow, which is done unto me, wherewith the LORD hath afflicted *me* in the day of His fierce anger.
	1	
2	12	Mine eyes do fail with tears, my bowels are troubled, my liver is poured upon the earth, for the destruction of the daughter of my people; because the children and the sucklings swoon in the streets of the city. They say to their mothers, **Where** *is* **corn and wine?** when they swooned as the wounded in the streets of the city, when their soul was poured out into their mothers' bosom.
	13*	**What thing shall I take to witness for thee? what thing shall I liken to thee, O daughter of Jerusalem? what shall I equal to thee, that I**

LAMENTATIONS:—II.-V.

may comfort thee, O virgin daughter of Zion? for thy breach is great like the sea: **who can heal thee?** Thy prophets have seen vain and foolish things for thee: and they have not discovered thine iniquity, to turn away thy captivity; but have seen for thee false burdens and causes of banishment. All that pass by clap *their* hands at thee; they hiss and wag their head at the daughter of Jerusalem, *saying*, Is **this the city that** *men* **call The perfection of beauty, The joy of the whole earth?** All thine enemies have opened their mouth against thee: they hiss and gnash the teeth: they say, We have swallowed *her* up: certainly this is the day that we looked for; we have found, we have seen it. — 2 15

Behold, O LORD, and consider to whom Thou hast done this. **Shall the women eat their fruit, and children of a span long? shall the priest and the prophet be slain in the sanctuary of the Lord?** — 20[2] / 8

Who is he *that* **saith, and it cometh to pass,** *when* **the Lord commandeth** it **not? Out of the mouth of the most High proceedeth not evil and good? Wherefore doth a living man complain, a man for the punishment of his sins?** Let us search and try our ways, and turn again to the LORD. — 3 37 / 38 / 39 / 3

Thou, O LORD, remainest for ever; Thy throne from generation to generation. **Wherefore dost Thou forget us for ever,** *and* **forsake us so long time?** Turn Thou us unto Thee, O LORD, and we shall be turned; renew our days as of old. — 5 20 / 1

Lamentations 13

EZEKIEL.

CHAP.	VER.	
8	6²	THEN said He unto me, Son of man, lift up thine eyes now the way toward the north. So I lifted up mine eyes the way toward the north, and behold northward at the gate of the altar this image of jealousy in the entry. He said furthermore unto me, **Son of man, seest thou what they do?** *even* **the great abominations that the house of Israel committeth here, that I should go far off from My sanctuary?** but turn thee yet again, *and* thou shalt see greater abominations. And He brought me to the door of the court; and when I looked, behold a hole in the wall. Then said He unto me, Son of man, dig now in the wall: and when I had digged in the wall, behold a door. And He said unto me, Go in, and behold the wicked abominations that they do here. So I went in and saw; and behold every form of creeping things, and abominable beasts, and all the idols of the house of Israel, pourtrayed upon the wall round about. And there stood before them seventy men of the ancients of the house of Israel, and in the midst of them stood Jaazaniah the son of Shaphan, with every man his censer in his hand; and a thick cloud of incense went up. Then said
	12	He unto me, **Son of man, hast thou seen what the ancients of the house of Israel do in the dark, every man in the chambers of his imagery?** for they say, The LORD seeth us not; the LORD hath forsaken the earth. He said also unto me, Turn thee yet again, *and* thou shalt see greater abominations that they do. Then He brought me to the door of the gate of the LORD's house which *was* toward the north; and, behold, there sat women weeping for Tammuz. Then said He
	15	unto me, **Hast thou seen** *this*, **O son of man?** turn thee yet again, *and* thou shalt see greater abominations than these. And He brought me into the inner court of the LORD's house, and, behold, at the door of the temple

EZEKIEL:—VIII.-XII.

of the LORD, between the porch and the altar, *were* about five and twenty men, with their backs toward the temple of the LORD, and their faces toward the east; and they worshipped the sun toward the east. Then He said unto me, **Hast thou seen** *this,* **O son of man? Is it a light thing to the house of Judah that they commit the abominations which they commit here?** for they have filled the land with violence, and have returned to provoke Me to anger: and, lo, they put the branch to their nose. Therefore will I also deal in fury: Mine eye shall not spare, neither will I have pity: and though they cry in Mine ears with a loud voice, *yet* will I not hear them.

CHAP.	VER.
8	17²
	6

And it came to pass, while they were slaying them, and I was left, that I fell upon my face, and cried, and said, Ah Lord GOD! **wilt Thou destroy all the residue of Israel in Thy pouring out of Thy fury upon Jerusalem?**

9	8
	1

And it came to pass, when I prophesied, that Pelatiah the son of Benaiah died. Then fell I down upon my face, and cried with a loud voice, and said, Ah Lord GOD! **wilt Thou make a full end of the remnant of Israel?**

11	13
	1

And in the morning came the word of the LORD unto me, saying, Son of man, hath not the house of Israel, the rebellious house, said unto thee, **What doest thou?** Say thou unto them, Thus saith the Lord GOD; This burden *concerneth* the prince in Jerusalem, and all the house of Israel that *are* among them. Say, I *am* your sign: like as I have done, so shall it be done unto them: they shall remove *and* go into captivity.

12	9

And the word of the LORD came unto me, saying, **Son of man, what** *is* **that proverb** *that* **ye have in the land of Israel,** saying, **The days are prolonged, and every vision faileth?** Tell them therefore, Thus

	22
	2

CHAP.	VER.	
		saith the Lord God; I will make this proverb to cease, and they shall no more use it as a proverb in Israel; but say unto them, The days are at hand, and the effect of every vision. For there shall be no more any vain vision nor flattering divination within the house of Israel.
13	7	**Have ye not seen a vain vision, and have ye not spoken a lying divination, whereas ye say, The** Lord **saith** *it;* **albeit I have not spoken?** Therefore thus saith the Lord God; Because ye have spoken vanity, and seen lies, therefore, behold, I *am* against you, saith the Lord God.
	12	Lo, when the wall is fallen, **shall it not be said unto you, Where** *is* **the daubing wherewith ye have daubed** *it?*
	18	Likewise, thou son of man, set thy face against the daughters of thy people, which prophesy out of their own heart; and prophesy thou against them, and say, Thus saith the Lord God; Woe to the *women* that sew pillows to all armholes, and make kerchiefs upon the head of every stature to hunt souls! **Will ye hunt the souls of My people, and will ye save the souls**
	19	**alive** *that come* **unto you?** And will ye pollute Me among My people for handfuls of barley and for pieces of bread, to slay the souls that should not
	4	die, and to save the souls alive that should not live, by your lying to My people that hear *your* lies?
14	3	And the word of the Lord came unto me, saying, Son of man, these men have set up their idols in their heart, and put the stumblingblock of their iniquity before their face: **should I be inquired of at all by them?**
		Or *if* I send a pestilence into that land, and pour out My fury upon it in blood, to cut off from it man and

	CHAP.	VER.

beast: though Noah, Daniel, and Job, *were* in it, *as* I live, saith the Lord God, they shall deliver neither son nor daughter; they shall *but* deliver their own souls by their righteousness. For thus saith the Lord God; **How much more when I send My four sore judgments upon Jerusalem, the sword, and the famine, and the noisome beast, and the pestilence, to cut off from it man and beast?** — 14, 21; 2

And the word of the Lord came unto me, saying, Son of man, **What is the vine tree more than any tree,** *or than* **a branch which is among the trees of the forest? Shall wood be taken thereof to do any work? or will** *men* **take a pin of it to hang any vessel thereon?** Behold, it is cast into the fire for fuel; the fire devoureth both the ends of it, and the midst of it is burned. **Is it meet for** *any* **work?** Behold, when it was whole, it was meet for no work: **how much less shall it be meet yet for** *any* **work, when the fire hath devoured it, and it is burned?** — 15, 2; 3²; 4; 5; 5

Moreover thou hast taken thy sons and thy daughters, whom thou hast borne unto Me, and these hast thou sacrificed unto them to be devoured. *Is this* **of thy whoredoms a small matter, that thou hast slain My children, and delivered them to cause them to pass through** *the fire* **for them?** — 16, 21; 1

Say thou, Thus saith the Lord God; **Shall it prosper? shall he not pull up the roots thereof, and cut off the fruit thereof, that it wither?** it shall wither in all the leaves of her spring, even without great power or many people to pluck it up by the roots thereof. **Yea, behold,** *being* **planted, shall it prosper? shall it not utterly wither, when the east wind toucheth it?** it shall wither in the furrows where it grew. Moreover the word of the Lord came unto me, — 17, 9²; 10²

CHAP.	VER.	
17	12	saying, Say now to the rebellious house, **Know ye not what these** *things mean?* tell *them,* Behold, the king of Babylon is come to Jerusalem, and hath taken the king thereof, and the princes thereof, and led them with him to Babylon; and hath taken of the king's seed, and made a covenant with him, and hath taken an oath of him : he hath also taken the mighty of the land : that the kingdom might be base, that it might not lift itself up, *but* that by keeping of his covenant it might stand. But he rebelled against him in sending his ambassadors into Egypt, that they might give him horses and much people.
	15³	**Shall he prosper? shall he escape that doeth such** *things?* **or shall he break the covenant, and be delivered?** *As* I live, saith the Lord GOD, surely in the place *where* the king *dwelleth* that made him king, whose oath he despised, and whose covenant he brake,
	8	*even* with him in the midst of Babylon he shall die.
18	2	The word of the LORD came unto me again, saying, **What mean ye, that ye use this proverb concerning the land of Israel, saying, The fathers have eaten sour grapes, and the children's teeth are set on edge?** *As* I live, saith the Lord GOD, ye shall not have *occasion* any more to use this proverb in Israel. Behold, all souls are Mine; as the soul of the father, so also the soul of the son is Mine : the soul that sinneth, it shall die.
	13	**If he beget a son** *that is* **a robber, a shedder of blood, and** *that* **doeth the like to** *any* **one of these** *things,* **and that doeth not any of those** *duties,* **but even hath eaten upon the mountains, and defiled his neighbour's wife, hath oppressed the poor and needy, hath spoiled by violence, hath not restored the pledge, and hath lifted up his eyes to the idols, hath committed abomination, hath given forth upon usury, and hath taken increase : shall he then live?** he shall not live . he hath done all these

abominations; he shall surely die; his blood shall be upon him.

Yet say ye, Why? doth not the son bear the iniquity of the father? When the son hath done that which is lawful and right, *and* hath kept all My statutes, and hath done them, he shall surely live.

Have I any pleasure at all that the wicked should die? saith the Lord God: *and* **not that he should return from his ways, and live? But when the righteous turneth away from his righteousness, and committeth iniquity,** *and* **doeth according to all the abominations that the wicked** *man* **doeth, shall he live?** All his righteousness that he hath done shall not be mentioned: in his trespass that he hath trespassed, and in his sin that he hath sinned, in them shall he die. Yet ye say, The way of the Lord is not equal. Hear now, O house of Israel; **Is not My way equal? are not your ways unequal?** When a righteous *man* turneth away from his righteousness, and committeth iniquity, and dieth in them; for his iniquity that he hath done shall he die.

Yet saith the house of Israel, The way of the Lord is not equal. **O house of Israel, are not My ways equal? are not your ways unequal?**

Cast away from you all your transgressions, whereby ye have transgressed; and make you a new heart and a new spirit: **for why will ye die, O house of Israel?** For I have no pleasure in the death of him that dieth, saith the Lord God: wherefore turn *yourselves*, and live ye.

Moreover take thou up a lamentation for the princes of Israel, and say, **What** *is* **thy mother?** A lioness: she lay down among lions, she nourished her whelps among young lions. And she brought up one of her

CHAP.	VER.
18	19²
	23²
	24
	25²
	29²
	31
	12
19	2
	1

CHAP.	VER
20	3
	4

whelps: it became a young lion, and it learned to catch the prey; it devoured men.

Then came the word of the LORD unto me, saying, Son of man, speak unto the elders of Israel, and say unto them, Thus saith the Lord GOD; **Are ye come to inquire of me?** *As* I live, saith the Lord GOD, I will not be inquired of by you. **Wilt thou judge them, son of man, wilt thou judge** *them?* cause them to know the abominations of their fathers: and say unto them, Thus saith the Lord GOD; In the day when I chose Israel, and lifted up Mine hand unto the seed of the house of Jacob, and made Myself known unto them in the land of Egypt, when I lifted up Mine hand unto them, saying, I *am* the LORD your God; in the day *that* I lifted up Mine hand unto them, to bring them forth of the land of Egypt into a land that I had espied for them, flowing with milk and honey, which *is* the glory of all lands: then said I unto them, Cast ye away every man the abominations of his eyes, and defile not yourselves with the idols of Egypt: I *am* the LORD your God.

---

29 Then I said unto them, **What** *is* **the high place whereunto ye go?** And the name thereof is called Bamah unto this day. Wherefore say unto the house of
30² Israel, Thus saith the Lord GOD, **Are ye polluted after the manner of your fathers? and commit ye whoredom after their abominations?** For when ye offer your gifts, when ye make your sons to pass through the fire, ye pollute yourselves with all
31 your idols, even unto this day and **shall I be inquired of by you, O house of Israel?** *As* I live, saith the Lord GOD, I will not be inquired of by you. And that which cometh into your mind shall not be at all, that ye say, We will be as the heathen, as the families of the countries, to serve wood and stone.

EZEKIEL:—XX., XXI.

	CHAP.	VER.
Moreover the word of the LORD came unto me, saying, Son of man, set thy face toward the south, and drop *thy word* toward the south, and prophesy against the forest of the south field; and say to the forest of the south, Hear the word of the LORD; Thus saith the Lord GOD; Behold I will kindle a fire in thee, and it shall devour every green tree in thee, and every dry tree: the flaming flame shall not be quenched, and all faces from the south to the north shall be burned therein And all flesh shall see that I the LORD have kindled it: it shall not be quenched. Then said I, Ah Lord GOD! they say of me, **Doth he not speak parables?**	20	49
		7
That all flesh may know that I the LORD have drawn forth My sword out of his sheath: it shall not return any more. Sigh therefore, thou son of man, with the breaking of *thy* loins, and with bitterness sigh before their eyes. And it shall be, when they say unto thee, **Wherefore sighest thou?** that thou shalt answer, For the tidings; because it cometh: and every heart shall melt, and all hands shall be feeble, and every spirit shall faint, and all knees shall be weak *as* water: behold, it cometh, and shall be brought to pass, saith the Lord GOD. Again the word of the LORD came unto me, saying, Son of man, prophesy, and say, Thus saith the LORD; Say, A sword, a sword is sharpened, and also furbished: it is sharpened to make a sore slaughter; it is furbished that it may glitter: **should we then make mirth?**	21	7
		10
it contemneth the rod of My son, *as* every tree. And He hath given it to be furbished, that it may be handled: this sword is sharpened, and it is furbished, to give it into the hand of the slayer. Cry and howl, son of man: for it shall be upon My people, it *shall be* upon all the princes of Israel: terrors by reason of the sword shall be upon My people: smite therefore upon *thy* thigh. Because *it is* a trial, and **what if** *the sword* **contemn even the rod?** it shall be no *more*, saith the Lord GOD.		13

CHAP.	VER.	
		And thou, son of man, prophesy and say, Thus saith the Lord God concerning the Ammonites, and concerning their reproach; even say thou, The sword, the sword *is* drawn: for the slaughter *it is* furbished, to consume because of the glittering: whiles they see vanity unto thee, whiles they divine a lie unto thee, to bring thee upon the necks of *them that are* slain, of the wicked, whose day is come, when their iniquity *shall have* an end. **Shall I cause** *it* **to return into his sheath?**
21	30	
	4	I will judge thee in the place where thou wast created, in the land of thy nativity.
22	2	Moreover the word of the Lord came unto me, saying, **Now, thou son of man, wilt thou judge, wilt thou judge the bloody city?** yea, thou shalt shew her all her abominations.
	14	Behold, therefore I have smitten Mine hand at thy dishonest gain which thou hast made, and at thy blood which hath been in the midst of thee. **Can thine heart endure, or can thine hands be strong, in the days that I shall deal with thee?** I the Lord have spoken *it*, and will do *it*. And I will scatter thee among the heathen, and disperse thee in the countries, and will consume thy filthiness out of thee.
	2	
23	36	The Lord said moreover unto me; **Son of man, wilt thou judge Aholah and Aholibah?** yea, declare unto them their abominations; that they have committed adultery, and blood *is* in their hands, and with their idols have they committed adultery, and have also caused their sons, whom they bare unto me, to pass for them through *the fire*, to devour *them*.
	43	Then said I unto *her that was* old in adulteries, **Will they now commit whoredoms with her, and she** *with them?* Yet they went in unto her, as they go in unto a woman that playeth the harlot: so went they in unto Aholah and unto Aholibah, the lewd women.
	2	

	CHAP.	VER.

And the people said unto me, **Wilt thou not tell us what these** *things are* **to us, that thou doest** *so?* — 24, 19

Thus Ezekiel is unto you a sign: according to all that he hath done shall ye do: and when this cometh, ye shall know that I *am* the Lord God. Also, thou son of man, *shall it* **not** *be* **in the day when I take from them their strength, the joy of their glory, the desire of their eyes, and that whereupon they set their minds, their sons and their daughters,** *that* **he that escapeth in that day shall come unto thee, to cause** *thee* **to hear** *it* **with** *thine* **ears?** In that day shall thy mouth be opened to him which is escaped, and thou shalt speak, and be no more dumb: and thou shalt be a sign unto them; and they shall know that I *am* the Lord. — 26; 2

Thus saith the Lord God to Tyrus; **Shall not the isles shake at the sound of thy fall, when the wounded cry, when the slaughter is made in the midst of thee?** — 26, 15; 1

And in their wailing they shall take up a lamentation for thee, and lament over thee, *saying,* **What** *city is* **like Tyrus, like the destroyed in the midst of the sea?** — 27, 32; 1

Therefore thus saith the Lord God; Because thou hast set thine heart as the heart of God; behold, therefore I will bring strangers upon thee, the terrible of the nations: and they shall draw their swords against the beauty of thy wisdom, and they shall defile thy brightness. They shall bring thee down to the pit, and thou shalt die the deaths of *them that are* slain in the midst of the seas. **Wilt thou yet say before him that slayeth thee, I** *am* **God?** but thou *shalt be* a man, and no God, in the hand of him that slayeth thee. — 28, 9; 1

CHAP.	VER.	
31	2	And it came to pass in the eleventh year, in the third *month*, in the first *day* of the month, *that* the word of the LORD came unto me, saying, Son of man, speak unto Pharaoh king of Egypt, and to his multitude; **Whom art thou like in thy greatness?**
	18	**To whom art thou thus like in glory and in greatness among the trees of Eden?** yet shalt thou be brought down with the trees of Eden unto the nether parts of the earth: thou shalt lie in the midst of the uncircumcised with *them that be* slain by the sword. This *is* Pharaoh and all his multitude, saith the Lord GOD.
	2	
32	19	It came to pass also in the twelfth year, in the fifteenth *day* of the month, *that* the word of the LORD came unto me, saying, Son of man, wail for the multitude of Egypt, and cast them down, *even* her, and the daughters of the famous nations, unto the nether parts of the earth, with them that go down into the pit. **Whom dost thou pass in beauty?** go down, and be thou laid with the uncircumcised. They shall fall in the midst of *them that are* slain by the sword: she is delivered to the sword: draw her and all her multitudes.
	1	
33	10	Nevertheless, if thou warn the wicked of his way to turn from it; if he do not turn from his way, he shall die in his iniquity; but thou hast delivered thy soul. Therefore, O thou son of man, speak unto the house of Israel; Thus ye speak, saying, **If our transgressions and our sins *be* upon us, and we pine away in them, how should we then live?** Say unto them, *As* I live, saith the Lord GOD, I have no pleasure in the death of the wicked; but that the wicked turn from his way and live: turn ye, turn ye from your evil ways; **for why will ye die, O house of Israel?**
	11	

Then the word of the LORD came unto me, saying, Son of man, they that inhabit those wastes of the land of Israel speak, saying, Abraham was one, and he inherited the land: but we *are* many; the land is given us for inheritance. Wherefore say unto them, Thus saith the Lord GOD; Ye eat with the blood, and lift up your eyes toward your idols, and shed blood: and **shall ye possess the land?** Ye stand upon your sword, ye work abomination, and ye defile every one his neighbour's wife: and **shall ye possess the land?** | 33 | 25

| | 26
| | 4

And the word of the LORD came unto me, saying, Son of man, prophesy against the shepherds of Israel, prophesy, and say unto them, Thus saith the Lord GOD unto the shepherds, Woe *be* to the shepherds of Israel that do feed themselves! **should not the shepherds feed the flocks?** Ye eat the fat, and ye clothe you with the wool, ye kill them that are fed: *but* ye feed not the flock. | 34 | 2

I will feed My flock, and I will cause them to lie down, saith the Lord GOD. I will seek that which was lost, and bring again that which was driven away, and will bind up *that which was* broken, and will strengthen that which was sick: but I will destroy the fat and the strong; I will feed them with judgment. And *as for* you, O My flock, thus saith the Lord GOD; Behold, I judge between cattle and cattle, between the rams and the he goats. *Seemeth it* **a small thing unto you to have eaten up the good pasture, but ye must tread down with your feet the residue of your pastures? and to have drunk of the deep waters, but ye must foul the residue with your feet?** And *as for* My flock, they eat that which ye have trodden with your feet; and they drink that which ye have fouled with your feet. | | 18[2]

| | 3

And He said unto me, **Son of man, can these bones live?** And I answered, O Lord GOD, Thou knowest. | 37 | 3

And when the children of thy people shall speak unto

CHAP.	VER.	
37	18	thee, saying, **Wilt thou not shew us what thou** *meanest* **by these?** say unto them, Thus saith the Lord GOD; Behold, I will take the stick of Joseph, which *is* in the hand of Ephraim, and the tribes of Israel his fellows, and will put them with him, *even* with the stick of Judah, and make them one stick, and they shall be one in Mine hand.
	2	

| 38 | 13³ | Sheba, and Dedan, and the merchants of Tarshish, with all the young lions thereof, shall say unto thee, **Art thou come to take a spoil? hast thou gathered thy company to take a prey? to carry away silver and gold, to take away cattle and goods, to take a great spoil?** Therefore, son of man, prophesy and say unto Gog, Thus saith the Lord GOD; In that day when My people of Israel dwelleth safely, **shalt thou not know** *it?* |
| | 14 | |

| | 17 | Thus saith the Lord GOD; *Art* **thou he of whom I have spoken in old time by My servants the prophets of Israel, which prophesied in those days** *many* **years that I would bring thee against them?** |
| | 5 | |

| 47 | 6 | And He said unto me, **Son of man, hast thou seen** *this?* Then He brought me, and caused me to return to the brink of the river. Now when I had returned, behold, at the bank of the river *were* very many trees on the one side and on the other. |
| | 1 | |

Ezekiel 81

DANIEL.

	CHAP.	VER.
Now God had brought Daniel into favour and tender love with the prince of the eunuchs. And the prince of the eunuchs said unto Daniel, I fear my lord the king, who hath appointed your meat and your drink: **for why should he see your faces worse liking than the children which** are **of your sort?** then shall ye make me endanger my head to the king.	1	10
		1

Then Daniel answered with counsel and wisdom to Arioch the captain of the king's guard, which was gone forth to slay the wise men of Babylon: He answered and said to Arioch the king's captain, **Why** is **the decree** so **hasty from the king?** Then Arioch made the thing known to Daniel. | **2** | 15 |

Then Arioch brought in Daniel before the king in haste, and said thus unto him, I have found a man of the captives of Judah, that will make known unto the king the interpretation. The king answered and said to Daniel, whose name was Belteshazzar, **Art thou able to make known unto me the dream which I have seen, and the interpretation thereof?** | | 26 |
| | | 2 |

Nebuchadnezzar spake and said unto them, Is it **true, O Shadrach, Meshach, and Abed-nego, do not ye serve my gods, nor worship the golden image which I have set up?** Now if ye be ready that at what time ye hear the sound of the cornet, flute, harp, sackbut, psaltery, and dulcimer, and all kinds of musick, ye fall down and worship the image which I have made; well: but if ye worship not, ye shall be cast the same hour into the midst of a burning fiery furnace; and **who** is **that God that shall deliver you out of my hands?** Shadrach, Meshach, and Abed-nego, answered | **3** | 14 |
| | | 15 |

DANIEL:—III., IV

CHAP.	VER.	
3	24	
	3	

and said to the king, O Nebuchadnezzar, we *are* not careful to answer thee in this matter.

Then Nebuchadnezzar the king was astonied, and rose up in haste, *and* spake, and said unto his counsellors, **Did not we cast three men bound into the midst of the fire?** They answered and said unto the king, True, O king. He answered and said, Lo, I see four men loose, walking in the midst of the fire, and they have no hurt; and the form of the fourth is like the Son of God.

| 4 | 30 |

All this came upon the king Nebuchadnezzar. At the end of twelve months he walked in the palace of the kingdom of Babylon. The king spake, and said, **Is not this great Babylon, that I have built for the house of the kingdom by the might of my power, and for the honour of my majesty?** While the word *was* in the king's mouth, there fell a voice from heaven, *saying*, O king Nebuchadnezzar, to thee it is spoken; The kingdom is departed from thee.

| | 35 |
| | 2 |

And at the end of the days, I Nebuchadnezzar lifted up mine eyes unto heaven, and mine understanding returned unto me, and I blessed the most High, and I praised and honoured Him that liveth for ever, whose dominion *is* an everlasting dominion, and His kingdom *is* from generation to generation; and all the inhabitants of the earth *are* reputed as nothing: and He doeth according to His will in the army of heaven, and *among* the inhabitants of the earth: and none can stay His hand, or say unto Him, **What doest Thou?** At the same time my reason returned unto me; and for the glory of my kingdom, mine honour and brightness returned unto me; and my counsellors and my lords sought unto me; and I was established in my kingdom, and excellent majesty was added unto me. Now I Nebuchadnezzar praise and extol and honour the King of heaven, all whose works *are* truth, and His ways judgment: and those that walk in pride He is able to abase.

	CHAP.	VER.

Then was Daniel brought in before the king. *And* the king spake and said unto Daniel, *Art* **thou that Daniel, which** *art* **of the children of the captivity of Judah, whom the king my father brought out of Jewry?** — 5, 13 / 1

Then these men assembled, and found Daniel praying and making supplication before his God. Then they came near, and spake before the king concerning the king's decree; **Hast thou not signed a decree, that every man that shall ask** *a petition* **of any God or man within thirty days, save of thee, O king, shall be cast into the den of lions?** The king answered and said, The thing *is* true, according to the law of the Medes and Persians, which altereth not. — 6, 12

Then the king arose very early in the morning, and went in haste unto the den of lions. And when he came to the den, he cried with a lamentable voice unto Daniel: *and* the king spake and said to Daniel, **O Daniel, servant of the living God, is thy God, whom thou servest continually, able to deliver thee from the lions?** Then said Daniel unto the king, O king, live for ever. My God hath sent His angel, and hath shut the lions' mouths, that they have not hurt me; forasmuch as before Him innocency was found in me; and also before thee, O king, have I done no hurt. — 20 / 2

Then I heard one saint speaking, and another saint said unto that certain *saint* which spake, **How long** *shall be* **the vision** *concerning* **the daily** *sacrifice,* **and the transgression of desolation, to give both the sanctuary and the host to be trodden under foot?** And he said unto me, Unto two thousand and three hundred days; then shall the sanctuary be cleansed. — 8, 13 / 1

For how can the servant of this my lord talk with this my lord? for as for me, straightway there — 10, 17

CHAP.	VER.	
10	20	remained no strength in me, neither is there breath left in me. Then there came again and touched me *one* like the appearance of a man, and he strengthened me, and said, O man greatly beloved, fear not: peace *be* unto thee, be strong, yea, be strong. And when he had spoken unto me, I was strengthened, and said, Let my lord speak; for thou hast strengthened me. Then said he, **Knowest thou wherefore I come unto thee?** and now will I return to fight with the prince of Persia: and when I am gone forth, lo, the prince of Grecia shall come. But I will shew thee that which is noted in the
	2	scripture of truth: and *there is* none that holdeth with me in these things, but Michael your prince.
12	6	And *one* said to the man clothed in linen, which *was* upon the waters of the river, **How long** *shall it be to* **the end of these wonders?** And I heard the man clothed in linen, which *was* upon the waters of the river, when he held up his right hand and his left hand unto heaven, and sware by Him that liveth for ever that *it shall be* for a time, times, and an half; and when he shall have accomplished to scatter the power of the holy people, all these *things* shall be finished. And I heard,
	8	but I understood not: then said I, O my Lord, **what** *shall be* **the end of these** *things?* And He said, Go thy way, Daniel: for the words *are* closed up and sealed till the time of the end.
	2	

Daniel 16

HOSEA.

CHAP.	VER.	
6	4²	O EPHRAIM, what shall I do unto thee? O Judah, what shall I do unto thee? for your
	2	goodness *is* as a morning cloud, and as the early dew it goeth away.

HOSEA:—VIII.-XIV.

	CHAP.	VER.
Thy calf, O Samaria, hath cast *thee* off; Mine anger is kindled against them: **how long** *will it be* **ere they attain to innocency?** For from Israel *was* it also: the workman made it; therefore it *is* not God: but the calf of Samaria shall be broken in pieces.	8	5
		1
What will ye do in the solemn day, and in the day of the feast of the LORD?	9	5
Give them, O LORD: **what wilt Thou give?** give them a miscarrying womb and dry breasts.		14
		2
For now they shall say, We have no king, because we feared not the LORD; **what then should a king do to us?**	10	3
		1
How shall I give thee up, Ephraim? *how* **shall I deliver thee, Israel? how shall I make thee as Admah?** *how* **shall I set thee as Zeboim?** Mine heart is turned within Me, My repentings are kindled together. I will not execute the fierceness of Mine anger, I will not return to destroy Ephraim: for I *am* God, and not man; the Holy One in the midst of thee: and I will not enter into the city.	11	8[4]
		4
Is there **iniquity** *in* **Gilead?** surely they are vanity: they sacrifice bullocks in Gilgal; yea, their altars *are* as heaps in the furrows of the fields.	12	11
		1
O Israel, thou hast destroyed thyself: but in Me *is* thine help. I will be thy king: **where** *is any other* **that may save thee in all thy cities?** and thy judges of whom thou saidst, **Give me a king and princes?** I gave thee a king in Mine anger, and took *him* away in My wrath.	13	10[a]
		2
Ephraim *shall say*, **What have I to do any more with idols?** I have heard *him*, and observed him: I	14	8

CHAP.	VER.	
14	9²	*am* like a green fir tree. From Me is thy fruit found. **Who** *is* **wise, and he shall understand these things?** **prudent, and he shall know them?** for the ways of the Lord *are* right, and the just shall walk in them: but the transgressors shall fall therein.
	3	

Hosea 16

JOEL.

CHAP.	VER.	
1	2	HEAR this, ye old men, and give ear, all ye inhabitants of the land. **Hath this been in your days, or even in the days of your fathers?** Tell ye your children of it, and *let* your children *tell* their children, and their children another generation.
	16	**Is not the meat cut off before our eyes,** *yea*, **joy and gladness from the house of our God?**
	2	
2	11	The earth shall quake before them; the heavens shall tremble: the sun and the moon shall be dark, and the stars shall withdraw their shining: and the Lord shall utter His voice before His army: for His camp *is* very great: for *He is* strong that executeth His word: for the day of the Lord *is* great and very terrible; and **who can abide it?** Therefore also now, saith the Lord, turn ye *even* to Me with all your heart, and with fasting, and with weeping, and with mourning: and rend your heart, and not your garments, and turn unto the Lord your God: for He *is* gracious and merciful, slow to anger, and of great kindness, and repenteth Him of the evil.
	14	**Who knoweth** *if* **He will return and repent, and leave a blessing behind Him;** *even* **a meat offering and a drink offering unto the** Lord **your God?**

Let the priests, the ministers of the LORD, weep between the porch and the altar, and let them say, Spare Thy people, O LORD, and give not Thine heritage to reproach, that the heathen should rule over them: **wherefore should they say among the people, Where** *is* **their God?**   2 17 / 3

Yea, **and what have ye to do with Me, O Tyre, and Zidon, and all the coasts of Palestine? will ye render Me a recompence?** and if ye recompense Me, swiftly *and* speedily will I return your recompence upon your own head; because ye have taken My silver and My gold, and have carried into your temples My goodly pleasant things: the children also of Judah and the children of Jerusalem have ye sold unto the Grecians, that ye might remove them far from their border.   3   4² / 2 / Joel 7

AMOS.

YET destroyed I the Amorite before them, whose height *was* like the height of the cedars, and he *was* strong as the oaks, yet I destroyed his fruit from above, and his roots from beneath. Also I brought you up from the land of Egypt, and led you forty years through the wilderness, to possess the land of the Amorite. And I raised up of your sons for prophets, and of your young men for Nazarites. *Is it* **not even thus, O ye children of Israel?** saith the LORD.   2 11 / 1

Hear this word that the LORD hath spoken against you, O children of Israel, against the whole family which I brought up from the land of Egypt, saying, You only have I known of all the families of the earth: there-

CHAP.	VER.	
3	3	fore I will punish you for all your iniquities. **Can two**
	4²	**walk together, except they be agreed? Will a lion roar in the forest, when he hath no prey? will a young lion cry out of his den, if he have taken nothing?** **Can a bird fall in a snare upon**
	5²	**the earth, where no gin** *is* **for him? shall** *one* **take up a snare from the earth, and have taken**
	6²	**nothing at all? Shall a trumpet be blown in the city, and the people not be afraid? shall there be evil in a city, and the** L<small>ORD</small> **hath not done** *it ?* Surely the Lord G<small>OD</small> will do nothing, but He revealeth
	8²	His secret unto His servants the prophets. **The lion hath roared, who will not fear? the** Lord G<small>OD</small>
	9	**hath spoken, who can but prophesy?**

And in all vineyards *shall be* wailing : for I will pass through thee, saith the L<small>ORD</small>. Woe unto you that

5	18	desire the day of the L<small>ORD</small>! **to what end** *is* **it for you?** the day of the L<small>ORD</small> *is* darkness, and not light. As if a man did flee from a lion, and a bear met him ; or went into the house, and leaned his hand on the wall,
	20²	and a serpent bit him. *Shall* **not the day of the** L<small>ORD</small> *be* **darkness, and not light? even very dark, and no brightness in it?**

	25	**Have ye offered unto Me sacrifices and offerings in the wilderness forty years, O house of Israel?** But ye have borne the tabernacle of your Moloch and Chiun your images, the star of your god, which ye made to yourselves. Therefore will I cause
	4	you to go into captivity beyond Damascus, saith the L<small>ORD</small>, whose name *is* The God of hosts.

Woe to them *that are* at ease in Zion, and trust in the mountain of Samaria, *which are* named chief of the nations, to whom the house of Israel came ! Pass ye unto Calneh, and see ; and from thence go ye to Hamath the great: then go down to Gath of the Philistines:

be they **better than these kingdoms? or their border greater than your border?** | 6 | 2²

And a man's uncle shall take him up, and he that burneth him, to bring out the bones out of the house, and shall say unto him that *is* by the sides of the house, *Is there* **yet** *any* **with thee?** and he shall say, No. Then shall he say, Hold thy tongue: for we may not make mention of the name of the LORD. For, behold, the LORD commandeth, and He will smite the great house with breaches, and the little house with clefts. | | 10

Shall horses run upon the rock? will *one* **plow** *there* **with oxen?** for ye have turned judgment into gall, and the fruit of righteousness into hemlock: ye which rejoice in a thing of nought, which say, **Have we not taken to us horns by our own strength?** But, behold, I will raise up against you a nation, O house of Israel, saith the LORD the God of hosts; and they shall afflict you from the entering in of Hemath unto the river of the wilderness. | | 12²

13

6

Thus hath the Lord GOD shewed unto me; and, behold, He formed grasshoppers in the beginning of the shooting up of the latter growth; and, lo, *it was* the latter growth after the king's mowings. And it came to pass, *that* when they had made an end of eating the grass of the land, then I said, O Lord GOD, forgive, I beseech Thee: **by whom shall Jacob arise?** for he *is* small. The LORD repented for this: It shall not be, saith the LORD. Thus hath the Lord GOD shewed unto me: and, behold, the Lord GOD called to contend by fire, and it devoured the great deep, and did eat up a part. Then said I, O Lord GOD, cease, I beseech Thee: **by whom shall Jacob arise?** for he *is* small. The LORD repented for this: This also shall not be, saith the Lord GOD. Thus He shewed me: and, behold, the Lord stood upon a wall *made* by a plumbline, with a plumbline in His hand. And the LORD said unto me, | 7 | 2

5

CHAP.	VER	
7	8	**Amos, what seest thou?** And I said, A plumbline. Then said the Lord, Behold, I will set a plumbline in the midst of My people Israel: I will not again pass by them any more: and the high places of Isaac shall be desolate, and the sanctuaries of Israel shall be laid waste; and I will rise against the house of Jeroboam with the sword.
	3	
8	2	Thus hath the Lord God shewed unto me: and behold a basket of summer fruit. And He said, **Amos, what seest thou?** And I said, A basket of summer fruit. Then said the Lord unto me, The end is come upon My people of Israel; I will not again pass by them any more. And the songs of the temple shall be howlings in that day. saith the Lord God: *there shall be many dead bodies in every place; they shall cast them forth with silence.*
	5[2]	Hear this, O ye that swallow up the needy, even to make the poor of the land to fail, saying, **When will the new moon be gone, that we may sell corn? and the sabbath, that we may set forth wheat, making the ephah small, and the shekel great,**
	6	**and falsifying the balances by deceit? That we may buy the poor for silver, and the needy for a pair of shoes;** *yea,* **and sell the refuse of the wheat?** The Lord hath sworn by the excellency of Jacob, Surely I will never forget any of their works.
	8	**Shall not the land tremble for this, and every one mourn that dwelleth therein?** and it shall rise up wholly as a flood; and it shall be cast out and drowned,
	5	as *by* the flood of Egypt.
9	7[3]	*Are* **ye not as children of the Ethiopians unto Me, O children of Israel?** saith the Lord. **Have not I brought up Israel out of the land of Egypt? and the Philistines from Caphtor, and the Syrians from Kir?**
	3	

Amos 31

OBADIAH.

THE pride of thine heart hath deceived thee, thou that dwellest in the clefts of the rock, whose habitation *is* high; that saith in his heart, **Who shall bring me down to the ground?** Though thou exalt *thyself* as the eagle, and though thou set thy nest among the stars, thence will I bring thee down, saith the Lord. **If thieves came to thee, if robbers by night, (how art thou cut off!) would they not have stolen till they had enough?** if the grapegatherers came to thee, would they not leave *some* grapes?

Shall I not in that day, saith the Lord, **even destroy the wise** *men* **out of Edom, and understanding out of the mount of Esau?** And thy mighty *men*, O Teman, shall be dismayed, to the end that every one of the mount of Esau may be cut off by slaughter.

CHAP.	VER.
1	3
	5²
	8
	4

Obadiah 4

JONAH.

BUT the Lord sent out a great wind into the sea, and there was a mighty tempest in the sea, so that the ship was like to be broken. Then the mariners were afraid, and cried every man unto his god, and cast forth the wares that *were* in the ship into the sea, to lighten *it* of them. But Jonah was gone down into the sides of the ship, and he lay, and was fast asleep. So the shipmaster came to him, and said unto him, **What meanest thou, O sleeper?** arise, call upon thy God, if so be that God will think upon us, that we perish not. And they said every one to his fellow, Come, and let us cast lots, that we

CHAP.	VER.
1	6

CHAP.	VER.	
1	8	may know for whose cause this evil *is* upon us. So they cast lots, and the lot fell upon Jonah. Then said they unto him, **Tell us, we pray thee, for whose cause this evil is upon us; What** *is* **thine occupation?** and **whence comest thou? what** *is* **thy country? and of what people** *art* **thou?** And he said unto them, I *am* an Hebrew; and I fear the LORD, the God of heaven, which hath made the sea and the dry *land*. Then were
	10	the men exceedingly afraid, and said unto him, **Why hast thou done this?** For the men knew that he fled from the presence of the LORD, because he had told them.
	11	Then said they unto him, **What shall we do unto thee, that the sea may be calm unto us?** for the sea wrought, and was tempestuous. And he said unto them, Take me up, and cast me forth into the sea; so
	7	shall the sea be calm unto you: for I know that for my sake this great tempest *is* upon you.
3	9	**Who can tell** *if* **God will turn and repent, and turn away from His fierce anger, that we perish not?** And God saw their works, that they turned from their evil way; and God repented of the evil, that He
	1	had said that He would do unto them; and He did *it* not.
4	2	But it displeased Jonah exceedingly, and he was very angry. And he prayed unto the LORD, and said, **I pray Thee, O** LORD, *was* **not this my saying, when I was yet in my country?** Therefore I fled before unto Tarshish: for I knew that Thou *art* a gracious God, and merciful, slow to anger, and of great kindness, and repentest Thee of the evil. Therefore now, O LORD, take, I beseech Thee, my life from me; for *it is* better
	4	for me to die than to live. Then said the LORD, **Doest thou well to be angry?**
	9	And God said to Jonah, **Doest thou well to be angry for the gourd?** And he said, I do well to be angry, *even* unto death. Then said the LORD, Thou hast had

pity on the gourd, for the which thou hast not laboured, neither madest it grow; which came up in a night, and perished in a night: **and should not I spare Nineveh, that great city, wherein are more than sixscore thousand persons that cannot discern between their right hand and their left hand; and** *also* **much cattle?**

CHAP.	VER.
4	11
	4

Jonah 12

MICAH.

FOR, behold, the LORD cometh forth out of His place, and will come down, and tread upon the high places of the earth. And the mountains shall be molten under Him, and the valleys shall be cleft, as wax before the fire, *and* as the waters *that are* poured down a steep place. For the transgression of Jacob *is* all this, and for the sins of the house of Israel. **What** *is* **the transgression of Jacob?** *is it* **not Samaria?** and **what** *are* **the high places of Judah?** *are they* **not Jerusalem?**

CHAP.	VER.
1	5⁴
	4

O *thou that art* **named the house of Jacob, is the spirit of the** LORD **straitened?** *are* **these His doings?** **do not My words do good to him that walketh uprightly?**

2	7³
	3

And I said, **Hear, I pray you, O heads of Jacob, and ye princes of the house of Israel; Is it not for you to know judgment?** Who hate the good, and love the evil; who pluck off their skin from off them, and their flesh from off their bones; who also eat the flesh of my people, and flay their skin from off them; and they break their bones, and chop them in pieces, as for the pot, and as flesh within the caldron.

3	1

CHAP.	VER.	
3	11	They build up Zion with blood, and Jerusalem with iniquity. The heads thereof judge for reward, and the priests thereof teach for hire, and the prophets thereof divine for money: yet will they lean upon the Lord, and say, *Is* **not the** Lord **among us?** none evil can come upon us.
	2	

4	9[3]	And thou, O tower of the flock, the strong hold of the daughter of Zion, unto thee shall it come, even the first dominion; the kingdom shall come to the daughter of Jerusalem. **Now why dost thou cry out aloud?** *is there* **no king in thee? is thy counsellor perished?** for pangs have taken thee as a woman in travail.
	3	

6	3[2]	**O My people, what have I done unto thee?** and **wherein have I wearied thee?** testify against Me.
	6[2]	**Wherewith shall I come before the** Lord, *and* **bow myself before the high God? shall I come before Him with burnt offerings, with calves of a year old? Will the** Lord **be pleased with thousands of rams,** *or* **with ten thousands of rivers of oil? shall I give my firstborn** *for* **my transgression, the fruit of my body** *for* **the sin of my soul?** He hath shewed thee, O man, what *is* good; **and what doth the** Lord **require of thee, but to do justly, and to love mercy, and to walk humbly with thy God?**
	7[2]	
	8	
	10	**Are there yet the treasures of wickedness in the house of the wicked, and the scant measure** *that is* **abominable? Shall I count** *them* **pure with the wicked balances, and with the bag of deceitful weights?**
	11	
	9	

Then *she that is* mine enemy shall see *it*, and shame

shall cover her which said unto me, **Where is the Lord thy God?** mine eyes shall behold her: now shall she be trodden down as the mire of the streets. | 7 | 10

Who *is* **a God like unto Thee, that pardoneth iniquity, and passeth by the transgression of the remnant of His heritage?** He retaineth not His anger for ever, because He delighteth *in* mercy. He will turn again, He will have compassion upon us; He will subdue our iniquities; and Thou wilt cast all their sins into the depths of the sea. | | 18

| | 2

Micah 23

NAHUM.

CHAP. VER.

Who can stand before His indignation? and **who can abide in the fierceness of His anger?** His fury is poured out like fire, and the rocks are thrown down by Him. The Lord *is* good, a strong hold in the day of trouble; and He knoweth them that trust in Him. | 1 | 6²

What do ye imagine against the Lord? He will make an utter end: affliction shall not rise up the second time. | | 9

| | 3

Where *is* **the dwelling of the lions, and the feedingplace of the young lions, where the lion,** *even* **the old lion, walked,** *and* **the lion's whelp, and none made** *them* **afraid?** | 2 | 11

| | 1

And it shall come to pass, *that* all they that look upon thee shall flee from thee, and say, Nineveh is laid waste: **who will bemoan her? whence shall I seek comforters for thee? Art thou better than populous No, that was situate among the rivers,** *that* had **the waters round about it, whose rampart** *was* **the sea,** *and* **her wall** *was* **from the sea?** | 3 | 7²

| | 8

CHAP.	VER.	
3	13	Thy shepherds slumber, O king of Assyria: thy nobles shall dwell *in the dust:* thy people is scattered upon the mountains, and no man gathereth *them.* There is no healing of thy bruise; thy wound is grievous: all that hear the bruit of thee shall clap the hands over thee: **for upon whom hath not thy wickedness passed continually?**
	4	

Nahum 8

HABAKKUK.

CHAP.	VER.	
1	3	O LORD, how long shall I cry, and Thou wilt not hear! *even* cry out unto Thee *of* violence, and Thou wilt not save! **Why dost Thou shew me iniquity, and cause** *me* **to behold grievance?** for spoiling and violence *are* before me: and there are *that* raise up strife and contention.
	12	*Art* **Thou not from everlasting, O** LORD **my God, mine Holy One?** we shall not die. O LORD, Thou hast ordained them for judgment; and, O mighty God, Thou hast established them for correction. *Thou art* of purer eyes than to behold evil, and canst not look on
	13	iniquity: **wherefore lookest Thou upon them that deal treacherously,** *and* **holdest Thy tongue when the wicked devoureth** *the man that is* **more righteous than he?** **And makest men as the**
	14	**fishes of the sea, as the creeping things,** *that have* **no ruler over them?** They take up all of them with the angle, they catch them in their net, and gather them in their drag: therefore they rejoice and are glad. Therefore they sacrifice unto their net, and burn incense unto their drag; because by them their portion
	17	*is* fat, and their meat plenteous. **Shall they therefore**
	5	**empty their net, and not spare continually to slay the nations?**

	CHAP.	VER.
Yea also, because he transgresseth by wine, *he is* a proud man, neither keepeth at home, who enlargeth his desire as hell, and *is* as death, and cannot be satisfied, but gathereth unto him all nations, and heapeth unto him all people: **shall not all these take up a parable against him, and a taunting proverb against him, and say, Woe to him that increaseth** *that which is* **not his!** how long? and to him that ladeth himself with thick clay! **Shall they not rise up suddenly that shall bite thee, and awake that shall vex thee, and thou shalt be for booties unto them?**	2	6
		7
Woe to him that buildeth a town with blood, and stablisheth a city by iniquity! **Behold,** *is it* **not of the** LORD **of hosts that the people shall labour in the very fire, and the people shall weary themselves for very vanity?** For the earth shall be filled with the knowledge of the glory of the LORD, as the waters cover the sea.		13
What profiteth the graven image that the maker thereof hath graven it; the molten image, and a teacher of lies, that the maker of his work trusteth therein, to make dumb idols?		18
		4
Was the LORD **displeased against the rivers?** *was* **Thine anger against the rivers?** *was* **Thy wrath against the sea, that Thou didst ride upon Thine horses** *and* **Thy chariots of salvation?**	3	8³
		3
	Habakkuk	12

ZEPHANIAH.

	Zephaniah	0

HAGGAI.

CHAP.	VER.	
1	4	THEN came the word of the LORD by Haggai the prophet, saying, *Is it* **time for you, O ye, to dwell in your cieled houses, and this house** *lie* **waste?**
	9	Thus saith the LORD of hosts; Consider your ways. Go up to the mountain, and bring wood, and build the house; and I will take pleasure in it, and I will be glorified, saith the LORD. Ye looked for much, and, lo, *it came* to little; and when ye brought *it* home, I did blow upon it. **Why?** saith the LORD of hosts. Because of Mine house that *is* waste, and ye run every man unto his own house
2	2	
2	3 3	In the seventh *month*, in the one and twentieth *day* of the month, came the word of the LORD by the prophet Haggai, saying, Speak now to Zerubbabel the son of Shealtiel, governor of Judah, and to Joshua the son of Josedech, the high priest, and to the residue of the people, saying, **Who** *is* **left among you that saw this house in her first glory?** and **how do ye see it now?** *is it* **not in your eyes in comparison of it as nothing?**
	12	In the four and twentieth *day* of the ninth *month*, in the second year of Darius, came the word of the LORD by Haggai the prophet, saying, Thus saith the LORD of hosts; Ask now the priests *concerning* the law, saying, **If one bear holy flesh in the skirt of his garment, and with his skirt do touch bread, or pottage, or wine, or oil, or any meat, shall it be holy?** And the
	13	priests answered and said, No Then said Haggai, **If** *one that is* **unclean by a dead body touch any of these, shall it be unclean?** And the priests answered and said, It shall be unclean.

	CHAP. VER.
Is the seed yet in the barn? yea, as yet the vine, and the fig tree, and the pomegranate, and the olive tree, hath not brought forth: from this day will I bless *you*.	**2** 19
	6
	Haggai 8

ZECHARIAH.

	CHAP. VER.
BE ye not as your fathers, unto whom the former prophets have cried, saying, Thus saith the LORD of hosts; Turn ye now from your evil ways, and *from* your evil doings: but they did not hear, nor hearken unto Me, saith the LORD. **Your fathers, where *are* they?** and **the prophets, do they live for ever? But My words and My statutes, which I commanded My servants the prophets, did they not take hold of your fathers?** and they returned and said, Like as the LORD of hosts thought to do unto us, according to our ways, and according to our doings, so hath He dealt with us.	**1** 5[2] 6
Upon the four and twentieth day of the eleventh month, which *is* the month Sebat, in the second year of Darius, came the word of the LORD unto Zechariah, the son of Berechiah, the son of Iddo the prophet, saying, I saw by night, and behold a man riding upon a red horse, and he stood among the myrtle trees that *were* in the bottom; and behind him *were there* red horses, speckled, and white. Then said I, **O my lord, what *are* these?** And the angel that talked with me said unto me, I will shew thee what these *be*	9
Then the angel of the LORD answered and said, **O LORD of hosts, how long wilt Thou not have mercy on Jerusalem and on the cities of Judah, against which Thou hast had indignation these**	12

CHAP.	VER.	
		threescore and ten years? And the Lord answered the angel that talked with me *with* good words *and* comfortable words.
1	19	Then lifted I up mine eyes, and saw, and behold four horns. And I said unto the angel that talked with me, **What** *be* **these?** And he answered me, These *are* the horns which have scattered Judah, Israel, and Jerusalem. And the Lord shewed me four carpenters. Then said I,
	21	**What come these to do?** And He spake, saying, These *are* the horns which have scattered Judah, so that no man did lift up his head: but these are come to fray
	7	them, to cast out the horns of the Gentiles, which lifted up *their* horn over the land of Judah to scatter it.
2	2	I lifted up mine eyes again, and looked, and behold a man with a measuring line in his hand. Then said I, **Whither goest thou?** And he said unto me, To measure Jerusalem, to see what *is* the breadth thereof,
	1	and what *is* the length thereof.
3	2	And he shewed me Joshua the high priest standing before the angel of the Lord, and Satan standing at his right hand to resist him. And the Lord said unto Satan, The Lord rebuke thee, O Satan; even the Lord that hath chosen Jerusalem rebuke thee: *is* **not this a brand**
	1	**plucked out of the fire?**
4	2	And the angel that talked with me came again, and waked me, as a man that is wakened out of his sleep, and said unto me, **What seest thou?** And I said, I have looked, and behold a candlestick all *of* gold, with a bowl upon the top of it, and his seven lamps thereon, and seven pipes to the seven lamps, which *are* upon the top thereof: and two olive trees by it, one upon the right *side* of the bowl, and the other upon the left *side* thereof. So I answered and spake to the angel that talked with me,
	4	saying, **What** *are* **these, my lord?** Then the angel that talked with me answered and said unto me,

ZECHARIAH:—IV., V.

	CHAP.	VER.
Knowest thou not what these be? And I said, No, my lord. Then he answered and spake unto me, saying, This *is* the word of the LORD unto Zerubbabel, saying, Not by might, nor by power, but by My spirit, saith the LORD of hosts.	**4**	5
Who *art* **thou, O great mountain?** before Zerubbabel *thou shalt become* a plain: and he shall bring forth the headstone *thereof with* shoutings, *crying*, Grace, grace unto it. Moreover the word of the LORD came unto me, saying, The hands of Zerubbabel have laid the foundation of this house; his hands shall also finish it; and thou shalt know that the LORD of hosts hath sent me unto you.		7
For who hath despised the day of small things? for they shall rejoice, and shall see the plummet in the hand of Zerubbabel *with* those seven; they *are* the eyes of the LORD, which run to and fro through the whole earth. Then answered I, and said unto him,		10
What *are* **these two olive trees upon the right** *side* **of the candlestick and upon the left** *side* **thereof?** And I answered again, and said unto him,		11
What *be these* **two olive branches which through the two golden pipes empty the golden** *oil* **out of themselves?** And he answered me and said,		12
Knowest thou not what these *be?* And I said, No, my lord.		13
Then said he, These *are* the two anointed ones, that stand by the Lord of the whole earth.		8

Then I turned, and lifted up mine eyes, and looked, and behold a flying roll. And he said unto me, **What seest thou?** And I answered, I see a flying roll; the length thereof *is* twenty cubits, and the breadth thereof ten cubits.

5 2

Then the angel that talked with me went forth, and said unto me, Lift up now thine eyes, and see what *is* this that goeth forth. And I said, **What** *is* **it?** And he said, This *is* an ephah that goeth forth. He said moreover, This *is* their resemblance through all the earth.

6

CHAP.	VER	
5	10	Then said I to the angel that talked with me, **Whither do these bear the ephah?** And he said unto me, To build it an house in the land of Shinar: and it shall be established, and set there upon her own base
	3	
6	4	Then I answered and said unto the angel that talked with me, **What are these, my lord?** And the angel answered and said unto me, These *are* the four spirits of the heavens, which go forth from standing before the Lord of all the earth.
	1	
7	3	And it came to pass in the fourth year of king Darius, *that* the word of the Lord came unto Zechariah in the fourth *day* of the ninth month, *even* in Chisleu; when they had sent unto the house of God Sherezer and Regem-melech, and their men, to pray before the Lord, *and* to speak unto the priests which *were* in the house of the Lord of hosts, and to the prophets, saying, **Should I weep in the fifth month, separating myself, as I have done these so many years?** Then came the word of the Lord of hosts unto me, saying, Speak unto all the people of the land, and to the priests, saying, **When ye fasted and mourned in the fifth and seventh** *month*, **even those seventy years, did ye at all fast unto Me,** *even* **to Me?** And when ye did eat, and when ye did drink, did not ye eat *for yourselves*, **and drink** *for yourselves?* Should ye not *hear* the words which the Lord hath cried by the former prophets, when Jerusalem was inhabited and in prosperity, and the cities thereof round about her, when *men* inhabited the south and the plain?
	5	
	6	
	7	
	4	
8	6	Thus saith the Lord of hosts; **If it be marvellous in the eyes of the remnant of this people in these days, should it also be marvellous in Mine eyes?** saith the Lord of hosts.
	1	

And it shall come to pass in that day, *that* the prophets shall be ashamed every one of his vision, when he hath prophesied; neither shall they wear a rough garment to deceive · but he shall say, I *am* no prophet, I *am* an husbandman ; for man taught me to keep cattle from my youth. And *one* shall say unto him, **What** *are* **these wounds in thine hands?** Then he shall answer, *Those* with which I was wounded *in* the house of my friends.

CHAP.	VER.
13	6
	1

Zechariah 27

MALACHI.

THE burden of the word of the LORD to Israel by Malachi I have loved you, saith the LORD. Yet ye say, **Wherein hast Thou loved us?** *Was* not **Esau Jacob's brother?** saith the LORD. yet I loved Jacob, and I hated Esau, and laid his mountains and his heritage waste for the dragons of the wilderness.

A son honoureth *his* father, and a servant his master : **if then I** *be* **a father, where** *is* **Mine honour?** and **if I** *be* **a master, where** *is* **My fear?** saith the LORD of hosts unto you, O priests, that despise My name. And ye say, **Wherein have we despised Thy name?** Ye offer polluted bread upon Mine altar ; and ye say, **Wherein have we polluted Thee?** In that ye say, The table of the LORD *is* contemptible. And **if ye offer the blind for sacrifice,** *is it* **not evil?** and **if ye offer the lame and sick,** *is it* **not evil?** offer it now unto thy governor , **will he be pleased with thee, or accept thy person?** saith the LORD of hosts. And now, I pray you, beseech God that He will be gracious unto us : this hath been by your means : **will He regard your persons?** saith the LORD of hosts. **Who** *is there* **even among you that would shut the doors** *for* **nought?** neither do ye kindle *fire* on Mine altar for nought.

CHAP.	VER.
1	2²
	3³
	7
	8³
	9
	10

CHAP.	VER	
1	13	I have no pleasure in you, saith the Lord of hosts, neither will I accept an offering at your hand.

Ye said also, Behold, what a weariness *is it !* and ye have snuffed at it, saith the Lord of hosts; and ye brought *that which was* torn, and the lame, and the sick; thus ye brought an offering: **should I accept this of your hand?** saith the Lord. |
	12	
2	10³	**Have we not all one father? hath not one God created us? why do we deal treacherously every man against his brother, by profaning the covenant of our fathers?**
	14	Yet ye say, **Wherefore?** Because the Lord hath been witness between thee and the wife of thy youth, against whom thou hast dealt treacherously · yet *is* she thy companion, and the wife of thy covenant. **And did not He make one?** Yet had He the residue of the spirit. **And wherefore one?** That He might seek a godly seed. Therefore take heed to your spirit, and let none deal treacherously against the wife of his youth. For the Lord, the God of Israel, saith that He hateth putting away : for *one* covereth violence with his garment, saith the Lord of hosts: therefore take heed to your spirit, that ye deal not treacherously. Ye have wearied the Lord with your words. Yet ye say, **Wherein have we wearied** *Him?* When ye say, Every one that doeth evil *is* good in the sight of the Lord, and He delighteth in them; or, **Where** *is* **the God of judgment?**
	15²	
	17²	
	8	
3	2²	Behold, I will send My messenger, and he shall prepare the way before Me: and the Lord, whom ye seek, shall suddenly come to His temple, even the Messenger of the covenant, whom ye delight in : behold, He shall come, saith the Lord of hosts. **But who may abide the day of His coming?** and **who shall stand when He appeareth?** for He *is* like a refiner's fire, and like fullers' soap : and He shall sit *as* a refiner and

MALACHI:—III.

	CHAP.	VER.

purifier of silver: and He shall purify the sons of Levi, and purge them as gold and silver, that they may offer unto the LORD an offering in righteousness.

Even from the days of your fathers ye are gone away from Mine ordinances, and have not kept *them*. Return unto Me, and I will return unto you, saith the LORD of hosts. But ye said, **Wherein shall we return? Will a man rob God?** Yet ye have robbed Me. But ye say, **Wherein have we robbed Thee?** In tithes and offerings.   3   7, 8²

Your words have been stout against Me, saith the LORD. Yet ye say, **What have we spoken** *so much* **against Thee?** Ye have said, It *is* vain to serve God: and **what profit** *is it* **that we have kept His ordinance, and that we have walked mournfully before the** LORD **of hosts?** And now we call the proud happy; yea, they that work wickedness are set up; yea, *they that* tempt God are even delivered.   13, 14, 7

Malachi 27

OLD TESTAMENT—Total 2274

THE NEW TESTAMENT.

SAINT MATTHEW.

	CHAP.	VER
NOW when Jesus was born in Bethlehem of Judæa in the days of Herod the king, behold, there came wise men from the east to Jerusalem, saying, **Where is He that is born King of the Jews?** for we have seen His star in the east, and are come to worship Him.	2	2
		1
But when he saw many of the Pharisees and Sadducees come to his baptism, he said unto them, **O generation of vipers, who hath warned you to flee from the wrath to come?**	3	7
Then cometh Jesus from Galilee to Jordan unto John, to be baptized of him. But John forbad Him, saying, I have need to be baptized of Thee, **and comest Thou to me?**		14
		2
Ye are the salt of the earth: but **if the salt have lost his savour, wherewith shall it be salted?** it is thenceforth good for nothing, but to be cast out, and to be trodden under foot of men.	5	13
Ye have heard that it hath been said, Thou shalt love thy neighbour, and hate thine enemy. But I say unto you, Love your enemies, bless them that curse you, do good to them that hate you, and pray for them which despitefully use you, and persecute you; that ye may be the children of your Father which is in heaven: for He maketh His sun to rise on the evil and on the good, and sendeth rain on the just and on the unjust. **For if ye love them which love you, what reward have ye? do not even the publicans the same?** And **if ye salute your brethren only, what do ye more** *than others?* **do not even the publicans so?** Be ye therefore perfect, even as your Father which is in heaven is perfect.		46[2]
		47[2]
		5

CHAP.	VER.	
6	25	No man can serve two masters: for either he will hate the one, and love the other; or else he will hold to the one, and despise the other. Ye cannot serve God and mammon. Therefore I say unto you, Take no thought for your life, what ye shall eat, or what ye shall drink; nor yet for your body, what ye shall put on. **Is not the life more than meat, and the body than raiment?** Behold the fowls of the air: for they sow not, neither do they reap, nor gather into barns, yet your heavenly Father feedeth them. **Are ye not much better than they? Which of you by taking thought can add one cubit unto his stature?** And **why take ye thought for raiment?** Consider the lilies of the field, how they grow; they toil not, neither do they spin: and yet I say unto you, That even Solomon in all his glory was not arrayed like one of these. Wherefore, **if God so clothe the grass of the field, which to day is, and to morrow is cast into the oven,** *shall He* **not much more** *clothe* **you, O ye of little faith?** Therefore take no thought, saying, **What shall we eat?** or, **What shall we drink?** or, **Wherewithal shall we be clothed?** (for after all these things do the Gentiles seek:) for your heavenly Father knoweth that ye have need of all these things. But seek ye first the kingdom of God, and His righteousness; and all these things shall be added unto you.
	26	
	27	
	28	
	30	
	31³	
	8	
7	3	And **why beholdest thou the mote that is in thy brother's eye, but considerest not the beam that is in thine own eye?** Or **how wilt thou say to thy brother, Let me pull out the mote out of thine eye; and, behold, a beam** *is* **in thine own eye?** Thou hypocrite, first cast out the beam out of thine own eye; and then shalt thou see clearly to cast out the mote out of thy brother's eye.
	4	

Ask, and it shall be given you; seek, and ye shall find; knock, and it shall be opened unto you: for every one that asketh receiveth; and he that seeketh findeth; and

	CHAP.	VER
to him that knocketh it shall be opened. Or **what man is there of you, whom if his son ask bread, will he give him a stone?** Or **if he ask a fish, will he give him a serpent? If ye then, being evil, know how to give good gifts unto your children, how much more shall your Father which is in heaven give good things to them that ask Him?**	**7**	9 10 11
Beware of false prophets, which come to you in sheep's clothing, but inwardly they are ravening wolves. Ye shall know them by their fruits. **Do men gather grapes of thorns, or figs of thistles?**		16
Not every one that saith unto Me, Lord, Lord, shall enter into the kingdom of heaven; but he that doeth the will of My Father which is in heaven. Many will say to Me in that day, Lord, Lord, **have we not prophesied in Thy name?** and **in Thy name have cast out devils?** and **in Thy name done many wonderful works?** And then will I profess unto them, I never knew you: depart from Me, ye that work iniquity.		22³ 9
And His disciples came to *Him*, and awoke Him, saying, Lord, save us: we perish. And He saith unto them, **Why are ye fearful, O ye of little faith?** Then He arose, and rebuked the winds and the sea; and there was a great calm.	**8**	26
And when He was come to the other side into the country of the Gergesenes, there met Him two possessed with devils, coming out of the tombs, exceeding fierce, so that no man might pass by that way. And, behold, they cried out, saying, **What have we to do with Thee, Jesus, Thou Son of God? art Thou come hither to torment us before the time?**	.	29² 3

And, behold, they brought to Him a man sick of the palsy, lying on a bed: and Jesus seeing their faith said unto the sick of the palsy; Son, be of good cheer; thy

CHAP.	VER.	
9	4 5	sins be forgiven thee. And, behold, certain of the scribes said within themselves, This *man* blasphemeth. And Jesus knowing their thoughts said, **Wherefore think ye evil in your hearts? For whether is easier, to say,** *Thy* **sins be forgiven thee; or to say, Arise, and walk?** But that ye may know that the Son of man hath power on earth to forgive sins, (then saith He to the sick of the palsy,) Arise, take up thy bed, and go unto thine house. And he arose, and departed to his house.
	11	And it came to pass, as Jesus sat at meat in the house, behold, many publicans and sinners came and sat down with Him and His disciples. And when the Pharisees saw *it*, they said unto His disciples, **Why eateth your Master with publicans and sinners?**
	14 15	Then came to Him the disciples of John, saying, **Why do we and the Pharisees fast oft, but Thy disciples fast not?** And Jesus said unto them, **Can the children of the bridechamber mourn, as long as the bridegroom is with them?** but the days will come, when the bridegroom shall be taken from them, and then shall they fast.
	28	And when Jesus departed thence, two blind men followed Him, crying, and saying, *Thou* Son of David, have mercy on us. And when He was come into the house, the blind men came to Him: and Jesus saith unto them, **Believe ye that I am able to do this?** They said unto Him, Yea, Lord. Then touched He their eyes, saying, According to your faith be it unto you. And their eyes were opened; and Jesus straitly charged them, saying, See *that* no man know *it*
	6	
10	25	The disciple is not above *his* master, nor the servant above his lord. It is enough for the disciple that he be as his master, and the servant as his lord. **If they have called the master of the house Beelzebub,**

how much more *shall they call* **them of his household?**

And fear not them which kill the body, but are not able to kill the soul: but rather fear Him which is able to destroy both soul and body in hell. **Are not two sparrows sold for a farthing?** and one of them shall not fall on the ground without your Father. But the very hairs of your head are all numbered. Fear ye not therefore, ye are of more value than many sparrows

10 29

2

Now when John had heard in the prison the works of Christ, he sent two of his disciples, and said unto Him, **Art Thou He that should come, or do we look for another?**

11 3

And as they departed, Jesus began to say unto the multitudes concerning John, **What went ye out into the wilderness to see? A reed shaken with the wind? But what went ye out for to see? A man clothed in soft raiment?** behold, they that wear soft *clothing* are in kings' houses. **But what went ye out for to see? A prophet?** yea, I say unto you, and more than a prophet For this is *he*, of whom it is written, Behold, I send my messenger before Thy face, which shall prepare Thy way before Thee.

7²

8²

9²

But whereunto shall I liken this generation? It is like unto children sitting in the markets, and calling unto their fellows, and saying, We have piped unto you, and ye have not danced, we have mourned unto you, and ye have not lamented.

16

8

At that time Jesus went on the sabbath day through the corn; and His disciples were an hungred, and began to pluck the ears of corn, and to eat. But when the Pharisees saw *it*, they said unto Him, Behold, Thy disciples do that which is not lawful to do upon the sabbath day. But He said unto them, **Have ye not**

12 4

CHAP.	VER.	
12	5	read what David did, when he was an hungred, and they that were with him; how he entered into the house of God, and did eat the shewbread, which was not lawful for him to eat, neither for them which were with him, but only for the priests? **Or have ye not read in the law, how that on the sabbath days the priests in the temple profane the sabbath, and are blameless?** But I say unto you, That in this place is *one* greater than the temple. But if ye had known what *this* meaneth, I will have mercy, and not sacrifice, ye would not have condemned the guiltless. For the Son of man is Lord even of the sabbath day.
	10	And, behold, there was a man which had *his* hand withered. And they asked Him, saying, **Is it lawful to heal on the sabbath days?** that they might accuse
	11	Him. And He said unto them, **What man shall there be among you, that shall have one sheep, and if it fall into a pit on the sabbath day, will he not**
	12	**lay hold on it, and lift** *it* **out? How much then is a man better than a sheep?** Wherefore it is lawful to do well on the sabbath days. Then saith He to the man, Stretch forth thine hand. And he stretched *it* forth, and it was restored whole, like as the other.
	23	Then was brought unto Him one possessed with a devil, blind, and dumb · and He healed him, insomuch that the blind and dumb both spake and saw. And all the people were amazed, and said, **Is not this the Son of David?** But when the Pharisees heard *it*, they said, This *fellow* doth not cast out devils, but by Beelzebub the prince of the devils. And Jesus knew their thoughts, and said unto them, Every kingdom divided against itself is brought to desolation; and every city or house divided against itself shall not stand and if Satan cast out
	26	Satan, he is divided against himself; **how shall then**
	27	**his kingdom stand? And if I by Beelzebub cast out devils, by whom do your children cast** *them*

	CHAP	VER

out? therefore they shall be your judges. But if I cast out devils by the Spirit of God, then the kingdom of God is come unto you. **Or else how can one enter into a strong man's house, and spoil his goods, except he first bind the strong man?** and then he will spoil his house. He that is not with Me is against Me; and he that gathereth not with Me scattereth abroad.   **12**   29

O generation of vipers, **how can ye, being evil, speak good things?** for out of the abundance of the heart the mouth speaketh.   34

While He yet talked to the people, behold, *His* mother and His brethren stood without, desiring to speak with Him. Then one said unto Him, Behold, Thy mother and Thy brethren stand without, desiring to speak with Thee. But He answered and said unto him that told Him, **Who is My mother?** and **who are My brethren?** And He stretched forth His hand toward His disciples, and said, Behold My mother and My brethren! For whosoever shall do the will of My Father which is in heaven, the same is My brother, and sister, and mother.   48²

12

And the disciples came, and said unto Him, **Why speakest Thou unto them in parables?** He answered and said unto them, Because it is given unto you to know the mysteries of the kingdom of heaven, but to them it is not given.   **13**   10

Another parable put He forth unto them, saying, The kingdom of heaven is likened unto a man which sowed good seed in his field: but while men slept, his enemy came and sowed tares among the wheat, and went his way. But when the blade was sprung up, and brought forth fruit, then appeared the tares also. So the servants of the householder came and said unto him, **Sir, didst not thou sow good seed in thy field? from whence then hath it tares?** He said unto them, An   27²

CHAP.	VER.	
13	28	enemy hath done this. The servants said unto him, **Wilt thou then that we go and gather them up?** But he said, Nay; lest while ye gather up the tares, ye root up also the wheat with them. Let both grow together until the harvest: and in the time of harvest I will say to the reapers, Gather ye together first the tares, and bind them in bundles to burn them: but gather the wheat into my barn.
	51	Jesus saith unto them, **Have ye understood all these things?** They say unto Him, Yea, Lord.
	54 55³ 56² 11	And when He was come into His own country, He taught them in their synagogue, insomuch that they were astonished, and said, **Whence hath this** man **this wisdom, and** these **mighty works?** **Is not this the carpenter's son?** **is not His mother called Mary?** **and His brethren, James, and Joses, and Simon, and Judas?** **And His sisters, are they not all with us?** **Whence then hath this** man **all these things?** And they were offended in Him. But Jesus said unto them, A prophet is not without honour, save in his own country, and in his own house
14	31 1	And He said, Come. And when Peter was come down out of the ship, he walked on the water, to go to Jesus. But when he saw the wind boisterous, he was afraid, and beginning to sink, he cried, saying, Lord, save me. And immediately Jesus stretched forth His hand, and caught him, and said unto him, **O thou of little faith, wherefore didst thou doubt?**
15	2 3	Then came to Jesus scribes and Pharisees, which were of Jerusalem, saying, **Why do Thy disciples transgress the tradition of the elders?** for they wash not their hands when they eat bread But He answered and said unto them, **Why do ye also transgress the commandment of God by your tradition?**

	CHAP	VER.

And He called the multitude, and said unto them, Hear, and understand: Not that which goeth into the mouth defileth a man; but that which cometh out of the mouth, this defileth a man. Then came His disciples, and said unto Him, **Knowest Thou that the Pharisees were offended, after they heard this saying?** But He answered and said, Every plant, which My heavenly Father hath not planted, shall be rooted up. Let them alone. they be blind leaders of the blind. And if the blind lead the blind, both shall fall into the ditch. Then answered Peter and said unto Him, Declare unto us this parable. And Jesus said, **Are ye also yet without understanding? Do not ye yet understand, that whatsoever entereth in at the mouth goeth into the belly, and is cast out into the draught?** But those things which proceed out of the mouth come forth from the heart; and they defile the man. For out of the heart proceed evil thoughts, murders, adulteries, fornications, thefts, false witness, blasphemies · these are *the things* which defile a man. but to eat with unwashen hands defileth not a man. **15** 12

16
17

Then Jesus called His disciples *unto Him*, and said, I have compassion on the multitude, because they continue with Me now three days, and have nothing to eat: and I will not send them away fasting, lest they faint in the way. And His disciples say unto Him, **Whence should we have so much bread in the wilderness, as to fill so great a multitude?** And Jesus saith unto them, **How many loaves have ye?** And they said, Seven, and a few little fishes.

33

34

7

The Pharisees also with the Sadducees came, and tempting desired Him that He would shew them a sign from heaven. He answered and said unto them, When it is evening, ye say, *It will be* fair weather · for the sky is red. And in the morning, *It will be* foul weather to day: for the sky is red and lowring. O *ye* hypocrites, ye can discern the face of the sky; **but can ye not** *discern* **16** 3

CHAP.	VER	
16	8	**the signs of the times?** A wicked and adulterous generation seeketh after a sign; and there shall no sign be given unto it, but the sign of the prophet Jonas And He left them, and departed. And when His disciples were come to the other side, they had forgotten to take bread. Then Jesus said unto them, Take heed and beware of the leaven of the Pharisees and of the Sadducees And they reasoned among themselves, saying. *It is* because we have taken no bread. *Which* when Jesus perceived, He said unto them, O ye of little faith, **why reason ye among yourselves, because ye have brought no**
	9	**bread? Do ye not yet understand, neither re-member the five loaves of the five thousand, and**
	10	**how many baskets ye took up? Neither the seven loaves of the four thousand, and how many**
	11	**baskets ye took up? How is it that ye do not understand that I spake** *it* **not to you concerning bread, that ye should beware of the leaven of the Pharisees and of the Sadducees?** Then understood they how that He bade *them* not beware of the leaven of bread, but of the doctrine of the Pharisees and of the Sadducees. When Jesus came into the coasts of Cæsarea
	13	Philippi, He asked His disciples, saying, **Whom do men say that I the Son of man am?** And they said, Some *say that Thou art* John the Baptist some, Elias: and others, Jeremias, or one of the prophets. He saith
	15	unto them, **But whom say ye that I am?** And Simon Peter answered and said, Thou art the Christ, the Son of the living God.
	26²	**For what is a man profited, if he shall gain the whole world, and lose his own soul? or what**
	9	**shall a man give in exchange for his soul?**
17	10	And His disciples asked Him, saying, **Why then say the scribes that Elias must first come?**
		And when they were come to the multitude, there came to Him a *certain* man, kneeling down to Him, and

SAINT MATTHEW:—XVII., XVIII. 251

| | CHAP. | VER. |

saying, Lord, have mercy on my son: for he is lunatick, and sore vexed: for ofttimes he falleth into the fire, and oft into the water. And I brought him to Thy disciples, and they could not cure him. Then Jesus answered and said, O faithless and perverse generation, **how long shall I be with you? how long shall I suffer you?** bring him hither to Me. And Jesus rebuked the devil, and he departed out of him: and the child was cured from that very hour. Then came the disciples to Jesus apart, and said, **Why could not we cast him out?** And Jesus said unto them, Because of your unbelief: for verily I say unto you, If ye have faith as a grain of mustard seed, ye shall say unto this mountain, Remove hence to yonder place; and it shall remove, and nothing shall be impossible unto you. Howbeit this kind goeth not out but by prayer and fasting. — **17** 17[2]

19

And when they were come to Capernaum, they that received tribute *money* came to Peter, and said, **Doth not your master pay tribute?** He saith, Yes. And when he was come into the house, Jesus prevented him, saying, **What thinkest thou, Simon? of whom do the kings of the earth take custom or tribute? of their own children, or of strangers?** Peter saith unto Him, Of strangers. Jesus saith unto him, Then are the children free. Notwithstanding, lest we should offend them, go thou to the sea, and cast an hook, and take up the fish that first cometh up; and when thou hast opened his mouth, thou shalt find a piece of money: that take, and give unto them for Me and thee. — 24

25[3]

8

At the same time came the disciples unto Jesus, saying, **Who is the greatest in the kingdom of heaven?** And Jesus called a little child unto Him, and set him in the midst of them, and said, Verily I say unto you, Except ye be converted, and become as little children, ye shall not enter into the kingdom of heaven. Whoso- — **18** 1

CHAP.	VER.	
		ever therefore shall humble himself as this little child, the same is greatest in the kingdom of heaven.
18	12²	**How think ye?** if a man have an hundred sheep, and one of them be gone astray, doth he not leave the ninety and nine, and goeth into the mountains, and seeketh that which is gone astray?
	21²	Then came Peter to Him, and said, Lord, **how oft shall my brother sin against me, and I forgive him? till seven times?** Jesus saith unto him, I say not unto thee, Until seven times: but, Until seventy times seven.
	33	Then his lord, after that he had called him, said unto him, O thou wicked servant, I forgave thee all that debt, because thou desiredst me · **shouldest not thou also have had compassion on thy fellowservant, even as I had pity on thee?**
	6	
19	3	The Pharisees also came unto Him, tempting Him, and saying unto Him, **Is it lawful for a man to put away his wife for every cause?** And He answered
	5	and said unto them, **Have ye not read, that He which made** *them* **at the beginning made them male and female,** and said, **For this cause shall a man leave father and mother, and shall cleave to his wife: and they twain shall be one flesh?** Wherefore they are no more twain, but one flesh. What therefore God hath joined together, let no man put
	7	asunder. They say unto Him, **Why did Moses then command to give a writing of divorcement, and to put her away?** He saith unto them, Moses because of the hardness of your hearts suffered you to put away your wives but from the beginning it was not so.
	16	And, behold, one came and said unto Him, **Good Master, what good thing shall I do, that I may**

have eternal life? And He said unto him, **Why callest thou Me good?** *there is* none good but one, *that is,* God but if thou wilt enter into life, keep the commandments. He saith unto Him, **Which?** Jesus said, Thou shalt do no murder, Thou shalt not commit adultery, Thou shalt not steal, Thou shalt not bear false witness, Honour thy father and *thy* mother: and, Thou shalt love thy neighbour as thyself. The young man saith unto Him, All these things have I kept from my youth up· **what lack I yet?** Jesus said unto him, If thou wilt be perfect, go *and* sell that thou hast, and give to the poor, and thou shalt have treasure in heaven: and come *and* follow Me. But when the young man heard that saying, he went away sorrowful: for he had great possessions Then said Jesus unto His disciples, Verily I say unto you, That a rich man shall hardly enter into the kingdom of heaven. And again I say unto you, It is easier for a camel to go through the eye of a needle, than for a rich man to enter into the kingdom of God. When His disciples heard *it,* they were exceedingly amazed, saying, **Who then can be saved?** But Jesus beheld *them,* and said unto them, With men this is impossible; but with God all things are possible. Then answered Peter and said unto Him, Behold, we have forsaken all, and followed Thee; **what shall we have therefore?** And Jesus said unto them, Verily I say unto you, That ye which have followed Me, in the regeneration when the Son of man shall sit in the throne of His glory, ye also shall sit upon twelve thrones, judging the twelve tribes of Israel. And every one that hath forsaken houses, or brethren, or sisters, or father, or mother, or wife, or children, or lands, for My name's sake, shall receive an hundredfold, and shall inherit everlasting life. But many *that are* first shall be last; and the last *shall be* first.

And about the eleventh hour he went out, and found others standing idle, and saith unto them, **Why stand ye here all the day idle?** They say unto him, Because no man hath hired us. He saith unto them, Go ye also into the vineyard; and whatsoever is right, *that* shall ye receive.

And when they came that *were hired* about the eleventh hour, they received every man a penny. But when the first came, they supposed that they should have received more; and they likewise received every man a penny. And when they had received *it*, they murmured against the goodman of the house, saying, These last have wrought *but* one hour, and thou hast made them equal unto us, which have borne the burden and heat of the day. But he answered one of them, and said, Friend, I do thee no wrong. **didst not thou agree with me for a penny?** Take *that* thine is, and go thy way: I will give unto this last, even as unto thee. **Is it not lawful for me to do what I will with mine own? Is thine eye evil, because I am good?** So the last shall be first, and the first last : for many be called, but few chosen.

Then came to Him the mother of Zebedee's children with her sons, worshipping *Him*, and desiring a certain thing of Him. And He said unto her, **What wilt thou?** She saith unto Him, Grant that these my two sons may sit, the one on Thy right hand, and the other on the left, in Thy kingdom. But Jesus answered and said, Ye know not what ye ask. **Are ye able to drink of the cup that I shall drink of, and to be baptized with the baptism that I am baptized with?** They say unto Him, We are able. And He saith unto them, Ye shall drink indeed of My cup, and be baptized with the baptism that I am baptized with: but to sit on My right hand, and on My left, is not Mine to give, but *it shall be given to them* for whom it is prepared of My Father.

And, behold, two blind men sitting by the way side, when they heard that Jesus passed by, cried out, saying, Have mercy on us, O Lord, *Thou* Son of David. And the multitude rebuked them, because they should hold their peace : but they cried the more, saying, Have mercy on us, O Lord, *Thou* Son of David. And Jesus stood still, and called them, and said, **What will ye that I shall do unto you?** They say unto Him, Lord, that our eyes may be opened. So Jesus had compassion *on them*, and touched their eyes · and immediately their eyes received sight, and they followed Him.   20   32

    7

And when He was come into Jerusalem, all the city was moved, saying, **Who is this?** And the multitude said, This is Jesus, the prophet of Nazareth of Galilee.   21   10

And when the chief priests and scribes saw the wonderful things that He did, and the children crying in the temple, and saying, Hosanna to the Son of David; they were sore displeased, and said unto Him, **Hearest Thou what these say?** And Jesus saith unto them, Yea, **have ye never read, Out of the mouth of babes and sucklings thou hast perfected praise?**   16[2]

And when He was come into the temple, the chief priests and the elders of the people came unto Him as He was teaching, and said, **By what authority doest thou these things?** and **who gave Thee this authority?** And Jesus answered and said unto them, I also will ask you one thing, which if ye tell Me, I in like wise will tell you by what authority I do these things. **The baptism of John, whence was it? from heaven, or of men?** And they reasoned with themselves, saying, If we shall say, From heaven, He will say unto us, **Why did ye not then believe him?** But if we shall say, Of men; we fear the people; for all hold John as a prophet. And they answered Jesus, and said, We cannot tell. And He said unto them, Neither tell I you by what authority I do these things. **But what think ye?** A *certain* man had two sons; and he came to the first, and said, Son, go work to day in my vineyard. He answered and said, I will not: but afterward he repented, and went. And he came to the second, and said likewise. And he answered and said, I *go*, sir. and   23[2]

    25[3]

    28

CHAP	VER	
21	31	went not. **Whether of them twain did the will of** *his* **father?** They say unto Him, The first. Jesus saith unto them, Verily I say unto you, That the publicans and the harlots go into the kingdom of God before you. For John came unto you in the way of righteousness, and ye believed him not: but the publicans and the harlots believed him: and ye, when ye had seen *it*, repented not afterward, that ye might believe him. Hear another parable: There was a certain householder, which planted a vineyard, and hedged it round about, and digged a winepress in it, and built a tower, and let it out to husbandmen, and went into a far country: and when the time of the fruit drew near, he sent his servants to the husbandmen, that they might receive the fruits of it. And the husbandmen took his servants, and beat one, and killed another, and stoned another. Again, he sent other servants more than the first: and they did unto them likewise. But last of all he sent unto them his son, saying, They will reverence my son. But when the husbandmen saw the son, they said among themselves, This is the heir; come, let us kill him, and let us seize on his inheritance. And they caught him, and cast *him*
	40	out of the vineyard, and slew *him*. **When the lord therefore of the vineyard cometh, what will he do unto those husbandmen?** They say unto him, He will miserably destroy those wicked men, and will let out *his* vineyard unto other husbandmen, which shall render him
	42	the fruits in their seasons. Jesus saith unto them, **Did ye never read in the scriptures, The stone which the builders rejected, the same is become the head**
	12	**of the corner: this is the Lord's doing, and it is marvellous in our eyes?**
22	12	And when the king came in to see the guests, He saw there a man which had not on a wedding garment: and He saith unto him, **Friend, how camest thou in hither not having a wedding garment?** And he was speechless. Then said the king to the servants, Bind him hand and foot, and take him away, and cast *him* into

outer darkness; there shall be weeping and gnashing of teeth. For many are called, but few *are* chosen. Then went the Pharisees, and took counsel how they might entangle Him in *His* talk. And they sent out unto Him their disciples with the Herodians, saying, Master, we know that Thou art true, and teachest the way of God in truth, neither carest Thou for any *man :* for Thou regardest not the person of men. Tell us therefore, **What thinkest Thou? Is it lawful to give tribute unto Cæsar, or not?** But Jesus perceived their wickedness, and said, **Why tempt ye Me,** *ye* **hypocrites?** Shew Me the tribute money. And they brought unto Him a penny. And He saith unto them, **Whose** *is* **this image and superscription?** They say unto Him, Cæsar's. Then saith He unto them, Render therefore unto Cæsar the things which are Cæsar's; and unto God the things that are God's. When they had heard *these words*, they marvelled, and left Him, and went their way.

22 17²

18

20

Therefore in the resurrection whose wife shall she be of the seven? for they all had her. Jesus answered and said unto them, Ye do err, not knowing the scriptures, nor the power of God. For in the resurrection they neither marry, nor are given in marriage, but are as the angels of God in heaven. But as touching the resurrection of the dead, **have ye not read that which was spoken unto you by God, saying, I am the God of Abraham, and the God of Isaac, and the God of Jacob?** God is not the God of the dead, but of the living.

28

32

Then one of them, *which was* a lawyer, asked *Him a question*, tempting Him, and saying, **Master, which** *is* **the great commandment in the law?** Jesus said unto him, Thou shalt love the Lord thy God with all thy heart, and with all thy soul, and with all thy mind. This is the first and great commandment. And the second *is* like unto it, Thou shalt love thy neighbour as

36

CHAP.	VER.	
22	42²	thyself. On these two commandments hang all the law and the prophets. While the Pharisees were gathered together, Jesus asked them, saying, **What think ye of Christ? whose son is He?** They say unto Him, *The Son* of David. He saith unto them, **How then doth David in spirit call Him Lord, saying, The** LORD **said unto my Lord, Sit thou on My right hand,**
	44	
	45	**till I make thine enemies thy footstool? If David then call Him Lord, how is He his son?** And no man was able to answer Him a word, neither durst any *man* from that day forth ask him any more *questions*.
	12	
23	17	Woe unto you, *ye* blind guides, which say, Whosoever shall swear by the temple, it is nothing; but whosoever shall swear by the gold of the temple, he is a debtor! *Ye* fools and blind: **for whether is greater, the gold, or the temple that sanctifieth the gold?** And, Whosoever shall swear by the altar, it is nothing; but whosoever sweareth by the gift that is upon it, he is guilty. *Ye* fools and blind: **for whether** *is* **greater, the gift, or the altar that sanctifieth the gift?**
	19	
	33	*Ye* serpents, *ye* generation of vipers, **how can ye escape the damnation of hell?**
	3	
24	2	And Jesus went out, and departed from the temple: and His disciples came to *Him* for to shew Him the buildings of the temple. And Jesus said unto them, **See ye not all these things?** verily I say unto you, There shall not be left here one stone upon another, that shall not be thrown down. And as He sat upon the mount of Olives, the disciples came unto Him privately, saying, **Tell us, when shall these things be?** and what *shall be* **the sign of Thy coming, and of the end of the world?**
	3²	
	45	**Who then is a faithful and wise servant, whom his lord hath made ruler over his household, to give them meat in due season?** Blessed *is* that
	4	

servant, whom his lord when he cometh shall find so doing.

Then shall the righteous answer Him saying, Lord, **when saw we Thee an hungered, and fed** *Thee?* **or thirsty, and gave** *Thee* **drink? When saw we Thee a stranger, and took** *Thee* **in? or naked, and clothed** *Thee?* Or **when saw we Thee sick, or in prison, and came unto Thee?** And the King shall answer and say unto them, Verily I say unto you, Inasmuch as ye have done *it* unto one of the least of these My brethren, ye have done *it* unto Me.

CHAP.	VER.
25	37[2]
	38[2]
	39

Then shall they also answer Him, saying, Lord, **when saw we Thee an hungred, or athirst, or a stranger, or naked, or sick, or in prison, and did not minister unto Thee?** Then shall He answer them, saying, Verily I say unto you, Inasmuch as ye did *it* not to one of the least of these, ye did *it* not to Me.

	44
	6

Now when Jesus was in Bethany, in the house of Simon the leper, there came unto Him a woman having an alabaster box of very precious ointment, and poured it on His head, as He sat *at meat*. But when His disciples saw *it*, they had indignation, saying, **To what purpose** *is* **this waste?** For this ointment might have been sold for much, and given to the poor. When Jesus understood *it*, He said unto them, **Why trouble ye the woman?** for she hath wrought a good work upon Me.

26	8
	10

Then one of the twelve, called Judas Iscariot, went unto the chief priests, and said *unto them*, **What will ye give me, and I will deliver Him unto you?** And they covenanted with him for thirty pieces of silver.

	15

Now the first *day* of the *feast of* unleavened bread the

CHAP.	VER.	
26	17	disciples came to Jesus, saying unto Him, **Where wilt Thou that we prepare for Thee to eat the passover?** And He said, Go into the city to such a man, and say unto him, The Master saith, My time is at hand; I will keep the passover at thy house with My disciples.
		Now when the even was come, He sat down with the twelve. And as they did eat, He said, Verily I say unto you, that one of you shall betray Me. And they were exceeding sorrowful, and began every one of them to say
	22	unto Him, **Lord, is it I?** And He answered and said, He that dippeth *his* hand with Me in the dish, the same shall betray Me. The Son of man goeth as it is written of Him: but woe unto that man by whom the Son of man is betrayed! it had been good for that man if he had not been born. Then Judas, which betrayed Him,
	25	answered and said, **Master, is it I?** He said unto him, Thou hast said.
	40	And He cometh unto the disciples, and findeth them asleep, and saith unto Peter, **What, could ye not watch with Me one hour?**
		And while He yet spake, lo, Judas, one of the twelve, came, and with him a great multitude with swords and staves, from the chief priests and elders of the people. Now he that betrayed Him gave them a sign, saying, Whomsoever I shall kiss, that same is He: hold Him fast. And forthwith he came to Jesus, and said, Hail, master; and kissed Him. And Jesus said unto him,
	50	**Friend, wherefore art thou come?** Then came they, and laid hands on Jesus, and took Him. And behold, one of them which were with Jesus stretched out *his* hand, and drew his sword, and struck a servant of the high priest's, and smote off his ear. Then said Jesus unto him, Put up again thy sword into his place: for all they that take the sword shall perish with the sword.
	53	**Thinkest thou that I cannot now pray to My**

	CHAP.	VER

Father, and He shall presently give **Me** more than twelve legions of angels? But how then shall the scriptures be fulfilled, that thus it must be? In that same hour said Jesus to the multitudes, **Are ye come out as against a thief with swords and staves for to take Me?** I sat daily with you teaching in the temple, and ye laid no hold on Me.   26   54

                                                                                           55

And the high priest arose, and said unto Him, **Answerest Thou nothing? what** *is it which* **these witness against Thee?** But Jesus held His peace. And the high priest answered and said unto Him, I adjure thee by the living God, that Thou tell us whether Thou be the Christ, the Son of God. Jesus saith unto him, Thou hast said: nevertheless I say unto you, Hereafter shall ye see the Son of man sitting on the right hand of power, and coming in the clouds of heaven. Then the high priest rent his clothes, saying, He hath spoken blasphemy; **what further need have we of witnesses?** behold, now ye have heard His blasphemy. **What think ye?** They answered and said, He is guilty of death. Then did they spit in His face, and buffeted Him; and others smote *Him* with the palms of their hands, saying, Prophesy unto us, Thou Christ, **Who is he that smote Thee?**   62[2]

                                                                                           65
                                                                                           66

                                                                                           68
                                                                                           16

Then Judas, which had betrayed Him, when he saw that He was condemned, repented himself, and brought again the thirty pieces of silver to the chief priests and elders, saying, I have sinned in that I have betrayed the innocent blood. And they said, **What** *is that* **to us?** see thou *to that*.   27   4

And Jesus stood before the governor: and the governor asked Him, saying, **Art Thou the King of the Jews?** And Jesus said unto him, Thou sayest. And when He was accused of the chief priests and elders, He answered nothing. Then said Pilate unto Him, **Hearest Thou**   11

                                                                                           13

CHAP.	VER.	
27	17²	not how many things they witness against **Thee?** And He answered him to never a word; insomuch that the governor marvelled greatly. Now at *that* feast the governor was wont to release unto the people a prisoner, whom they would. And they had then a notable prisoner, called Barabbas. Therefore when they were gathered together, Pilate said unto them, **Whom will ye that I release unto you? Barabbas, or Jesus which is called Christ?** For he knew that for envy they had delivered Him.
	21	The governor answered and said unto them, **Whether of the twain will ye that I release unto you?**
	22	They said, Barabbas. Pilate saith unto them, **What shall I do then with Jesus which is called Christ?** *They* all say unto him, Let Him be crucified. And the
	23	governor said, **Why, what evil hath He done?** But they cried out the more, saying, Let Him be crucified.
	46²	And about the ninth hour Jesus cried with a loud voice, saying, **Eli, Eli, lama sabachthani?** that is to say, **My God, My God, why hast Thou forsaken Me?**
10		

Saint Matthew 177

SAINT MARK.

CHAP.	VER.	
1	24²	AND there was in their synagogue a man with an unclean spirit; and he cried out, saying, Let *us* alone, **what have we to do with Thee, Thou Jesus of Nazareth? art Thou come to destroy us?** I know Thee who Thou art, the Holy One of God. And Jesus rebuked him, saying, Hold thy peace, and come out of him. And when the unclean spirit had torn him, and

cried with a loud voice, he came out of him. And they were all amazed, insomuch that they questioned among themselves, saying, **What thing is this? what new doctrine** *is* **this?** for with authority commandeth He even the unclean spirits, and they do obey Him.

1 27²

4

And they come unto Him, bringing one sick of the palsy, which was borne of four. And when they could not come nigh unto Him for the press, they uncovered the roof where He was : and when they had broken *it* up, they let down the bed wherein the sick of the palsy lay. When Jesus saw their faith, He said unto the sick of the palsy, Son, thy sins be forgiven thee. But there were certain of the scribes sitting there, and reasoning in their hearts, **Why doth this** *man* **thus speak blasphemies? who can forgive sins but God only?** And immediately when Jesus perceived in His spirit that they so reasoned within themselves, He said unto them, **Why reason ye these things in your hearts? Whether is it easier to say to the sick of the palsy,** *Thy* **sins be forgiven thee; or to say, Arise, and take up thy bed, and walk?** But that ye may know that the Son of man hath power on earth to forgive sins, (He saith to the sick of the palsy,) I say unto thee, Arise, and take up thy bed, and go thy way into thine house. And immediately he arose, took up the bed, and went forth before them all; insomuch that they were all amazed, and glorified God, saying, We never saw it on this fashion.

2   7²

8
9

And when the scribes and Pharisees saw Him eat with publicans and sinners, they said unto His disciples, **How is it that He eateth and drinketh with publicans and sinners?** When Jesus heard *it*, He saith unto them, They that are whole have no need of the physician, but they that are sick : I came not to call the righteous, but sinners to repentance. And the disciples of John and of the Pharisees used to fast: and they come and say unto Him, **Why**

16

18

CHAP.	VER.	
2	19	do the disciples of John and of the Pharisees fast, but Thy disciples fast not? And Jesus said unto them, **Can the children of the bridechamber fast, while the bridegroom is with them?** as long as they have the bridegroom with them, they cannot fast. But the days will come, when the bridegroom shall be taken away from them, and then shall they fast in those days.
	24	And it came to pass, that He went through the corn fields on the sabbath day; and His disciples began, as they went, to pluck the ears of corn. And the Pharisees said unto Him, **Behold, why do they on the sabbath day that which is not lawful?** And He said unto
	25	them, **Have ye never read what David did, when he had need, and was an hungred, he, and they**
	26	**that were with him? How he went into the house of God in the days of Abiathar the high priest, and did eat the shewbread, which is not lawful to eat but for the priests, and gave also to them which were with him?** And He said unto them, The sabbath was made for man, and not man for
	10	the sabbath. Therefore the Son of man is Lord also of the sabbath.
3	4²	And He entered again into the synagogue; and there was a man there which had a withered hand. And they watched Him, whether He would heal him on the sabbath day; that they might accuse Him. And He saith unto the man which had the withered hand, Stand forth. And He saith unto them, **Is it lawful to do good on the sabbath days, or to do evil? to save life, or to kill?** But they held their peace. And when He had looked round about on them with anger, being grieved for the hardness of their hearts, He saith unto the man, Stretch forth thine hand. And he stretched *it* out: and his hand was restored whole as the other.

And the scribes which came down from Jerusalem said, He hath Beelzebub, and by the prince of the devils

	CHAP.	VER.

casteth He out devils. And He called them *unto Him*, and said unto them in parables, **How can Satan cast out Satan?** And if a kingdom be divided against itself, that kingdom cannot stand. And if a house be divided against itself, that house cannot stand. And if Satan rise up against himself, and be divided, he cannot stand, but hath an end **3 23**

There came then His brethren and His mother, and, standing without, sent unto Him, calling Him. And the multitude sat about Him, and they said unto Him, Behold, Thy mother and Thy brethren without seek for Thee. And He answered them, saying, **Who is My mother, or My brethren?** And He looked round about on them which sat about Him, and said, Behold My mother and My brethren! For whosoever shall do the will of God, the same is My brother, and My sister, and mother. **33**

4

And He said unto them, **Know ye not this parable?** and **how then will ye know all parables?** **4 13²**

And He said unto them, **Is a candle brought to be put under a bushel, or under a bed? and not to be set on a candlestick?** For there is nothing hid, which shall not be manifested; neither was any thing kept secret, but that it should come abroad. **21²**

And He said, **Whereunto shall we liken the kingdom of God?** or **with what comparison shall we compare it?** **30²**

And there arose a great storm of wind, and the waves beat into the ship, so that it was now full. And He was in the hinder part of the ship, asleep on a pillow. and they awake Him, and say unto Him, **Master, carest Thou not that we perish?** And He arose, and rebuked the wind, and said unto the sea, Peace, be still. And the wind ceased and there was a great calm. And **38**

CHAP	VER.	
4	40	He said unto them, **Why are ye so fearful? how is it that ye have no faith?** And they feared exceed-
	41	ingly, and said one to another, **What manner of man**
	10	**is this, that even the wind and the sea obey Him?**

And when He was come out of the ship, immediately there met Him out of the tombs a man with an unclean spirit, who had *his* dwelling among the tombs; and no man could bind him, no, not with chains. because that he had been often bound with fetters and chains, and the chains had been plucked asunder by him, and the fetters broken in pieces : neither could any *man* tame him. And always, night and day, he was in the mountains, and in the tombs, crying, and cutting himself with stones. But when he saw Jesus afar off, he ran and worshipped Him. and cried with a loud voice, and said,

| 5 | 7 | **What have I to do with Thee, Jesus,** *Thou* **Son of the most high God?** I adjure Thee by God, that Thou torment me not. For He said unto him, Come out of the man, *thou* unclean spirit. And He asked him, |
| | 9 | **What** *is* **thy name?** And he answered, saying, My name *is* Legion · for we are many. |

And Jesus, immediately knowing in Himself that virtue had gone out of Him, turned Him about in the
| | 30 | press, and said, **Who touched My clothes?** And His disciples said unto Him, Thou seest the multitude |
| | 31 | thronging Thee, **and sayest Thou, Who touched Me?** |

While He yet spake, there came from the ruler of the synagogue's *house certain* which said, Thy daughter is
| | 35 | dead : **why troublest thou the Master any further?** As soon as Jesus heard the word that was spoken, He saith unto the ruler of the synagogue, Be not afraid, only believe. And He suffered no man to follow Him, save Peter, and James, and John the brother of James. And He cometh to the house of the ruler of the synagogue, and seeth the tumult, and them that wept and wailed |

SAINT MARK:—V.-VII.

	CHAP.	VER.
greatly. And when He was come in, He saith unto them, **Why make ye this ado, and weep?** the damsel is not dead, but sleepeth.	**5**	39
		6
And when the sabbath day was come, He began to teach in the synagogue. and many hearing *Him* were astonished, saying, **From whence hath this** *man* **these things?** and **what wisdom** *is* **this which is given unto Him, that even such mighty works are wrought by His hands? Is not this the carpenter, the son of Mary, the brother of James, and Joses, and of Juda, and Simon?** and **are not His sisters here with us?** And they were offended at Him | **6** | 2^2 3^2 |
And when the daughter of the said Herodias came in, and danced, and pleased Herod and them that sat with him, the king said unto the damsel, Ask of me whatsoever thou wilt, and I will give *it* thee. And he sware unto her, Whatsoever thou shalt ask of me, I will give *it* thee, unto the half of my kingdom. And she went forth, and said unto her mother, **What shall I ask?** And she said, The head of John the Baptist. | | 24 |
And when the day was now far spent, His disciples came unto Him, and said, This is a desert place, and now the time *is* far passed: send them away, that they may go into the country round about, and into the villages, and buy themselves bread: for they have nothing to eat. He answered and said unto them, Give ye them to eat. And they say unto Him, **Shall we go and buy two hundred pennyworth of bread, and give them to eat?** He saith unto them, **How many loaves have ye?** go and see. And when they knew, they say, Five, and two fishes. | | 37 38 **7** |
Then the Pharisees and scribes asked Him, **Why walk not Thy disciples according to the tradition of the elders, but eat bread with unwashen** | **7** | 5 |

CHAP	VER	
		hands? He answered and said unto them, Well hath Esaias prophesied of you hypocrites, as it is written, This people honoureth Me with *their* lips, but their heart is far from Me.
7	18 19	And when He was entered into the house from the people, His disciples asked Him concerning the parable. And He saith unto them, **Are ye so without understanding also? Do ye not perceive, that whatsoever thing from without entereth into the man, *it* cannot defile him; because it entereth not into his heart, but into the belly, and goeth out into the draught, purging all meats?** And he said, That which cometh out of the man, that defileth the man.
	3	
8	4 5	In those days the multitude being very great, and having nothing to eat, Jesus called His disciples *unto Him*, and saith unto them, I have compassion on the multitude, because they have now been with Me three days, and have nothing to eat: and if I send them away fasting to their own houses, they will faint by the way: for divers of them came from far. And His disciples answered Him, **From whence can a man satisfy these *men* with bread here in the wilderness?** And He asked them, **How many loaves have ye?** And they said, Seven.
	12	And the Pharisees came forth, and began to question with Him, seeking of Him a sign from heaven, tempting Him. And He sighed deeply in His spirit, and saith, **Why doth this generation seek after a sign?** verily I say unto you, There shall no sign be given unto this generation.
		Now *the disciples* had forgotten to take bread, neither had they in the ship with them more than one loaf. And He charged them, saying, Take heed, beware of the leaven of the Pharisees, and *of* the leaven of Herod. And they reasoned among themselves, saying, *It is* be-

cause we have no bread. And when Jesus knew *it*, He saith unto them, **Why reason ye, because ye have no bread? perceive ye not yet, neither understand? have ye your heart yet hardened? Having eyes, see ye not?** and **having ears, hear ye not? and do ye not remember?** When I brake the five loaves among five thousand, **how many baskets full of fragments took ye up?** They say unto Him, Twelve. And when the seven among four thousand, **how many baskets full of fragments took ye up?** And they said, Seven. And He said unto them, **How is it that ye do not understand?**

8 17³
18³
19
20
21

And Jesus went out, and His disciples, into the towns of Cæsarea Philippi: and by the way He asked His disciples, saying unto them, **Whom do men say that I am?** And they answered, John the Baptist: but some *say*, Elias; and others, One of the prophets. And He saith unto them, **But whom say ye that I am?** And Peter answereth and saith unto Him, Thou art the Christ. And He charged them that they should tell no man of Him.

27
29

For what shall it profit a man, if he shall gain the whole world, and lose his own soul? Or what shall a man give in exchange for his soul?

36
37
16

And they asked Him, saying, **Why say the scribes that Elias must first come?** And He answered and told them, Elias verily cometh first, and restoreth all things; and how it is written of the Son of man, that He must suffer many things, and be set at nought. But I say unto you, That Elias is indeed come, and they have done unto him whatsoever they listed, as it is written of him.

9 11

And when He came to *His* disciples, He saw a great multitude about them, and the scribes questioning with them. And straightway all the people, when they beheld Him, were greatly amazed, and running to *Him* saluted

CHAP.	VER.	
9	16	Him. And He asked the scribes, **What question ye with them?** And one of the multitude answered and said, Master, I have brought unto Thee my son, which hath a dumb spirit; and wheresoever he taketh him, he teareth him: and he foameth, and gnasheth with his teeth, and pineth away: and I spake to Thy disciples that they should cast him out; and they could not. He
	19²	answereth him, and saith, O faithless generation, **how long shall I be with you? how long shall I suffer you?** bring him unto Me And they brought him unto Him: and when he saw Him, straightway the spirit tare him; and he fell on the ground, and wallowed foaming.
	21	And He asked his father, **How long is it ago since this came unto him?** And he said, Of a child.
	28	And when He was come into the house, His disciples asked Him privately, **Why could not we cast him out?** And He said unto them, This kind can come forth by nothing, but by prayer and fasting.
	33	And He came to Capernaum: and being in the house He asked them, **What was it that ye disputed among yourselves by the way?** But they held their peace: for by the way they had disputed among themselves, who *should be* the greatest.
	50	Salt *is* good: **but if the salt have lost his saltness, wherewith will ye season it?** Have salt in yourselves, and have peace one with another
	8	
10	2	And the Pharisees came to Him, and asked Him, **Is it lawful for a man to put away** *his* **wife?** tempting
	3	Him. And He answered and said unto them, **What did Moses command you?** And they said, Moses suffered to write a bill of divorcement, and to put *her* away.

And when He was gone forth into the way, there came one running, and kneeled to Him, and asked Him, Good

SAINT MARK:—X., XI. 271

| | CHAP | VER. |

Master, **what shall I do that I may inherit eternal life?** And Jesus said unto him, **Why callest thou Me good?** *there is* none good but one, *that is*, God. | **10** | 17
| | | 18

It is easier for a camel to go through the eye of a needle, than for a rich man to enter into the kingdom of God. And they were astonished out of measure, saying among themselves, **Who then can be saved?** And Jesus looking upon them saith, With men *it is* impossible, but not with God: for with God all things are possible. | | 26

And James and John, the sons of Zebedee, come unto Him, saying, Master, we would that Thou shouldest do for us whatsoever we shall desire. And He said unto them, **What would ye that I should do for you?** They said unto Him, Grant unto us that we may sit, one on Thy right hand, and the other on Thy left hand, in Thy glory. But Jesus said unto them, Ye know not what ye ask: **can ye drink of the cup that I drink of? and be baptized with the baptism that I am baptized with?** And they said unto Him, We can. And Jesus said unto them, Ye shall indeed drink of the cup that I drink of; and with the baptism that I am baptized withal shall ye be baptized: but to sit on My right hand and on My left hand is not Mine to give; but *it shall be given to them* for whom it is prepared. | | 36

| | | 38²

And Jesus answered and said unto him, **What wilt thou that I should do unto thee?** The blind man said unto Him, Lord, that I might receive my sight. | | 51
| | | 9

And when they came nigh to Jerusalem, unto Bethphage and Bethany, at the mount of Olives, He sendeth forth two of His disciples, and saith unto them, Go your way into the village over against you: and as soon as ye be entered into it, ye shall find a colt tied, whereon never man sat; loose him, and bring *him*. And if any man say unto you, **Why do ye this?** say ye that the Lord hath need | **11** | 3

CHAP.	VER.	
11	5	of him; and straightway he will send him hither. And they went their way, and found the colt tied by the door without in a place where two ways met; and they loose him. And certain of them that stood there said unto them, **What do ye, loosing the colt?** And they said unto them even as Jesus had commanded: and they let them go.
	17	And He taught, saying unto them, **Is it not written, My house shall be called of all nations the house of prayer?** but ye have made it a den of thieves.
	28²	And they come again to Jerusalem: and as He was walking in the temple, there come to Him the chief priests, and the scribes, and the elders, and say unto Him, **By what authority doest Thou these things? and who gave Thee this authority to do these things?** And Jesus answered and said unto them, I will also ask of you one question, and answer Me, and I will tell you by what authority I do these things.
	30	**The baptism of John, was** *it* **from heaven or of men?** answer Me. And they reasoned with themselves, saying,
	31	If we shall say, From heaven; He will say, **Why then did ye not believe him?** But if we shall say, Of men; they feared the people: for all *men* counted John, that he was a prophet indeed. And they answered and
	7	said unto Jesus, We cannot tell. And Jesus answering saith unto them, Neither do I tell you by what authority I do these things.
12	9	**What shall therefore the lord of the vineyard do?** he will come and destroy the husbandmen, and will
	11	give the vineyard unto others. And **have ye not read this scripture; The stone which the builders rejected is become the head of the corner: this was the Lord's doing, and it is marvellous in our eyes?**
		And they send unto Him certain of the Pharisees and

SAINT MARK :—XII.

of the Herodians, to catch Him in *His* words. And when they were come, they say unto Him, Master, we know that Thou art true, and carest for no man: for Thou regardest not the person of men, but teachest the way of God in truth: **Is it lawful to give tribute to Cæsar, or not? Shall we give, or shall we not give?** But He, knowing their hypocrisy, said unto them, **Why tempt ye Me?** bring Me a penny, that I may see *it*. And they brought *it* And He saith unto them, **Whose** *is* **this image and superscription?** And they said unto Him, Cæsar's. And Jesus answering said unto them, Render to Cæsar the things that are Cæsar's, and to God the things that are God's. And they marvelled at Him.

12   14
15²

16

And the seven had her, and left no seed: last of all the woman died also. **In the resurrection therefore, when they shall rise, whose wife shall she be of them?** for the seven had her to wife. And Jesus answering said unto them, **Do ye not therefore err, because ye know not the scriptures, neither the power of God?** For when they shall rise from the dead, they neither marry, nor are given in marriage; but are as the angels which are in heaven. And as touching the dead, that they rise: **have ye not read in the book of Moses, how in the bush God spake unto him, saying, I** *am* **the God of Abraham, and the God of Isaac, and the God of Jacob?** He is not the God of the dead, but the God of the living: ye therefore do greatly err. And one of the scribes came, and having heard them reasoning together, and perceiving that He had answered them well, asked Him, **Which is the first commandment of all?** And Jesus answered him, The first of all the commandments *is*, Hear, O Israel; The Lord our God is one Lord: and thou shalt love the Lord thy God with all thy heart, and with all thy soul, and with all thy mind, and with all thy strength: this *is* the first commandment.

23

24

26

28

CHAP.	VER.	
12	35	And Jesus answered and said, while He taught in the temple, **How say the scribes that Christ is the Son of David?** For David himself said by the Holy Ghost, The LORD said to my Lord, Sit thou on My right hand, till I make thine enemies thy footstool. David therefore
	37	himself calleth Him Lord; and **whence is He** *then*
	12	**his son?** And the common people heard Him gladly.

13	2	And as He went out of the temple, one of His disciples saith unto Him, Master, see what manner of stones and what buildings *are here!* And Jesus answering said unto him, **Seest thou these great buildings?** there shall not be left one stone upon another, that shall not be thrown down. And as He sat upon the mount of Olives over against the temple, Peter and James and John and
	4²	Andrew asked Him privately, **Tell us, when shall these things be?** and **what** *shall be* **the sign when all these things shall be fulfilled?** And Jesus answering them began to say, Take heed lest any *man*
	3	deceive you. for many shall come in My name, saying, I am *Christ;* and shall deceive many.

14	4	And being in Bethany in the house of Simon the leper, as He sat at meat, there came a woman having an alabaster box of ointment of spikenard very precious; and she brake the box, and poured *it* on His head. And there were some that had indignation within themselves, and said, **Why was this waste of the ointment made?** For it might have been sold for more than three hundred pence, and have been given to the poor. And they murmured against her. And Jesus said, Let
	6	her alone, **why trouble ye her?** she hath wrought a good work on Me.
	12	And the first day of unleavened bread, when they killed the passover, His disciples said unto Him, **Where wilt Thou that we go and prepare that Thou mayest eat the passover?** And He sendeth forth two of His disciples, and saith unto them, Go ye into the

city, and there shall meet you a man bearing a pitcher of water: follow him. And wheresoever he shall go in, say ye to the goodman of the house, The Master saith, **Where is the guestchamber, where I shall eat the passover with My disciples?** And he will shew you a large upper room furnished *and* prepared: there make ready for us.

    14   14

And in the evening He cometh with the twelve. And as they sat and did eat, Jesus said, Verily I say unto you, One of you which eateth with Me shall betray Me. And they began to be sorrowful, and to say unto Him one by one, *Is* **it I?** and another *said, Is* **it I?** And He answered and said unto them, *It is* one of the twelve, that dippeth with Me in the dish.

    19^2

And He cometh, and findeth them sleeping, and saith unto Peter, **Simon, sleepest thou? couldest not thou watch one hour?** Watch ye and pray, lest ye enter into temptation. The spirit truly *is* ready, but the flesh *is* weak.

    37^2

And Jesus answered and said unto them, **Are ye come out, as against a thief, with swords and** *with* **staves to take Me?** I was daily with you in the temple teaching, and ye took Me not: but the scriptures must be fulfilled.

    48

And the high priest stood up in the midst, and asked Jesus, saying, **Answerest Thou nothing? what** *is* *it which* **these witness against Thee?** But He held His peace, and answered nothing. Again the high priest asked Him, and said unto Him, **Art Thou the Christ, the Son of the Blessed?** And Jesus said, I am. and ye shall see the Son of man sitting on the right hand of power, and coming in the clouds of heaven. Then the high priest rent his clothes, and saith, **What need we any further witnesses?** Ye have heard the blasphemy. **what think ye?** And they all condemned Him to be guilty of death.

    60^2

    61

    63

    64

    14

CHAP.	VER.	
15	2	And Pilate asked Him, **Art Thou the King of the Jews?** And He answering said unto him, Thou sayest it. And the chief priests accused Him of many things: but He answered nothing. And Pilate asked Him again,
	4	saying, **Answerest Thou nothing?** behold how many things they witness against Thee. But Jesus yet answered nothing; so that Pilate marvelled. Now at *that* feast he released unto them one prisoner, whomsoever they desired. And there was *one* named Barabbas, *which lay* bound with them that had made insurrection with him, who had committed murder in the insurrection. And the multitude crying aloud began to desire *him to do* as he had ever done unto them. But Pilate answered them,
	9	saying, **Will ye that I release unto you the King of the Jews?** For he knew that the chief priests had delivered Him for envy. But the chief priests moved the people, that he should rather release Barabbas unto them. And Pilate answered and said again unto them,
	12	**What will ye then that I shall do** *unto Him* **whom ye call the King of the Jews?** And they cried out
	14	again, Crucify Him. Then Pilate said unto them, **Why, what evil hath He done?** And they cried out the more exceedingly, Crucify Him.
	34²	And at the ninth hour Jesus cried with a loud voice, saying, **Eloi, Eloi, lama sabachthani?** which is, being interpreted, **My God, My God, why hast Thou forsaken Me?**
	7	
16	3	And when the sabbath was past, Mary Magdalene, and Mary the *mother* of James, and Salome, had bought sweet spices, that they might come and anoint Him. And very early in the morning the first *day* of the week, they came unto the sepulchre at the rising of the sun. And they said among themselves, **Who shall roll us away the stone from the door of the sepulchre?**
	1	And when they looked, they saw that the stone was rolled away: for it was very great.

Saint Mark 121

SAINT LUKE.

	CHAP.	VER.

AND Zacharias said unto the angel, **Whereby shall I know this?** for I am an old man, and my wife well stricken in years. And the angel answering said unto him, I am Gabriel, that stand in the presence of God; and am sent to speak unto thee, and to shew thee these glad tidings. — **1** 18

Then said Mary unto the angel, **How shall this be, seeing I know not a man?** And the angel answered and said unto her, The Holy Ghost shall come upon thee, and the power of the Highest shall overshadow thee: therefore also that holy thing which shall be born of thee shall be called the Son of God. — 34

And whence *is* **this to me, that the mother of my Lord should come to me?** — 43 / 3

And all that heard Him were astonished at His understanding and answers. And when they saw Him, they were amazed: and His mother said unto Him, Son, **why hast Thou thus dealt with us?** behold, Thy father and I have sought Thee sorrowing. And He said unto them, **How is it that ye sought Me? wist ye not that I must be about My Father's business?** And they understood not the saying which He spake unto them. — **2** 48 / 49² / 3

Then said he to the multitude that came forth to be baptized of him, **O generation of vipers, who hath warned you to flee from the wrath to come?** — **3** 7

And now also the axe is laid unto the root of the trees: every tree therefore which bringeth not forth good fruit is hewn down, and cast into the fire. And the people asked him, saying, **What shall we do then?** — 10

CHAP.	VER.	
3	12	He answereth and saith unto them, He that hath two coats, let him impart to him that hath none; and he that hath meat, let him do likewise. Then came also publicans to be baptized, and said unto him, **Master, what shall we do?** And he said unto them, Exact no more than that which is appointed you. And the soldiers
	14	likewise demanded of him, saying, **And what shall we do?** And he said unto them, Do violence to no
	4	man, neither accuse *any* falsely; and be content with your wages

| 4 | 22 | And all bare Him witness, and wondered at the gracious words which proceeded out of His mouth. And they said, **Is not this Joseph's son?** |

| | 34² | And in the synagogue there was a man, which had a spirit of an unclean devil, and cried out with a loud voice, saying, Let *us* alone; **what have we to do with Thee,** *Thou* **Jesus of Nazareth? art Thou** |
| | 3 | **come to destroy us?** I know Thee who Thou art; the Holy One of God. |

5	21²	And, behold, men brought in a bed a man which was taken with a palsy · and they sought *means* to bring him in, and to lay *him* before Him. And when they could not find by what *way* they might bring him in because of the multitude, they went upon the housetop, and let him down through the tiling with *his* couch into the midst before Jesus. And when He saw their faith, He said unto him, Man, thy sins are forgiven thee. And the scribes and the Pharisees began to reason, saying, **Who is this which speaketh blasphemies? Who can forgive sins, but God alone?** But when Jesus perceived their
	22	thoughts, He answering said unto them, **What reason**
	23	**ye in your hearts? Whether is easier, to say, Thy sins be forgiven thee; or to say, Rise up and walk?** But that ye may know that the Son of man hath power upon earth to forgive sins (He said unto the sick of the palsy), I say unto thee, Arise, and take up

thy couch, and go into thine house. And immediately he rose up before them, and took up that whereon he lay, and departed to his own house, glorifying God.

And Levi made Him a great feast in his own house: and there was a great company of publicans and of others that sat down with them. But their scribes and Pharisees murmured against His disciples, saying, **Why do ye eat and drink with publicans and sinners?** And Jesus answering said unto them, They that are whole need not a physician; but they that are sick. I came not to call the righteous, but sinners to repentance. And they said unto Him, **Why do the disciples of John fast often, and make prayers, and likewise** *the disciples* **of the Pharisees; but thine eat and drink?** And He said unto them, **Can ye make the children of the bridechamber fast, while the bridegroom is with them?** But the days will come, when the bridegroom shall be taken away from them, and then shall they fast in those days.

And it came to pass on the second sabbath after the first, that He went through the corn fields; and His disciples plucked the ears of corn, and did eat, rubbing *them* in *their* hands. And certain of the Pharisees said unto them, **Why do ye that which is not lawful to do on the sabbath days?** And Jesus answering them said, **Have ye not read so much as this, what David did, when himself was an hungred, and they which were with him; how he went into the house of God, and did take and eat the shewbread, and gave also to them that were with him; which it is not lawful to eat but for the priests alone?** And he said unto them, That the Son of man is Lord also of the sabbath.

Then said Jesus unto them, I will ask you one thing; **Is it lawful on the sabbath days to do good, or to do evil? to save life, or to destroy** *it*? And looking

CHAP.	VER.
5	30
	33
	34
7	
6	2
	4
	9²

CHAP.	VER.	
		round about upon them all, He said unto the man, Stretch forth thy hand. And he did so: and his hand was restored whole as the other.
6	32	**For if ye love them which love you, what thank have ye?** for sinners also love those that love them.
	33	**And if ye do good to them which do good to you, what thank have ye?** for sinners also do even the same.
	34	**And if ye lend** *to them* **of whom ye hope to receive, what thank have ye?** for sinners also lend to sinners, to receive as much again. But love ye your enemies, and do good, and lend, hoping for nothing again; and your reward shall be great, and ye shall be the children of the Highest: for He is kind unto the unthankful and *to* the evil.
	39[2]	And He spake a parable unto them, **Can the blind lead the blind? shall they not both fall into the ditch?** The disciple is not above his master but every one that is perfect shall be as his master. **And why beholdest thou the mote that is in thy brother's eye, but perceivest not the beam that is in thine own eye? Either how canst thou say to thy brother, Brother, let me pull out the mote that is in thine eye, when thou thyself beholdest not the beam that is in thine own eye?** Thou hypocrite, cast out first the beam out of thine own eye, and then shalt thou see clearly to pull out the mote that is in thy brother's eye.
	41	
	42	
	46	And **why call ye Me, Lord, Lord, and do not the things which I say?**
	12	
7	19[2]	And John calling *unto him* two of his disciples sent *them* to Jesus, saying, **Art thou He that should come? or look we for another?** When the men were come unto Him, they said, John Baptist hath sent us unto Thee, saying, **Art Thou He that should come? or look we for another?**
	20[2]	

SAINT LUKE :—VII., VIII.

	CHAP	VER
And when the messengers of John were departed, He began to speak unto the people concerning John, **What went ye out into the wilderness for to see? A reed shaken with the wind? But what went ye out for to see? A man clothed in soft raiment?** Behold, they which are gorgeously apparelled, and live delicately, are in kings' courts. **But what went ye out for to see? A prophet?** Yea, I say unto you, and much more than a prophet. This is *he*, of whom it is written, Behold, I send my messenger before Thy face, which shall prepare Thy way before Thee.	7	24[2] 25[2] 26[2]
And the Lord said, **Whereunto then shall I liken the men of this generation? and to what are they like?** They are like unto children sitting in the marketplace, and calling one to another, and saying, We have piped unto you, and ye have not danced; we have mourned to you, and ye have not wept		31[2]
And Jesus answering said unto him, Simon, I have somewhat to say unto thee. And he saith, Master, say on. There was a certain creditor which had two debtors the one owed five hundred pence, and the other fifty And when they had nothing to pay, he frankly forgave them both **Tell Me therefore, which of them will love him most?** Simon answered and said, I suppose that *he*, to whom he forgave most. And He said unto him, Thou hast rightly judged. And He turned to the woman, and said unto Simon, **Seest thou this woman?** I entered into thine house, thou gavest Me no water for My feet: but she hath washed My feet with tears, and wiped *them* with the hairs of her head.		42 44
And He said unto her, Thy sins are forgiven. And they that sat at meat with Him began to say within themselves, **Who is this that forgiveth sins also?** And He said to the woman, Thy faith hath saved thee; go in peace.		49 15
And His disciples asked Him, saying, **What might**	8	9

CHAP.	VER.	
		this parable be? And He said, Unto you it is given to know the mysteries of the kingdom of God: but to others in parables; that seeing they might not see, and hearing they might not understand.
		Now it came to pass on a certain day, that He went into a ship with His disciples: and He said unto them, Let us go over unto the other side of the lake. And they launched forth. But as they sailed He fell asleep. and there came down a storm of wind on the lake; and they were filled *with water*, and were in jeopardy. And they came to Him, and awoke Him, saying, Master, Master, we perish. Then He arose, and rebuked the wind and the raging of the water: and they ceased, and there was
8	25	a calm. And He said unto them, **Where is your faith?** And they being afraid wondered, saying one to another, What manner of man is this! for He commandeth even the winds and water, and they obey Him.
	*	And when He went forth to land, there met Him out of the city a certain man, which had devils long time, and ware no clothes, neither abode in *any* house, but in the tombs. When he saw Jesus, he cried out, and fell
	28	down before Him, and with a loud voice said, **What have I to do with Thee, Jesus,** *Thou* **Son of God most high?** I beseech Thee, torment me not. (For He had commanded the unclean spirit to come out of the man. For oftentimes it had caught him: and he was kept bound with chains and in fetters; and he brake the bands, and was driven of the devil into the wilderness)
	30	And Jesus asked him, saying, **What is thy name?** And he said, Legion: because many devils were entered into him.
	45²	And Jesus said, **Who touched Me?** When all denied, Peter and they that were with him said, Master, the multitude throng Thee and press *Thee*, **and sayest**
	6	**Thou, Who touched Me?**
		Now Herod the tetrarch heard of all that was done by

Him: and he was perplexed, because that it was said of some, that John was risen from the dead; and of some, that Elias had appeared; and of others, that one of the old prophets was risen again. And Herod said, John have I beheaded: but **who is this, of whom I hear such things?** And he desired to see Him.   9

And it came to pass, as He was alone praying, His disciples were with Him: and He asked them, saying, **Whom say the people that I am?** They answering said, John the Baptist; but some *say*, Elias; and others *say*, that one of the old prophets is risen again. He said unto them, **But whom say ye that I am?** Peter answering said, The Christ of God   18

   20

For what is a man advantaged, if he gain the whole world, and lose himself, or be cast away?   25

And, behold, a man of the company cried out, saying, Master, I beseech Thee, look upon my son: for he is mine only child. And, lo, a spirit taketh him, and he suddenly crieth out, and it teareth him that he foameth again, and bruising him hardly departeth from him. And I besought Thy disciples to cast him out, and they could not. And Jesus answering said, O faithless and perverse generation, **how long shall I be with you, and suffer you?** Bring thy son hither. And as he was yet a coming, the devil threw him down, and tare *him*. And Jesus rebuked the unclean spirit, and healed the child, and delivered him again to his father.   41

And sent messengers before His face: and they went, and entered into a village of the Samaritans, to make ready for Him. And they did not receive Him, because His face was as though He would go to Jerusalem. And when His disciples James and John saw *this*, they said, **Lord, wilt Thou that we command fire to come down from heaven, and consume them, even as Elias did?** But He turned, and rebuked them, and   54

   6

SAINT LUKE:—X.

CHAP.	VER	
		said, Ye know not what manner of spirit ye are of. For the Son of man is not come to destroy men's lives, but to save *them*. And they went to another village.
10	25	And, behold, a certain lawyer stood up, and tempted Him, saying, **Master, what shall I do to inherit**
	26²	**eternal life?** He said unto him, **What is written in the law? how readest thou?** And he answering said, Thou shalt love the Lord thy God with all thy heart, and with all thy soul, and with all thy strength, and with all thy mind; and thy neighbour as thyself. And He said unto him, Thou hast answered right: this do, and thou shalt live. But he, willing to justify him-
	29	self, said unto Jesus, **And who is my neighbour?** And Jesus answering said, A certain *man* went down from Jerusalem to Jericho, and fell among thieves, which stripped him of his raiment, and wounded *him*, and departed, leaving *him* half dead. And by chance there came down a certain priest that way: and when he saw him, he passed by on the other side. And likewise a Levite, when he was at the place, came and looked on *him*, and passed by on the other side. But a certain Samaritan, as he journeyed, came where he was · and when he saw him, he had compassion *on him*, and went to *him*, and bound up his wounds, pouring in oil and wine, and set him on his own beast, and brought him to an inn, and took care of him. And on the morrow when he departed, he took out two pence, and gave *them* to the host, and said unto him, Take care of him; and what- soever thou spendest more, when I come again, I will
	36	repay thee. **Which now of these three, thinkest thou, was neighbour unto him that fell among the thieves?** And he said, He that shewed mercy on him. Then said Jesus unto him, Go, and do thou like- wise.
	40	But Martha was cumbered about much serving, and came to Him, and said, **Lord, dost Thou not care**
	6	**that my sister hath left me to serve alone?** bid

her therefore that she help me. And Jesus answered and said unto her, Martha, Martha, thou art careful and troubled about many things: but one thing is needful: and Mary hath chosen that good part, which shall not be taken away from her.

And He said unto them, **Which of you shall have a friend, and shall go unto him at midnight, and say unto him, Friend, lend me three loaves; for a friend of mine in his journey is come to me, and I have nothing to set before him?** And he from within shall answer and say, Trouble me not: the door is now shut, and my children are with me in bed; I cannot rise and give thee. I say unto you, Though he will not rise and give him, because he is his friend, yet because of his importunity he will rise and give him as many as he needeth.   11   6

If a son shall ask bread of any of you that is a father, will he give him a stone? or **if** *he ask* **a fish, will he for a fish give him a serpent?** or **if he shall ask an egg, will he offer him a scorpion?** If ye then, being evil, know how to give good gifts unto your children: **how much more shall** *your* **heavenly Father give the Holy Spirit to them that ask Him?**   11²   12   13

And others, tempting *Him*, sought of Him a sign from heaven. But He, knowing their thoughts, said unto them, Every kingdom divided against itself is brought to desolation; and a house *divided* against a house falleth. **If Satan also be divided against himself, how shall his kingdom stand?** because ye say that I cast out devils through Beelzebub. And **if I by Beelzebub cast out devils, by whom do your sons cast** *them* **out?** therefore shall they be your judges.   18   19

And as He spake, a certain Pharisee besought Him to dine with him: and He went in, and sat down to meat.

CHAP.	VER.	
11	40	And when the Pharisee saw *it*, he marvelled that He had not first washed before dinner. And the Lord said unto him, Now do ye Pharisees make clean the outside of the cup and the platter; but your inward part is full of ravening and wickedness. *Ye* fools, **did not He that made that which is without make that which is within also?** But rather give alms of such
	8	things as ye have; and, behold, all things are clean unto you.
12	6	**Are not five sparrows sold for two farthings, and not one of them is forgotten before God?** But even the very hairs of your head are all numbered. Fear not therefore: ye are of more value than many sparrows.
	14	And one of the company said unto Him, Master, speak to my brother, that he divide the inheritance with me. And He said unto him, **Man, who made Me a judge or a divider over you?** And He said unto them, Take heed, and beware of covetousness: for a man's life consisteth not in the abundance of the things which he possesseth. And He spake a parable unto them, saying, The ground of a certain rich man brought forth plenti-
	17	fully: and he thought within himself, saying, **What shall I do, because I have no room where to bestow my fruits?** And he said, This will I do: I will pull down my barns, and build greater; and there will I bestow all my fruits and my goods. And I will say to my soul, Soul, thou hast much goods laid up for many years; take thine ease, eat, drink, *and* be merry. But God said unto him, *Thou* fool, this night thy soul
	20	shall be required of thee: then **whose shall those things be, which thou hast provided?** So *is* he that layeth up treasure for himself, and is not rich toward God.

Consider the ravens: for they neither sow nor reap; which neither have storehouse nor barn; and God feedeth them: **how much more are ye better than the fowls?** And **which of you with taking thought can add to his stature one cubit? If ye then be not able to do that thing which is least, why take ye thought for the rest?** Consider the lilies how they grow: they toil not, they spin not; and yet I say unto you, that Solomon in all his glory was not arrayed like one of these. If then God so clothe the grass, which is to day in the field, and to morrow is cast into the oven; **how much more** *will He clothe* **you, O ye of little faith?**

	CHAP.	VER
	12	24
		25
		26
		28

Then Peter said unto Him, Lord, **speakest Thou this parable unto us, or even to all?** And the Lord said, **Who then is that faithful and wise steward, whom** *his* **lord shall make ruler over his household, to give** *them their* **portion of meat in due season?** Blessed *is* that servant, whom his lord when he cometh shall find so doing.

41
42

I am come to send fire on the earth, and **what will I, if it be already kindled?** But I have a baptism to be baptized with; and how am I straitened till it be accomplished! **Suppose ye that I am come to give peace on earth?** I tell you, Nay; but rather division; for from henceforth there shall be five in one house divided, three against two, and two against three · the father shall be divided against the son, and the son against the father; the mother against the daughter, and the daughter against the mother; the mother-in-law against her daughter-in-law, and the daughter-in-law against her mother-in-law

49

51

Ye hypocrites, ye can discern the face of the sky and of the earth, **but how is it that ye do not discern this time?** Yea, and **why even of yourselves judge ye not what is right?**

56
57

14

There were present at that season some that told Him

SAINT LUKE:—XIII.

CHAP	VER.	
13	2	of the Galilæans, whose blood Pilate had mingled with their sacrifices. And Jesus answering said unto them, **Suppose ye that these Galilæans were sinners above all the Galilæans, because they suffered such things?** I tell you, Nay: but, except ye repent, ye shall all likewise perish. Or those eighteen, upon
	4	whom the tower in Siloam fell, and slew them, **think ye that they were sinners above all men that dwelt in Jerusalem?** I tell you, Nay: but, except ye repent, ye shall all likewise perish. He spake also this parable; A certain *man* had a fig tree planted in his vineyard; and he came and sought fruit thereon, and found none. Then said he unto the dresser of his vineyard, Behold, these three years I come seeking fruit
	7	on this fig tree, and find none cut it down; **why cumbereth it the ground?** And he answering said unto him, Lord, let it alone this year also, till I shall dig about it, and dung *it:* and if it bear fruit, *well·* and if not, *then* after that thou shalt cut it down.
	15	And the ruler of the synagogue answered with indignation, because that Jesus had healed on the sabbath day, and said unto the people, There are six days in which men ought to work: in them therefore come and be healed, and not on the sabbath day. The Lord then answered him, and said, *Thou* hypocrite, **doth not each one of you on the sabbath loose his ox or** *his* **ass from the stall, and lead** *him* **away to watering?**
	16	**And ought not this woman, being a daughter of Abraham, whom Satan hath bound, lo, these eighteen years, be loosed from this bond on the sabbath day?**
	18[2]	Then said He, **Unto what is the kingdom of God like?** and **whereunto shall I resemble it?** It is like a grain of mustard seed which a man took, and cast into his garden; and it grew, and waxed a great tree, and the fowls of the air lodged in the branches of it.
	20	And again He said, **Whereunto shall I liken the**

SAINT LUKE:—XIII., XIV.

	CHAP.	VER.

kingdom of God? It is like leaven, which a woman took and hid in three measures of meal, till the whole was leavened.

Then said one unto Him, **Lord, are there few that be saved?** And He said unto them, Strive to enter in at the strait gate; for many, I say unto you, will seek to enter in and shall not be able. | 13 | 23 |
| | | 9 |

And, behold, there was a certain man before Him which had the dropsy. And Jesus answering spake unto the lawyers and Pharisees, saying, **Is it lawful to heal on the sabbath day?** And they held their peace. And He took *him*, and healed him, and let him go; and answered them, saying, **Which of you shall have an ass or an ox fallen into a pit, and will not straightway pull him out on the sabbath day?** And they could not answer Him again to these things. | 14 | 3 |
| | | 5 |

And whosoever doth not bear his cross, and come after Me, cannot be My disciple. For **which of you, intending to build a tower, sitteth not down first, and counteth the cost, whether he have** *sufficient* **to finish** *it?* Lest haply, after he hath laid the foundation, and is not able to finish *it*, all that behold *it* begin to mock him, saying, This man began to build, and was not able to finish. **Or what king, going to make war against another king, sitteth not down first, and consulteth whether he be able with ten thousand to meet him that cometh against him with twenty thousand?** Or else, while the other is yet a great way off, he sendeth an ambassage, and desireth conditions of peace. So likewise, whosoever he be of you that forsaketh not all that he hath, he cannot be My disciple. Salt *is* good: but **if the salt have lost his savour, wherewith shall it be seasoned?** It is neither fit for the land, nor yet for the dunghill; *but* men cast it out. He that hath ears to hear, let him hear. | | 28 |
		31
		34
		5

CHAP	VER.	
15	4	**What man of you, having an hundred sheep, if he lose one of them, doth not leave the ninety and nine in the wilderness, and go after that which is lost, until he find it?** And when he hath found *it*, he layeth *it* on his shoulders, rejoicing.
	8	**Either what woman having ten pieces of silver, if she lose one piece, doth not light a candle, and sweep the house, and seek diligently till she find** *it?* And when she hath found *it*, she calleth *her* friends and *her* neighbours together, saying, Rejoice with me; for I have found the piece which I had lost. Likewise, I say unto you, there is joy in the presence of the angels of God over one sinner that repenteth.
	2	
16	2	And He said also unto His disciples, There was a certain rich man, which had a steward; and the same was accused unto him that he had wasted his goods. And he called him, and said unto him, **How is it that I hear this of thee?** give an account of thy stewardship; for thou mayest be no longer steward. Then the
	3	steward said within himself, **What shall I do?** for my lord taketh away from me the stewardship: I cannot dig, to beg I am ashamed. I am resolved what to do, that, when I am put out of the stewardship, they may receive me into their houses. So he called every one of
	5	his lord's debtors *unto him*, and said unto the first, **How much owest thou unto my lord?** And he said, An hundred measures of oil. And he said unto him, Take thy bill, and sit down quickly, and write fifty. Then said
	7	he to another, **And how much owest thou?** And he said, An hundred measures of wheat. And he said unto him, Take thy bill, and write fourscore. And the lord commended the unjust steward, because he had done wisely: for the children of this world are in their generation wiser than the children of light. And I say unto you, Make to yourselves friends of the mammon of unrighteousness; that, when ye fail, they may receive you into everlasting habitations. He that is faithful in

that which is least is faithful also in much : and he that is unjust in the least is unjust also in much. **If therefore ye have not been faithful in the unrighteous mammon, who will commit to your trust the true** *riches ?* And **if ye have not been faithful in that which is another man's, who shall give you that which is your own ?**

But which of you, having a servant plowing or feeding cattle, will say unto him by and by, when he is come from the field, Go and sit down to meat ? And will not rather say unto him, Make ready wherewith I may sup, and gird thyself, and serve me, till I have eaten and drunken; and afterward thou shalt eat and drink ? Doth he thank that servant because he did the things that were commanded him ? I trow not. So likewise ye, when ye shall have done all those things which are commanded you, say, We are unprofitable servants : we have done that which was our duty to do.

And Jesus answering said, **Were there not ten cleansed ? but where** *are* **the nine ?** There are not found that returned to give glory to God, save this stranger. And He said unto him, Arise, go thy way· thy faith hath made thee whole.

Two *men* shall be in the field; the one shall be taken, and the other left. And they answered and said unto Him, **Where, Lord ?** And He said unto them, Wheresoever the body *is,* thither will the eagles be gathered together.

And shall not God avenge His own elect, which cry day and night unto Him, though He bear long with them ? I tell you that He will avenge them speedily. Nevertheless when the Son of man cometh, **shall He find faith on the earth ?**

And a certain ruler asked Him, saying, Good Master,

CHAP.	VER.
16	11
	12
	6
17	7
	8
	9
	17[2]
	37
	6
18	7
	8

CHAP.	VER
18	18
	19

what shall I do to inherit eternal life? And Jesus said unto him, **Why callest thou Me good?** none *is* good, save one, *that is*, God. Thou knowest the commandments, Do not commit adultery, Do not kill, Do not steal, Do not bear false witness, Honour thy father and thy mother.

	26

And when Jesus saw that he was very sorrowful, He said, How hardly shall they that have riches enter into the kingdom of God! For it is easier for a camel to go through a needle's eye, than for a rich man to enter into the kingdom of God. And they that heard *it* said, **Who then can be saved?**

	41
	6

And Jesus stood, and commanded him to be brought unto Him: and when he was come near, He asked him, saying, **What wilt thou that I shall do unto thee?** And he said, Lord, that I may receive my sight.

19	23

And another came, saying, Lord, behold, *here is* thy pound, which I have kept laid up in a napkin: for I feared thee, because thou art an austere man: thou takest up that thou layedst not down, and reapest that thou didst not sow. And he saith unto him, Out of thine own mouth will I judge thee, *thou* wicked servant. Thou knewest that I was an austere man, taking up that I laid not down, and reaping that I did not sow: **wherefore then gavest not thou my money into the bank, that at my coming I might have required mine own with usury?** And he said unto them that stood by, Take from him the pound, and give *it* to him that hath ten pounds.

	31

And it came to pass, when He was come nigh to Bethphage and Bethany, at the mount called *the mount* of Olives, He sent two of His disciples, saying, Go ye into the village over against *you;* in the which at your entering ye shall find a colt tied, whereon yet never man sat: loose him, and bring *him hither.* And if any man ask you, **Why do ye loose** *him?* thus shall ye say unto him, Because the Lord hath need of him. And they that were sent went their way, and found even as He had said unto them And as they were loosing the colt, the owners thereof said unto them, **Why loose ye the colt?** And they said, The Lord hath need of him.

And it came to pass, *that* on one of those days, as He taught the people in the temple, and preached the gospel, the chief priests and the scribes came upon *Him* with the elders, and spake unto Him, saying, **Tell us, by what authority doest Thou these things?** or **who is he that gave Thee this authority?** And He answered and said unto them, I will also ask you one thing; and answer Me: **The baptism of John, was it from heaven, or of men?** And they reasoned with themselves, saying, If we shall say, From heaven; He will say, **Why then believed ye him not?** But and if we say, Of men; all the people will stone us: for they be persuaded that John was a prophet. And they answered, that they could not tell whence *it was*. And Jesus said unto them, Neither tell I you by what authority I do these things. Then began He to speak to the people this parable, A certain man planted a vineyard, and let it forth to husbandmen, and went into a far country for a long time And at the season he sent a servant to the husbandmen, that they should give him of the fruit of the vineyard: but the husbandmen beat him, and sent *him* away empty. And again he sent another servant: and they beat him also, and entreated *him* shamefully, and sent *him* away empty. And again he sent a third: and they wounded him also, and cast *him* out. Then said the lord of the vineyard, **What shall I do?** I will send my beloved son: it may be they will reverence *him* when they see him. But when the husbandmen saw him, they reasoned among themselves, saying, This is the heir: come, let us kill him, that the inheritance may be ours. So they cast him out of the vineyard, and killed *him*. **What therefore shall the lord of the vineyard do unto them?** He shall come and destroy

CHAP.	VER.
19	33
	3
20	2²
	4
	5
	13
	15

CHAP.	VER.	
20	17	these husbandmen, and shall give the vineyard to others. And when they heard *it*, they said, God forbid. And He beheld them, and said, **What is this then that is written, The stone which the builders rejected, the same is become the head of the corner?** Whosoever shall fall upon that stone shall be broken ; but on whomsoever it shall fall, it will grind him to powder
		And they asked Him, saying, Master, we know that Thou sayest and teachest rightly, neither acceptest Thou the person *of any*, but teachest the way of God truly
	22	**Is it lawful for us to give tribute unto Cæsar, or no?** But He perceived their craftiness, and said unto
	23	them, **Why tempt ye Me?** Shew me a penny.
	24	**Whose image and superscription hath it?** They answered and said, Cæsar's. And He said unto them, Render therefore unto Cæsar the things which be Cæsar's, and unto God the things which be God's.
	33	Last of all the woman died also. **Therefore in the resurrection whose wife of them is she?** for seven had her to wife. And Jesus answering said unto them, The children of this world marry, and are given in marriage . but they which shall be accounted worthy to obtain that world, and the resurrection from the dead, neither marry, nor are given in marriage : neither can they die any more : for they are equal unto the angels; and are the children of God, being the children of the resurrection.
	41	And He said unto them, **How say they that Christ is David's son?** And David himself saith in the book of Psalms, The LORD said unto my Lord, Sit Thou on my right hand, till I make Thine enemies Thy footstool.
	44	David therefore calleth Him Lord, **how is He then**
	13	**his son?**
		And as some spake of the temple, how it was adorned with goodly stones and gifts, He said, *As for* these things which ye behold, the days will come, in the which

there shall not be left one stone upon another, that shall not be thrown down. And they asked Him, saying, **Master, but when shall these things be?** and **what sign** *will there be* **when these things shall come to pass?**

CHAP.	VER.
21	7²
	2

Then came the day of the unleavened bread, when the passover must be killed. And He sent Peter and John, saying, Go and prepare us the passover, that we may eat. And they said unto Him, **Where wilt Thou that we prepare?** And He said unto them, Behold, when ye are entered into the city, there shall a man meet you, bearing a pitcher of water, follow him into the house where he entereth in. And ye shall say unto the goodman of the house, The Master saith unto thee, **Where is the guestchamber, where I shall eat the passover with My disciples?** And he shall shew you a large upper room furnished : there make ready.

22	9
	11

For whether *is* **greater, he that sitteth at meat, or he that serveth?** *is* **not he that sitteth at meat?** but I am among you as he that serveth.

27²

And He said unto them, **When I sent you without purse, and scrip, and shoes, lacked ye any thing?** And they said, Nothing.

35

And when He rose up from prayer, and was come to His disciples, He found them sleeping for sorrow, and said unto them, **Why sleep ye?** rise and pray, lest ye enter into temptation. And while He yet spake, behold a multitude, and he that was called Judas, one of the twelve, went before them, and drew near unto Jesus to kiss Him. But Jesus said unto him, **Judas, betrayest thou the Son of man with a kiss?** When they which were about Him saw what would follow, they said unto Him, **Lord, shall we smite with the sword?** And one of them smote the servant of the high priest, and cut off his right ear. And Jesus answered and said,

46

48

49

CHAP.	VER.	
22	52	Suffer ye thus far. And He touched his ear, and healed him. Then Jesus said unto the chief priests, and captains of the temple, and the elders, which were come to Him, **Be ye come out, as against a thief, with swords and staves?** When I was daily with you in the temple, ye stretched forth no hands against Me: but this is your hour, and the power of darkness.
	64	And the men that held Jesus mocked Him, and smote *Him*. And when they had blindfolded Him, they struck Him on the face, and asked Him, saying, **Prophesy, who is it that smote Thee?** And many other things blasphemously spake they against Him. And as soon as it was day, the elders of the people and the chief priests and the scribes came together, and led Him into their
	67	council, saying, **Art Thou the Christ?** tell us. And He said unto them, If I tell you, ye will not believe· and if I also ask *you*, ye will not answer Me, nor let *Me* go. Hereafter shall the Son of man sit on the right
	70	hand of the power of God. Then said they all, **Art Thou then the Son of God?** And He said unto
	71	them, Ye say that I am. And they said, **What need
	13	we any further witness?** for we ourselves have heard of His own mouth.
23	3	And Pilate asked Him, saying, **Art Thou the King of the Jews?** And He answered him and said, Thou sayest *it*.
	22	Pilate therefore, willing to release Jesus, spake again to them. But they cried, saying, Crucify *Him*, crucify Him. And he said unto them the third time, **Why, what evil hath He done?** I have found no cause of death in Him: I will therefore chastise Him, and let *Him* go.
	31	**For if they do these things in a green tree, what shall be done in the dry?**

And one of the malefactors which were hanged railed

on Him, saying, If Thou be Christ, save Thyself and us. But the other answering rebuked him, saying, **Dost not thou fear God, seeing thou art in the same condemnation?** And we indeed justly; for we receive the due reward of our deeds: but this man hath done nothing amiss.

23 40

4

Now upon the first *day* of the week, very early in the morning, they came unto the sepulchre, bringing the spices which they had prepared, and certain *others* with them. And they found the stone rolled away from the sepulchre. And they entered in, and found not the body of the Lord Jesus. And it came to pass, as they were much perplexed thereabout, behold, two men stood by them in shining garments: and as they were afraid, and bowed down *their* faces to the earth, they said unto them, **Why seek ye the living among the dead?** He is not here, but is risen: remember how He spake unto you when He was yet in Galilee, saying, The Son of man must be delivered into the hands of sinful men, and be crucified, and the third day rise again.

24 5

And, behold, two of them went that same day to a village called Emmaus, which was from Jerusalem *about* threescore furlongs. And they talked together of all these things which had happened. And it came to pass, that, while they communed *together* and reasoned, Jesus Himself drew near, and went with them. But their eyes were holden that they should not know Him. And He said unto them, **What manner of communications** *are* **these that ye have one to another, as ye walk, and are sad?** And the one of them, whose name was Cleopas, answering said unto Him, **Art Thou only a stranger in Jerusalem, and hast not known the things which are come to pass there in these days?** And He said unto them, **What things?** And they said unto Him, Concerning Jesus of Nazareth, which was a prophet mighty in deed and word before God and all the people: and how the chief priests and our rulers

17

18

19

CHAP.	VER.	
		delivered Him to be condemned to death, and have crucified Him. But we trusted that it had been He which should have redeemed Israel· and beside all this, to day is the third day since these things were done.
24	26	Then he said unto them, O fools, and slow of heart to believe all that the prophets have spoken: **Ought not Christ to have suffered these things, and to enter into His glory?** And beginning at Moses and all the prophets, He expounded unto them in all the scriptures the things concerning Himself.
	32	And their eyes were opened, and they knew Him; and He vanished out of their sight. And they said one to another, **Did not our heart burn within us, while He talked with us by the way, and while He opened to us the scriptures?**
	38²	And as they thus spake, Jesus Himself stood in the midst of them, and saith unto them, Peace *be* unto you. But they were terrified and affrighted, and supposed that they had seen a spirit. And He said unto them, **Why are ye troubled? and why do thoughts arise in your hearts?** Behold My hands and My feet, that it is I Myself: handle Me, and see; for• a spirit hath not flesh and bones, as ye see Me have. And when He had thus spoken, He shewed them *His* hands and *His* feet
	41	And while they yet believed not for joy, and wondered, He said unto them, **Have ye here any meat?** And they gave Him a piece of a broiled fish, and of an honeycomb. And He took *it*, and did eat before them.
	9	

Saint Luke 165

SAINT JOHN.

	CHAP.	VER
AND this is the record of John, when the Jews sent priests and Levites from Jerusalem to ask him, **Who art thou?** And he confessed, and denied not; but confessed, I am not the Christ. And they asked him, **What then? Art thou Elias?** And he saith, I am not. **Art thou that prophet?** And he answered, No. Then said they unto him, **Who art thou?** that we may give an answer to them that sent us. **What sayest thou of thyself?** He said, I *am* the voice of one crying in the wilderness, Make straight the way of the Lord, as said the prophet Esaias. And they which were sent were of the Pharisees. And they asked him, and said unto him, **Why baptizest thou then, if thou be not that Christ, nor Elias, neither that prophet?** John answered them, saying, I baptize with water. but there standeth one among you, whom ye know not, He it is, who coming after me is preferred before me, whose shoe's latchet I am not worthy to unloose.	1	19 21³ 22² 25

Again the next day after John stood, and two of his disciples; and looking upon Jesus as He walked, he saith, Behold the Lamb of God! And the two disciples heard him speak, and they followed Jesus. Then Jesus turned, and saw them following, and saith unto them, **What seek ye?** They said unto Him, **Rabbi** (which is to say, being interpreted, Master), **where dwellest Thou?** He saith unto them, Come and see. They came and saw where He dwelt, and abode with Him that day: for it was about the tenth hour.   38²

Philip findeth Nathanael, and saith unto him, We have found Him, of whom Moses in the law, and the prophets, did write, Jesus of Nazareth, the son of

CHAP.	VER.	
1	46	Joseph. And Nathanael said unto him, **Can there any good thing come out of Nazareth?** Philip saith unto him, Come and see. Jesus saw Nathanael coming to Him, and saith of him, Behold an Israelite indeed, in whom is no guile! Nathanael saith unto Him,
	48	**Whence knowest Thou me?** Jesus answered and said unto him, Before that Philip called thee, when thou wast under the fig tree, I saw thee. Nathanael answered and saith unto Him, Rabbi, Thou art the Son of God; Thou art the King of Israel. Jesus answered and said
	50	unto him, **Because I said unto thee, I saw thee under the fig tree, believest thou?** thou shalt see greater things than these. And He saith unto him, Verily, verily, I say unto you, Hereafter ye shall see
	12	heaven open, and the angels of God ascending and descending upon the Son of man.

And when they wanted wine, the mother of Jesus saith unto Him, They have no wine. Jesus saith unto

2	4	her, **Woman, what have I to do with thee?** Mine hour is not yet come.
	18	Then answered the Jews and said unto Him, **What sign shewest Thou unto us, seeing that Thou doest these things?** Jesus answered and said unto them, Destroy this temple, and in three days I will raise it up. Then said the Jews, Forty and six years was this
	20	temple in building, **and wilt Thou rear it up in three**
	3	**days?** But He spake of the temple of His body.

There was a man of the Pharisees, named Nicodemus, a ruler of the Jews: the same came to Jesus by night, and said unto Him, Rabbi, we know that Thou art a teacher come from God: for no man can do these miracles that Thou doest, except God be with him. Jesus answered and said unto him, Verily, verily, I say unto thee, Except a man be born again, he cannot see the

| 3 | 4² | kingdom of God. Nicodemus saith unto Him, **How can a man be born when he is old? can he enter** |

SAINT JOHN:—III., IV.   301

	CHAP.	VER.

the second time into his mother's womb, and be born? Jesus answered, Verily, verily, I say unto thee, Except a man be born of water and *of* the Spirit, he cannot enter into the kingdom of God.

Nicodemus answered and said unto Him, **How can these things be?** Jesus answered and said unto him, **Art thou a master of Israel, and knowest not these things?** Verily, verily, I say unto thee, We speak that we do know, and testify that we have seen; and ye receive not our witness. If I have told you earthly things, and ye believe not, **how shall ye believe, if I tell you** *of* **heavenly things?**

    3   9
         10
         12
         5

There cometh a woman of Samaria to draw water: Jesus saith unto her, Give Me to drink. (For His disciples were gone away unto the city to buy meat.) Then saith the woman of Samaria unto Him, **How is it that Thou, being a Jew, askest drink of me, which am a woman of Samaria?** for the Jews have no dealings with the Samaritans. Jesus answered and said unto her, If thou knewest the gift of God, and who it is that saith to thee, Give Me to drink; thou wouldest have asked of Him, and He would have given thee living water. The woman saith unto Him, Sir, Thou hast nothing to draw with, and the well is deep: **from whence then hast Thou that living water? Art Thou greater than our father Jacob, which gave us the well, and drank thereof himself, and his children, and his cattle?** Jesus answered and said unto her, Whosoever drinketh of this water shall thirst again: but whosoever drinketh of the water that I shall give him shall never thirst; but the water that I shall give him shall be in him a well of water springing up into everlasting life.

    4   9
         11
         12

And upon this came His disciples, and marvelled that He talked with the woman yet no man said, **What seekest Thou?** or, **Why talkest Thou with her?** The woman then left her waterpot, and went her way

         27[2]

CHAP.	VER.	
4	29	into the city, and saith to the men, Come, see a man, which told me all things that ever I did: **is not this the Christ?**
	33	In the mean while His disciples prayed Him, saying, Master, eat. But He said unto them, I have meat to eat that ye know not of. Therefore said the disciples one to another, **Hath any man brought Him** *ought* **to eat?** Jesus saith unto them, My meat is to do the
	35	will of Him that sent Me, and to finish His work. **Say not ye, There are yet four months, and** *then* **cometh harvest?** behold, I say unto you, Lift up your
	8	eyes, and look on the fields; for they are white already to harvest.
5	6	And a certain man was there, which had an infirmity, thirty and eight years. When Jesus saw him lie, and knew that he had been now a long time *in that case*, He saith unto him, **Wilt thou be made whole?** The impotent man answered Him, Sir, I have no man, when the water is troubled, to put me into the pool · but while I am coming, another steppeth down before me. Jesus saith unto him, Rise, take up thy bed, and walk. And immediately the man was made whole, and took up his bed, and walked : and on the same day was the sabbath. The Jews therefore said unto him that was cured, It is the sabbath day: it is not lawful for thee to carry *thy* bed. He answered them, He that made me whole, the same said unto me, Take up thy bed, and walk. Then
	12	asked they him, **What man is that which said unto thee, Take up thy bed, and walk?** And he that was healed wist not who it was : for Jesus had conveyed Himself away, a multitude being in *that* place.
	44	**How can ye believe, which receive honour one of another, and seek not the honour that** *cometh* **from God only?** Do not think that I will accuse you to the Father : there is *one* that accuseth you, *even* Moses, in whom ye trust. For had ye believed Moses,

SAINT JOHN:—V., VI.

	CHAP.	VER.
ye would have believed Me: for he wrote of Me. But if ye believe not his writings, **how shall ye believe My words?**	5	47
		4
When Jesus then lifted up *His* eyes, and saw a great company come unto Him, He saith unto Philip, **Whence shall we buy bread, that these may eat?** And this He said to prove him: for He Himself knew what he would do. Philip answered Him, Two hundred pennyworth of bread is not sufficient for them, that every one of them may take a little. One of His disciples, Andrew, Simon Peter's brother, saith unto Him, There is a lad here, which hath five barley loaves, and two small fishes: **but what are they among so many?** And Jesus said, Make the men sit down. Now there was much grass in the place. So the men sat down, in number about five thousand.	6	5
		9
When the people therefore saw that Jesus was not there, neither His disciples, they also took shipping, and came to Capernaum, seeking for Jesus. And when they had found Him on the other side of the sea, they said unto Him, **Rabbi, when camest Thou hither?** Jesus answered them and said, Verily, verily, I say unto you, Ye seek Me, not because ye saw the miracles, but because ye did eat of the loaves, and were filled. Labour not for the meat which perisheth, but for that meat which endureth unto everlasting life, which the Son of man shall give unto you· for Him hath God the Father sealed. Then said they unto Him, **What shall we do, that we might work the works of God?** Jesus answered and said unto them, This is the work of God, that ye believe on Him whom He hath sent. They said therefore unto Him, **What sign shewest Thou then, that we may see, and believe Thee? what dost Thou work?**		25
		28
		30

The Jews then murmured at Him, because He said, I am the bread which came down from heaven. And they

CHAP.	VER.	
6	42²	said, **Is not this Jesus, the son of Joseph, whose father and mother we know? how is it then that He saith, I came down from heaven?** Jesus therefore answered and said unto them, Murmur not among yourselves. No man can come to Me, except the Father which hath sent Me draw him: and I will raise him up at the last day.
	52	I am the living bread which came down from heaven: if any man eat of this bread, he shall live for ever: and the bread that I will give is My flesh, which I will give for the life of the world. The Jews therefore strove among themselves, saying, **How can this man give us** *His* **flesh to eat?** Then Jesus said unto them, Verily, verily, I say unto you, Except ye eat the flesh of the Son of man, and drink His blood, ye have no life in you.
	60 61 62	Many therefore of His disciples, when they had heard *this*, said, This is an hard saying; **who can hear it?** When Jesus knew in Himself that His disciples murmured at it, He said unto them, **Doth this offend you?** *What* **and if ye shall see the Son of man ascend up where He was before?** It is the spirit that quickeneth; the flesh profiteth nothing: the words that I speak unto you, *they* are spirit, and *they* are life.
	67 68 70 15	From that *time* many of His disciples went back, and walked no more with Him. Then said Jesus unto the twelve, **Will ye also go away?** Then Simon Peter answered Him, **Lord, to whom shall we go?** Thou hast the words of eternal life. And we believe and are sure that Thou art that Christ, the Son of the living God. Jesus answered them, **Have not I chosen you twelve, and one of you is a devil?** He spake of Judas Iscariot *the son* of Simon: for he it was that should betray Him, being one of the twelve.

Then the Jews sought Him at the feast, and said,

SAINT JOHN:—VII.

| | CHAP. | VER. |

Where is He? And there was much murmuring among the people concerning Him: for some said, He is a good man: others said, Nay; but He deceiveth the people.   7   11

Now about the midst of the feast Jesus went up into the temple, and taught. And the Jews marvelled, saying, **How knoweth this man letters, having never learned?** Jesus answered them, and said, My doctrine is not Mine, but His that sent Me. If any man will do His will, he shall know of the doctrine, whether it be of God, or *whether* I speak of Myself. He that speaketh of himself seeketh his own glory: but He that seeketh His glory that sent Him, the same is true, and no unrighteousness is in Him. **Did not Moses give you the law, and *yet* none of you keepeth the law? Why go ye about to kill Me?** The people answered and said, Thou hast a devil: **who goeth about to kill Thee?** Jesus answered and said unto them, I have done one work, and ye all marvel. Moses therefore gave unto you circumcision (not because it is of Moses, but of the fathers); and ye on the sabbath day circumcise a man. If a man on the sabbath day receive circumcision, that the law of Moses should not be broken; **are ye angry at Me, because I have made a man every whit whole on the sabbath day?** Judge not according to the appearance, but judge righteous judgment. Then said some of them of Jerusalem, **Is not this He, whom they seek to kill?** But, lo, He speaketh boldly, and they say nothing unto Him. **Do the rulers know indeed that this is the very Christ?**

15

19^2

20

23

25

26

And many of the people believed on Him, and said, **When Christ cometh, will He do more miracles than these which this *man* hath done?** The Pharisees heard that the people murmured such things concerning Him; and the Pharisees and the chief priests sent officers to take Him. Then said Jesus unto them, Yet a little while am I with you, and *then* I go unto Him

31

CHAP.	VER.	
7	35²	that sent Me. Ye shall seek Me, and shall not find *Me*: and where I am, *thither* ye cannot come. Then said the Jews among themselves, **Whither will He go, that we shall not find Him?** **will He go unto the dispersed among the Gentiles, and teach the Gentiles?** **What** *manner* **of saying is this that He said, Ye shall seek Me, and shall not find** *Me*: **and where I am,** *thither* **ye cannot come?**
	36	
	41	Many of the people therefore, when they heard this saying, said, Of a truth this is the Prophet. Others said, This is the Christ. But some said, **Shall Christ come out of Galilee?** **Hath not the scripture said, That Christ cometh of the seed of David, and out of the town of Bethlehem, where David was?** So there was a division among the people because of Him. And some of them would have taken Him; but no man laid hands on Him. Then came the officers to the chief priests and Pharisees; and they said unto them, **Why have ye not brought Him?** The officers answered, Never man spake like this man. Then answered them the Pharisees, **Are ye also deceived?** **Have any of the rulers or of the Pharisees believed on Him?** But this people who knoweth not the law are cursed. Nicodemus saith unto them (he that came to Jesus by night, being one of them), **Doth our law judge** *any* **man, before it hear him, and know what he doeth?** They answered and said unto him, **Art thou also of Galilee?** Search, and look: for out of Galilee ariseth no prophet. And every man went unto his own house. Jesus went unto the Mount of Olives.
	42	
	45	
	47	
	48	
	51	
	52	
	19	
8	5	They say unto Him, Master, this woman was taken in adultery, in the very act. Now Moses in the law commanded us, that such should be stoned: but **what sayest Thou?** This they said, tempting Him, that they might have to accuse Him. But Jesus stooped down, and with *His* finger wrote on the ground, *as though He heard them not.* So when they continued ask-

SAINT JOHN:—VIII.

ing Him, He lifted up Himself, and said unto them, He that is without sin among you, let him first cast a stone at her. And again He stooped down, and wrote on the ground. And they which heard *it*, being convicted by *their own* conscience, went out one by one, beginning at the eldest, *even* unto the last : and Jesus was left alone, and the woman standing in the midst When Jesus had lifted up Himself, and saw none but the woman, He said unto her, **Woman, where are those thine accusers? hath no man condemned thee ?** She said, No man, Lord. And Jesus said unto her, Neither do I condemn thee go, and sin no more. | 8 | 10²

It is also written in your law, that the testimony of two men is true. I am one that bear witness of Myself, and the Father that sent Me beareth witness of Me. Then said they unto Him, **Where is Thy Father?** Jesus answered, Ye neither know Me, nor My Father if ye had known Me, ye should have known My Father also. | | 19

Then said Jesus again unto them, I go My way, and ye shall seek Me, and shall die in your sins : whither I go, ye cannot come. Then said the Jews, **Will He kill Himself?** because He saith, Whither I go, ye cannot come And He said unto them, Ye are from beneath ; I am from above : ye are of this world ; I am not of this world. I said therefore unto you, that ye shall die in your sins for if ye believe not that I am *He*, ye shall die in your sins. Then said they unto Him, **Who art Thou ?** And Jesus saith unto them, Even *the same* that I said unto you from the beginning. | | 22

| | 25

Then said Jesus to those Jews which believed on Him, If ye continue in My word, *then* are ye My disciples indeed ; and ye shall know the truth, and the truth shall make you free. They answered Him, We be Abraham's seed, and were never in bondage to any man : **how sayest Thou, ye shall be made free ?** Jesus | | 33

CHAP. VER

CHAP.	VER
8	43
	46²
	48
	53²
	57
	14

answered them, Verily, verily, I say unto you, Whosoever committeth sin is the servant of sin. And the servant abideth not in the house for ever : *but* the Son abideth ever. If the Son therefore shall make you free, ye shall be free indeed.

Jesus said unto them, If God were your Father, ye would love Me : for I proceeded forth and came from God ; neither came I of Myself, but He sent Me. **Why do ye not understand My speech ?** *even* because ye cannot hear My word.

And because I tell *you* the truth, ye believe Me not. **Which of you convinceth Me of sin ?** And if I say the truth, **why do ye not believe Me ?** He that is of God heareth God's words : ye therefore hear *them* not, because ye are not of God. Then answered the Jews, and said unto Him, **Say we not well that Thou art a Samaritan, and hast a devil ?** Jesus answered, I have not a devil ; but I honour My Father, and ye do dishonour Me. And I seek not Mine own glory : there is One that seeketh and judgeth. Verily, verily, I say unto you, If a man keep My saying, he shall never see death. Then said the Jews unto Him, Now we know that Thou hast a devil. Abraham is dead, and the prophets ; and Thou sayest, If a man keep My saying, he shall never taste of death. **Art Thou greater than our father Abraham, which is dead ?** and the prophets are dead : **whom makest Thou Thyself ?** Jesus answered, If I honour Myself, My honour is nothing : it is My Father that honoureth Me ; of whom ye say, that He is your God : yet ye have not known Him ; but I know Him : and if I should say, I know Him not, I shall be a liar like unto you : but I know Him, and keep His saying. Your father Abraham rejoiced to see My day : and he saw *it*, and was glad. Then said the Jews unto Him, **Thou art not yet fifty years old, and hast Thou seen Abraham ?** Jesus said unto them, Verily, verily, I say unto you, Before Abraham was, I am.

SAINT JOHN:—IX.

	CHAP.	VER.

And as *Jesus* passed by, He saw a man which was blind from *his* birth. And His disciples asked Him, saying, **Master, who did sin, this man, or his parents, that he was born blind?** Jesus answered, Neither hath this man sinned, nor his parents: but that the works of God should be made manifest in him. — 9 2

The neighbours therefore, and they which before had seen him that he was blind, said, **Is not this he that sat and begged?** Some said, This is he: others *said*, He is like him: *but* he said, I am *he*. Therefore said they unto him, **How were thine eyes opened?** He answered and said, A man that is called Jesus made clay, and anointed mine eyes, and said unto me, Go to the pool of Siloam, and wash: and I went and washed, and I received sight. Then said they unto him, **Where is He?** He said, I know not. — 8, 10, 12

Therefore said some of the Pharisees, This man is not of God, because He keepeth not the sabbath day. Others said, **How can a man that is a sinner do such miracles?** And there was a division among them. They say unto the blind man again, **What sayest thou of Him, that He hath opened thine eyes?** He said, He is a prophet. But the Jews did not believe concerning him, that he had been blind, and received his sight, until they called the parents of him that had received his sight. And they asked them, saying, **Is this your son, who ye say was born blind? how then doth he now see?** — 16, 17, 19²

Then said they to him again, **What did He to thee? how opened He thine eyes?** He answered them, I have told you already, and ye did not hear. **wherefore would ye hear** *it* **again? will ye also be His disciples?** Then they reviled him, and said, Thou art His disciple; but we are Moses' disciples. We know that God spake unto Moses. *as for* this *fellow*, we know not from whence He is. — 26², 27²

CHAP.	VER	
9	34	If this man were not of God, He could do nothing. They answered and said unto him, Thou wast altogether born in sins, and **dost thou teach us?** And they cast him out. Jesus heard that they had cast him out; and
	35	when He had found him, He said unto him, **Dost thou believe on the Son of God?** He answered and said,
	36	**Who is He, Lord, that I might believe on Him?** And Jesus said unto him, Thou hast both seen Him, and it is He that talketh with thee. And he said, Lord, I believe. And he worshipped Him. And Jesus said, For judgment I am come into this world, that they which see not might see ; and that they which see might be made blind. And *some* of the Pharisees which were with Him
	40	heard these words, and said unto Him, **Are we blind also?** Jesus said unto them, If ye were blind, ye should
	16	have no sin : but now ye say, We see; therefore your sin remaineth.

There was a division therefore again among the Jews for these sayings. And many of them said, He hath a

10	20	devil, and is mad; **why hear ye Him?** Others said,
	21	These are not the words of him that hath a devil. **Can a devil open the eyes of the blind?**

	24	Then came the Jews round about Him, and said unto Him, **How long dost Thou make us to doubt?** If Thou be the Christ, tell us plainly. Jesus answered them, I told you, and ye believed not : the works that I do in My Father's name, they bear witness of Me.

	32	Then the Jews took up stones again to stone Him. Jesus answered them, Many good works have I shewed you from My Father; **for which of those works do ye stone Me?** The Jews answered Him, saying, For a good work we stone Thee not ; but for blasphemy ; and because that Thou, being a man, makest Thyself God.
	34	Jesus answered them, **Is it not written in your law, I said, Ye are gods?** If He called them gods, unto whom the word of God came, and the scripture cannot

	CHAP.	VER.

be broken; **say ye of Him, whom the Father hath sanctified, and sent into the world, Thou blasphemest; because I said, I am the Son of God?** If I do not the works of My Father, believe Me not. But if I do, though ye believe not Me, believe the works: that ye may know, and believe, that the Father *is* in Me, and I in Him. — 10 — 36 / 6

Then after that saith He to *His* disciples, Let us go into Judæa again. *His* disciples say unto Him, Master, the Jews of late sought to stone Thee; and **goest Thou thither again?** Jesus answered, **Are there not twelve hours in the day?** If any man walk in the day, he stumbleth not, because he seeth the light of this world. But if a man walk in the night, he stumbleth, because there is no light in him. — 11 — 8 / 9

Jesus said unto her, I am the resurrection, and the life: he that believeth in Me, though he were dead, yet shall he live: and whosoever liveth and believeth in Me shall never die. **Believest thou this?** She saith unto Him, Yea, Lord: I believe that Thou art the Christ, the Son of God, which should come into the world. — 26

Then when Mary was come where Jesus was, and saw Him, she fell down at His feet, saying unto Him, Lord, if Thou hadst been here, my brother had not died. When Jesus therefore saw her weeping, and the Jews also weeping which came with her, He groaned in the spirit, and was troubled, and said, **Where have ye laid him?** They said unto Him, Lord, come and see. Jesus wept. Then said the Jews, Behold how He loved him! And some of them said, **Could not this man, which opened the eyes of the blind, have caused that even this man should not have died?** Jesus therefore again groaning in Himself cometh to the grave. It was a cave, and a stone lay upon it. Jesus said, Take ye away the stone. Martha, the sister of him that was dead, saith unto Him, Lord, by this time he stinketh: for he — 34 / 37

CHAP	VER	
11	40	hath been *dead* four days. Jesus saith unto her, **Said I not unto thee, that, if thou wouldest believe, thou shouldest see the glory of God?**
	47	Then gathered the chief priests and the Pharisees a council, and said, **What do we?** for this man doeth many miracles. If we let Him thus alone, all *men* will believe on Him: and the Romans shall come and take away both our place and nation.
	56	And the Jews' passover was nigh at hand · and many went out of the country up to Jerusalem before the passover, to purify themselves. Then sought they for Jesus, and spake among themselves, as they stood in the temple, **What think ye, that He will not come to the feast?** Now both the chief priests and the Pharisees
	8	had given a commandment, that, if any man knew where He were, he should shew *it*, that they might take Him
12	5	Then took Mary a pound of ointment of spikenard, very costly, and anointed the feet of Jesus, and wiped His feet with her hair: and the house was filled with the odour of the ointment. Then saith one of His disciples, Judas Iscariot, Simon's *son*, which should betray Him, **Why was not this ointment sold for three hundred pence, and given to the poor?**
	19	The people therefore that was with Him when He called Lazarus out of his grave, and raised him from the dead, bare record. For this cause the people also met Him, for that they heard that He had done this miracle. The Pharisees therefore said among themselves, **Perceive ye how ye prevail nothing?** behold, the world is gone after Him.
	27	Now is My soul troubled; and **what shall I say?** Father, save Me from this hour: but for this cause came I unto this hour. Father, glorify Thy name.

And I, if I be lifted up from the earth, will draw all *men* unto Me. This He said, signifying what death He should die. The people answered Him, We have heard out of the law that Christ abideth for ever: and **how sayest Thou, The Son of man must be lifted up? who is this Son of man?** | 12 | 34²

But though He had done so many miracles before them, yet they believed not on Him: that the saying of Esaias the prophet might be fulfilled, which he spake, **Lord, who hath believed our report? and to whom hath the arm of the** Lord **been revealed?** | | 38²
| | 7

After that He poureth water into a bason, and began to wash the disciples' feet, and to wipe *them* with the towel wherewith He was girded. Then cometh He to Simon Peter: and Peter saith unto Him, **Lord, dost Thou wash my feet?** Jesus answered and said unto him, What I do thou knowest not now; but thou shalt know hereafter. | 13 | 6

So after He had washed their feet, and had taken His garments, and was set down again, He said unto them, **Know ye what I have done to you?** Ye call Me Master and Lord: and ye say well; for *so* I am. If I then, *your* Lord and Master, have washed your feet; ye also ought to wash one another's feet. For I have given you an example, that ye should do as I have done to you. | | 12

When Jesus had thus said, He was troubled in spirit, and testified, and said, Verily, verily, I say unto you, that one of you shall betray Me. Then the disciples looked one on another, doubting of whom He spake. Now there was leaning on Jesus' bosom one of His disciples, whom Jesus loved. Simon Peter therefore beckoned to him, that he should ask who it should be of whom He spake. He then lying on Jesus' breast saith unto Him, **Lord, who is it?** Jesus answered, He it is, to whom I shall give a sop, when I have dipped *it*. And when He had | | 25

CHAP.	VER	
		dipped the sop, He gave *it* to Judas Iscariot, *the son* of Simon.
13	36	Simon Peter said unto Him, **Lord, whither goest Thou?** Jesus answered him, Whither I go, thou canst not follow Me now; but thou shalt follow Me afterwards.
	37	Peter said unto Him, Lord, **why cannot I follow Thee now?** I will lay down my life for Thy sake.
	38	Jesus answered him, **Wilt thou lay down thy life for My sake?** Verily, verily, I say unto thee, The cock shall not crow, till thou hast denied Me thrice.
	6	
14	5	Thomas saith unto Him, Lord, we know not whither Thou goest; and **how can we know the way?** Jesus saith unto him, I am the way, the truth, and the life: no man cometh unto the Father, but by Me. If ye had known Me, ye should have known My Father also: and from henceforth ye know Him, and have seen Him. Philip saith unto Him, Lord, shew us the Father, and it sufficeth us. Jesus saith unto him, **Have I been so long time with you, and yet hast thou not known Me, Philip?** he that hath seen Me hath seen the Father; and **how sayest thou** *then,* **Shew us the Father? Believest thou not that I am in the Father, and the Father in Me?** the words that I speak unto you I speak not of Myself: but the Father that dwelleth in Me, He doeth the works.
	9²	
	10	
	22	Judas saith unto Him, not Iscariot, Lord, **how is it that Thou wilt manifest Thyself unto us, and not unto the world?**
	5	
16	5	But now I go My way to Him that sent Me; and none of you asketh Me, **Whither goest Thou?** But because I have said these things unto you, sorrow hath filled your heart.
	17	Then said *some* of His disciples among themselves, **What is this that He saith unto us, A little while,**

	CHAP.	VER.
and ye shall not see **Me**: and again, a little while, and ye shall see **Me**: and, **Because I go to the Father?** They said therefore, **What is this that He saith, A little while?** we cannot tell what He saith.	**16**	18
Now Jesus knew that they were desirous to ask Him, and said unto them, **Do ye inquire among yourselves of that I said, A little while, and ye shall not see Me: and again, a little while, and ye shall see Me?** Verily, verily, I say unto you, That ye shall weep and lament, but the world shall rejoice: and ye shall be sorrowful, but your sorrow shall be turned into joy.		19
Jesus answered them, **Do ye now believe?** Behold, the hour cometh, yea, is now come, that ye shall be scattered, every man to his own, and shall leave Me alone: and yet I am not alone, because the Father is with Me.		31
		5
Jesus therefore, knowing all things that should come upon Him, went forth, and said unto them, **Whom seek ye?** They answered Him, Jesus of Nazareth. Jesus saith unto them, I am *He*. And Judas also, which betrayed Him, stood with them. As soon then as He had said unto them, I am *He*, they went backward, and fell to the ground. Then asked He them again, **Whom seek ye?** And they said, Jesus of Nazareth. Jesus answered, I have told you that I am *He*: if therefore ye seek Me, let these go their way: that the saying might be fulfilled, which He spake, Of them which thou gavest Me have I lost none. Then Simon Peter having a sword drew it, and smote the high priest's servant, and cut off his right ear. The servant's name was Malchus. Then said Jesus unto Peter, Put up thy sword into the sheath: **the cup which My Father hath given Me, shall I not drink it?**	**18**	4
		7
		11
But Peter stood at the door without. Then went out that other disciple, which was known unto the high priest, and spake unto her that kept the door, and brought in Peter. Then saith the damsel that kept the		

CHAP.	VER.	
18	17	door unto Peter, **Art not thou also** *one* **of this man's disciples?** He saith, I am not.
		The high priest then asked Jesus of His disciples, and of His doctrine. Jesus answered him, I spake openly to the world; I ever taught in the synagogue, and in the temple, whither the Jews always resort; and in secret
	21	have I said nothing. **Why askest thou Me?** ask them which heard Me, what I have said unto them: behold, they know what I said. And when He had thus spoken, one of the officers which stood by struck Jesus
	22	with the palm of his hand, saying, **Answerest Thou the high priest so?** Jesus answered him, If I have
	23	spoken evil, bear witness of the evil: but if well, **why smitest thou Me?** Now Annas had sent Him bound unto Caiaphas the high priest. And Simon Peter stood and warmed himself. They said therefore unto him,
	25	**Art not thou also** *one* **of His disciples?** He denied *it*, and said, I am not. One of the servants of the high priest, being *his* kinsman whose ear Peter cut off, saith,
	26	**Did not I see thee in the garden with Him?** Peter then denied again: and immediately the cock crew. Then led they Jesus from Caiaphas unto the hall of judgment: and it was early, and they themselves went not into the judgment hall, lest they should be defiled; but that they might eat the passover. Pilate
	29	then went out unto them, and said, **What accusation bring ye against this man?** They answered and said unto him, If He were not a malefactor, we would not have delivered Him up unto thee.
		Then Pilate entered into the judgment hall again, and
	33	called Jesus, and said unto Him, **Art Thou the King**
	34	**of the Jews?** Jesus answered him, **Sayest thou this thing of thyself, or did others tell it thee of**
	35[2]	**Me?** Pilate answered, **Am I a Jew?** Thine own nation and the chief priests have delivered Thee unto me: **what hast Thou done?** Jesus answered, My kingdom is not of this world. if My kingdom were of

this world, then would My servants fight, that I should
not be delivered to the Jews: but now is My kingdom
not from hence. Pilate therefore said unto Him, **Art
Thou a king then?** Jesus answered, Thou sayest
that I am a king. To this end was I born, and for this
cause came I into the world, that I should bear witness
unto the truth. Every one that is of the truth heareth
My voice. Pilate saith unto Him, **What is truth?**
And when he had said this, he went out again unto the
Jews, and saith unto them, I find in Him no fault *at all*.
But ye have a custom, that I should release unto you one
at the passover: **will ye therefore that I release
unto you the King of the Jews?** Then cried they
all again, saying, Not this man, but Barabbas. Now
Barabbas was a robber.

When Pilate therefore heard that saying, he was the
more afraid; and went again into the judgment hall, and
saith unto Jesus, **Whence art Thou?** But Jesus gave
him no answer. Then saith Pilate unto Him, **Speakest
Thou not unto me? knowest Thou not that I
have power to crucify Thee, and have power to
release Thee?** Jesus answered, Thou couldest have
no power *at all* against Me, except it were given thee
from above: therefore he that delivered Me unto thee
hath the greater sin.

And it was the preparation of the passover, and about
the sixth hour: and he saith unto the Jews, Behold your
King! But they cried out, Away with *Him*, away with
Him, crucify Him. Pilate saith unto them, **Shall I
crucify your King?** The chief priests answered, We
have no king but Cæsar.

But Mary stood without at the sepulchre weeping: and
as she wept, she stooped down, *and looked* into the
sepulchre, and seeth two angels in white sitting, the one
at the head, and the other at the feet, where the body of
Jesus had lain. And they say unto her, Woman, **why**

CHAP	VER.
18	37
	38
	39
	17
19	9
	10²
	15
	4
20	13

CHAP	VER	
20	15²	**weepest thou?** She saith unto them, Because they have taken away my Lord, and I know not where they have laid Him. And when she had thus said, she turned herself back, and saw Jesus standing, and knew not that it was Jesus. Jesus saith unto her, Woman, **why weepest thou? whom seekest thou?** She, supposing Him to be the gardener, saith unto Him, Sir, if Thou have borne Him hence, tell me where Thou hast laid Him, and I will take Him away. Jesus saith unto her, Mary. She turned herself, and saith unto Him, Rabboni, which is to say, Master.
	3	
21	5	But when the morning was now come, Jesus stood on the shore · but the disciples knew not that it was Jesus. Then Jesus saith unto them, Children, **have ye any meat?** They answered Him, No. And He said unto them, Cast the net on the right side of the ship, and ye shall find. They cast therefore, and now they were not able to draw it for the multitude of fishes.
	12	Jesus saith unto them, Come *and* dine. And none of the disciples durst ask Him, **Who art Thou?** knowing that it was the Lord. Jesus then cometh, and taketh bread, and giveth them, and fish likewise.
	15	So when they had dined, Jesus saith to Simon Peter, Simon, *son* of Jonas, **lovest thou Me more than these?** He saith unto Him, Yea, Lord; Thou knowest that I love Thee. He saith unto him, Feed My lambs. He saith to him again the second time, Simon, *son* of Jonas,
	16	**lovest thou Me?** He saith unto Him, Yea, Lord; Thou knowest that I love Thee. He saith unto him, Feed My sheep. He saith unto him the third time,
	17²	Simon, *son* of Jonas, **lovest thou Me?** Peter was grieved because He said unto him the third time, **Lovest thou Me?** And he said unto Him, Lord, Thou knowest all things; Thou knowest that I love Thee. Jesus saith unto him, Feed My sheep.

Then Peter, turning about, seeth the disciple whom

Jesus loved following; which also leaned on His breast at supper, and said, Lord, **which is he that betrayeth Thee?** Peter seeing him saith to Jesus, Lord, **and what** *shall* **this man** *do?* Jesus saith unto him, If I will that he tarry till I come, **what** *is that* **to thee?** follow thou Me. Then went this saying abroad among the brethren, that that disciple should not die: yet Jesus said not unto him, He shall not die; but, If I will that he tarry till I come, **what** *is that* **to thee?**

CHAP	VER.
21	20
	21
	22
	23
	10

Saint John 167

THE
ACTS OF THE APOSTLES.

WHEN they therefore were come together, they asked of Him, saying, Lord, **wilt Thou at this time restore again the kingdom to Israel?** And He said unto them, It is not for you to know the times or the seasons, which the Father hath put in His own power.

And while they looked stedfastly toward heaven as He went up, behold, two men stood by them in white apparel; which also said, Ye men of Galilee, **why stand ye gazing up into heaven?** this same Jesus, which is taken up from you into heaven, shall so come in like manner as ye have seen Him go into heaven.

And there were dwelling at Jerusalem Jews, devout men, out of every nation under heaven. Now when this was noised abroad, the multitude came together, and were confounded, because that every man heard them speak in his own language. And they were all amazed

CHAP.	VER.
1	6
	11
	2

CHAP.	VER.	
2	7	and marvelled, saying one to another, Behold, **are not**
	8	**all these which speak Galilæans? And how hear we every man in our own tongue, wherein we were born?**
	12	And they were all amazed, and were in doubt, saying one to another, **What meaneth this?** Others mocking said, These men are full of new wine.
	37	Now when they heard *this*, they were pricked in their heart, and said unto Peter and to the rest of the apostles, Men *and* brethren, **what shall we do?** Then Peter said unto them, Repent, and be baptized every one of you in the name of Jesus Christ for the remission of sins,
	4	and ye shall receive the gift of the Holy Ghost.
3	12[2]	And as the lame man which was healed held Peter and John, all the people ran together unto them in the porch that is called Solomon's, greatly wondering. And when Peter saw *it*, he answered unto the people, Ye men of Israel, **why marvel ye at this? or why look ye so earnestly on us, as though by our own power or holiness we had made this man to walk?**
	2	
4	7	And it came to pass on the morrow, that their rulers, and elders, and scribes, and Annas the high priest, and Caiaphas, and John, and Alexander, and as many as were of the kindred of the high priest, were gathered together at Jerusalem. And when they had set them in the midst, they asked, **By what power, or by what name, have ye done this?**

Now when they saw the boldness of Peter and John, and perceived that they were unlearned and ignorant men, they marvelled; and they took knowledge of them, that they had been with Jesus. And beholding the man which was healed standing with them, they could say nothing against it. But when they had commanded them to go aside out of the council, they conferred among

THE ACTS OF THE APOSTLES:—IV., V.

themselves, saying, **What shall we do to these men?** for that indeed a notable miracle hath been done by them *is* manifest to all them that dwell in Jerusalem; and we cannot deny *it*.

And being let go, they went to their own company, and reported all that the chief priests and elders had said unto them. And when they heard that, they lifted up their voice to God with one accord, and said, Lord, Thou *art* God, which hast made heaven, and earth, and the sea, and all that in them is: who by the mouth of Thy servant David hast said, **Why did the heathen rage, and the people imagine vain things?**

But a certain man named Ananias, with Sapphira his wife, sold a possession, and kept back *part* of the price, his wife also being privy *to it*, and brought a certain part, and laid *it* at the apostles' feet. But Peter said, **Ananias, why hath Satan filled thine heart to lie to the Holy Ghost, and to keep back** *part* **of the price of the land? Whiles it remained, was it not thine own?** and **after it was sold, was it not in thine own power? why hast thou conceived this thing in thine heart?** thou hast not lied unto men, but unto God. And Ananias hearing these words fell down, and gave up the ghost: and great fear came on all them that heard these things. And the young men arose, wound him up, and carried *him* out, and buried *him*. And it was about the space of three hours after, when his wife, not knowing what was done, came in. And Peter answered unto her, **Tell me whether ye sold the land for so much?** And she said, Yea, for so much. Then Peter said unto her, **How is it that ye have agreed together to tempt the Spirit of the Lord?** behold, the feet of them which have buried thy husband *are* at the door, and shall carry thee out. Then fell she down straightway at his feet, and yielded up the ghost: and the young men came in, and found her dead, and, carrying *her* forth, buried *her* by her husband.

CHAP.	VER.
4	16
	25
	3
5	3
	4,3
	8
	9

CHAP.	VER.	
5	28	And when they had brought them, they set *them* before the council: and the high priest asked them, saying, **Did not we straitly command you that ye should not teach in this name?** and, behold, ye have filled Jerusalem with your doctrine, and intend to bring this man's blood upon us.
	7	
7	1	Then said the high priest, **Are these things so?**
	26	And the next day he shewed himself unto them as they strove, and would have set them at one again, saying, Sirs, ye are brethren; **why do ye wrong one to another?** But he that did his neighbour wrong thrust
	27	him away, saying, **Who made thee a ruler and a**
	28	**judge over us? Wilt thou kill me, as thou diddest the Egyptian yesterday?** Then fled Moses at this saying, and was a stranger in the land of Madian, where he begat two sons.
	35	This Moses whom they refused, saying, **Who made thee a ruler and a judge?** the same did God send *to be* a ruler and a deliverer by the hand of the angel which appeared to him in the bush.
	42	Then God turned, and gave them up to worship the host of heaven; as it is written in the book of the prophets, O ye house of Israel, **have ye offered to Me slain beasts and sacrifices** *by the space of* **forty years in the wilderness?**
	49²	Howbeit the most High dwelleth not in temples made with hands; as saith the prophet, Heaven *is* My throne, and earth *is* My footstool: **what house will ye build Me?** saith the Lord: or **what** *is* **the place of My**
	50	**rest? Hath not My hand made all these things?** Ye stiffnecked and uncircumcised in heart and ears, ye do always resist the Holy Ghost: as your fathers *did*, so
	52	do ye. **Which of the prophets have not your fathers persecuted?** and they have slain them which
	10	shewed before of the coming of the Just One; of whom ye

have been now the betrayers and murderers: who have received the law by the disposition of angels, and have not kept it.

Then the Spirit said unto Philip, Go near, and join thyself to this chariot. And Philip ran thither to *him*, and heard him read the prophet Esaias, and said, **Understandest thou what thou readest?** And he said, **How can I, except some man should guide me?** And he desired Philip that he would come up and sit with him. The place of the scripture which he read was this, He was led as a sheep to the slaughter; and like a lamb dumb before his shearer, so opened He not His mouth: in His humiliation His judgment was taken away: and **who shall declare His generation?** for His life is taken from the earth. And the eunuch answered Philip, and said, I pray thee, **of whom speaketh the prophet this? of himself, or of some other man?** Then Philip opened his mouth, and began at the same scripture, and preached unto him Jesus. And as they went on *their* way, they came unto a certain water: and the eunuch said, See, *here is* water; **what doth hinder me to be baptized?** And Philip said, If thou believest with all thine heart, thou mayest. And he answered and said, I believe that Jesus Christ is the Son of God.

CHAP.	VER.
8	30
	31
	33
	34[2]
	36
	6

And as he journeyed, he came near Damascus: and suddenly there shined round about him a light from heaven: and he fell to the earth, and heard a voice saying unto him, **Saul, Saul, why persecutest thou Me?** And he said, **Who art Thou, Lord?** And the Lord said, I am Jesus whom thou persecutest: *it is* hard for thee to kick against the pricks. And he trembling and astonished said, **Lord, what wilt Thou have me to do?** And the Lord *said* unto him, Arise, and go into the city, and it shall be told thee what thou must do.

9	4
	5
	6

And straightway he preached Christ in the synagogues,

CHAP.	VER.	
9	21	that He is the Son of God. But all that heard *him* were amazed, and said ; **Is not this he that destroyed them which called on this name in Jerusalem, and came hither for that intent, that he might bring them bound unto the chief priests ?** But Saul increased the more in strength, and confounded the
	4	Jews which dwelt at Damascus, proving that this is very Christ.
10	4	He saw in a vision evidently about the ninth hour of the day an angel of God coming in to him, and saying unto him, Cornelius. And when he looked on him, he was afraid, and said, **What is it, Lord ?** and he said unto him, Thy prayers and thine alms are come up for a memorial before God.
	21	Then Peter went down to the men which were sent unto him from Cornelius ; and said, Behold, I am he whom ye seek : **what *is* the cause wherefore ye are come ?** And they said, Cornelius the centurion, a just man, and one that feareth God, and of good report among all the nation of the Jews, was warned from God by an holy angel to send for thee into his house, and to hear words of thee.
	29	But Peter took him up, saying, Stand up ; I myself also am a man. And as he talked with him, he went in, and found many that were come together. And he said unto them, Ye know how that it is an unlawful thing for a man that is a Jew to keep company, or come unto one of another nation ; but God hath shewed me that I should not call any man common or unclean. Therefore came I *unto you* without gainsaying, as soon as I was sent for : I ask therefore **for what intent ye have sent for me ?**
	47	Then answered Peter, **Can any man forbid water, that these should not be baptized, which have**
	4	**received the Holy Ghost as well as we ?** And he

THE ACTS OF THE APOSTLES:—XI.-XIV.

	CHAP.	VER.

commanded them to be baptized in the name of the Lord. Then prayed they him to tarry certain days.

Forasmuch then as God gave them the like gift as *He did* unto us, who believed on the Lord Jesus Christ; **what was I, that I could withstand God?**   11   17

                         1

But Elymas the sorcerer (for so is his name by interpretation) withstood them, seeking to turn away the deputy from the faith. Then Saul (who also *is called* Paul), filled with the Holy Ghost, set his eyes on him, and said, O full of all subtilty and all mischief, *thou* child of the devil, *thou* enemy of all righteousness, **wilt thou not cease to pervert the right ways of the Lord?**   13   10

Of this man's seed hath God according to *His* promise raised unto Israel a Saviour, Jesus: when John had first preached before His coming the baptism of repentance to all the people of Israel. And as John fulfilled his course, he said, **Whom think ye that I am?** I am not *He*. But, behold, there cometh one after me, whose shoes of *His* feet I am not worthy to loose.   25

                         2

Which when the apostles, Barnabas and Paul, heard *of*, they rent their clothes, and ran in among the people, crying out, and saying, **Sirs, why do ye these things?** We also are men of like passions with you, and preach unto you that ye should turn from these vanities unto the living God, which made heaven, and earth, and the sea, and all things that are therein: who in times past suffered all nations to walk in their own ways.   14   15

                         1

And when there had been much disputing, Peter rose up, and said unto them, Men *and* brethren, ye know how that a good while ago God made choice among us, that the Gentiles by my mouth should hear the word of the gospel, and believe. And God, which knoweth the hearts, bear them witness, giving them the Holy Ghost, even as

CHAP.	VER
15	10
	1
16	30
	37
	2
17	18
	19
	2

He did unto us; and put no difference between us and them, purifying their hearts by faith. Now therefore **why tempt ye God, to put a yoke upon the neck of the disciples, which neither our fathers nor we were able to bear?** But we believe that through the grace of the Lord Jesus Christ we shall be saved, even as they.

And the keeper of the prison awaking out of his sleep, and seeing the prison doors open, he drew out his sword, and would have killed himself, supposing that the prisoners had been fled. But Paul cried with a loud voice, saying, Do thyself no harm : for we are all here. Then he called for a light, and sprang in, and came trembling, and fell down before Paul and Silas, and brought them out, and said, **Sirs, what must I do to be saved?** And they said, Believe on the Lord Jesus Christ, and thou shalt be saved, and thy house.

But Paul said unto them, They have beaten us openly uncondemned, being Romans, and have cast *us* into prison; and **now do they thrust us out privily?** nay verily; but let them come themselves and fetch us out.

Then certain philosophers of the Epicureans, and of the Stoicks, encountered him. And some said, **What will this babbler say?** other some, He seemeth to be a setter forth of strange gods : because he preached unto them Jesus, and the resurrection. And they took him, and brought him unto Areopagus, saying, **May we know what this new doctrine, whereof thou speakest,** *is?* For thou bringest certain strange things to our ears : we would know therefore what these things mean.

And it came to pass, that, while Apollos was at Corinth, Paul having passed through the upper coasts came to Ephesus : and finding certain disciples, he said

THE ACTS OF THE APOSTLES:—XIX., XXI.

	CHAP.	VER.
unto them, **Have ye received the Holy Ghost since ye believed?** And they said unto him, We have not so much as heard whether there be any Holy Ghost. And he said unto them, **Unto what then were ye baptized?** And they said, Unto John's baptism.	19	2
		3

Then certain of the vagabond Jews, exorcists, took upon them to call over them which had evil spirits the name of the Lord Jesus, saying, We adjure you by Jesus whom Paul preacheth. And there were seven sons of *one* Sceva, a Jew, *and* chief of the priests, which did so. And the evil spirit answered and said, Jesus I know, and Paul I know; but **who are ye?** And the man in whom the evil spirit was leaped on them, and overcame them, and prevailed against them, so that they fled out of that house naked and wounded.

15

And when the townclerk had appeased the people, he said, *Ye* men of Ephesus, **what man is there that knoweth not how that the city of the Ephesians is a worshipper of the great goddess Diana, and of the** *image* **which fell down from Jupiter?** Seeing then that these things cannot be spoken against, ye ought to be quiet, and to do nothing rashly.

35

4

Then Paul answered, **What mean ye to weep and to break mine heart?** for I am ready not to be bound only, but also to die at Jerusalem for the name of the Lord Jesus.

21 13

What is it therefore? the multitude must needs come together: for they will hear that thou art come.

22

And as Paul was to be led into the castle, he said unto the chief captain, **May I speak unto thee?** Who said, **Canst thou speak Greek? Art not thou that Egyptian, which before these days madest an uproar, and leddest out into the wilderness four thousand men that were murderers?**

37²
38

5

CHAP.	VER.	
22	7	And it came to pass, that, as I made my journey, and was come nigh unto Damascus about noon, suddenly there shone from heaven a great light round about me. And I fell unto the ground, and heard a voice saying unto me, **Saul, Saul, why persecutest thou Me?**
	8	And I answered, **Who art Thou, Lord?** And He said unto me, I am Jesus of Nazareth, whom thou persecutest. And they that were with me saw indeed the light, and were afraid; but they heard not the voice
	10	of Him that spake to me. And I said, **What shall I do, Lord?** And the Lord said unto me, Arise, and go into Damascus; and there it shall be told thee of all things which are appointed for thee to do.

And one Ananias, a devout man according to the law, having a good report of all the Jews which dwelt *there*, came unto me, and stood, and said unto me, Brother Saul, receive thy sight. And the same hour I looked up upon him. And he said, The God of our fathers hath chosen thee, that thou shouldest know His will, and see that Just One, and shouldest hear the voice of His mouth. For thou shalt be His witness unto all men of what thou hast seen and heard. And now **why tarriest thou?** arise, and be baptized, and wash away thy sins, calling on the name of the Lord.

	16	(see above)
	25	The chief captain commanded him to be brought into the castle, and bade that he should be examined by scourging; that he might know wherefore they cried so against him. And as they bound him with thongs, Paul said unto the centurion that stood by, **Is it lawful for you to scourge a man that is a Roman, and uncondemned?** When the centurion heard *that*, he went and told the chief captain, saying, Take heed what thou doest: for this man is a Roman. Then the chief
	27	captain came, and said unto him, Tell me, **art thou a Roman?** He said, Yea.
	6	And Paul, earnestly beholding the council, said, Men *and* brethren, I have lived in all good conscience before

THE ACTS OF THE APOSTLES:—XXIII.-XXVI.

| | CHAP. | VER. |

God until this day. And the high priest Ananias commanded them that stood by him to smite him on the mouth. Then said Paul unto him, God shall smite thee, *thou* whited wall: for **sittest thou to judge me after the law, and commandest me to be smitten contrary to the law?** And they that stood by said, **Revilest thou God's high priest?** Then said Paul, I wist not, brethren, that he was the high priest; for it is written, Thou shalt not speak evil of the ruler of thy people. — 23, 3; 4

Then Paul called one of the centurions unto *him*, and said, Bring this young man unto the chief captain: for he hath a certain thing to tell him. So he took him, and brought *him* to the chief captain, and said, Paul the prisoner called me unto *him*, and prayed me to bring this young man unto thee, who hath something to say unto thee. Then the chief captain took him by the hand, and went *with him* aside privately, and asked *him*, **What is that thou hast to tell me?** — 19; 3

But Festus, willing to do the Jews a pleasure, answered Paul, and said, **Wilt thou go up to Jerusalem, and there be judged of these things before me?** Then said Paul, I stand at Cæsar's judgment seat, where I ought to be judged: to the Jews have I done no wrong, as thou very well knowest. For if I be an offender, or have committed any thing worthy of death, I refuse not to die. but if there be none of these things whereof these accuse me, no man may deliver me unto them. I appeal unto Cæsar Then Festus, when he had conferred with the council, answered, **Hast thou appealed unto Cæsar?** unto Cæsar shalt thou go. — 25, 9; 12; 2

And now I stand and am judged for the hope of the promise made of God unto our fathers: unto which *promise* our twelve tribes, instantly serving *God* day and night, hope to come. For which hope's sake, king Agrippa, I am accused of the Jews. **Why should** — 26, 8

CHAP.	VER.	
		it be thought a thing incredible with you, that God should raise the dead?
26	14	At midday, O king, I saw in the way a light from heaven, above the brightness of the sun, shining round about me and them which journeyed with me. And when we were all fallen to the earth, I heard a voice speaking unto me, and saying in the Hebrew tongue, **Saul, Saul, why persecutest thou Me?** *it is* hard
	15	for thee to kick against the pricks. And I said, **Who art Thou, Lord?** And He said, I am Jesus whom thou persecutest.
	27	**King Agrippa, believest thou the prophets?** I know that thou believest. Then Agrippa said unto Paul, Almost thou persuadest me to be a Christian.
	4	

The Acts 75

THE EPISTLE OF PAUL THE APOSTLE
TO THE
ROMANS.

CHAP.	VER	
2	3	BUT we are sure that the judgment of God is according to truth against them which commit such things. **And thinkest thou this, O man, that judgest them which do such things, and doest the same, that thou shalt escape the judgment
	4	of God?** Or despisest thou the riches of His goodness and forbearance and longsuffering; not knowing that the goodness of God leadeth thee to repentance?
	21²	Thou therefore which teachest another, **teachest**

	CHAP.	VER.
thou not thyself? thou that preachest a man should not steal, **dost thou steal?** Thou that sayest a man should not commit adultery, **dost thou commit adultery?** thou that abhorrest idols, **dost thou commit sacrilege?** Thou that makest thy boast of the law, through breaking the law **dishonourest thou God?**	2	22[2] 23
Therefore if the uncircumcision keep the righteousness of the law, **shall not his uncircumcision be counted for circumcision? And shall not uncircumcision which is by nature,** if it fulfil the law, **judge thee, who by the letter and circumcision dost transgress the law?**		26 27 9
What advantage then hath the Jew? or **what profit** *is there* **of circumcision?** Much every way: chiefly, because that unto them were committed the oracles of God. **For what if some did not believe? shall their unbelief make the faith of God without effect?** God forbid: yea, let God be true, but every man a liar; as it is written, That Thou mightest be justified in Thy sayings, and mightest overcome when Thou art judged. But if our unrighteousness commend the righteousness of God, **what shall we say?** *Is* **God unrighteous who taketh vengeance?** (I speak as a man) God forbid: for then **how shall God judge the world?** For if the truth of God hath more abounded through my lie unto His glory; **why yet am I also judged as a sinner? And not** *rather* (as we be slanderously reported, and as some affirm that we say), **Let us do evil, that good may come?** whose damnation is just. **What then? are we better** *than they?* No, in no wise: for we have before proved both Jews and Gentiles, that they are all under sin; as it is written, There is none righteous, no, not one.	3	1[2] 3[2] 5[2] 6 7 8 9[2]
Where *is* **boasting then?** It is excluded. **By what law? of works?** Nay: but by the law of		27[3]

CHAP.	VER	
3	29[2]	faith. Therefore we conclude that a man is justified by faith without the deeds of the law. **Is He the God of the Jews only?** *is He* **not also of the Gentiles?** Yes, of the Gentiles also: seeing *it is* one God, which shall justify the circumcision by faith, and uncircum-
	31	cision through faith. **Do we then make void the law through faith?** God forbid. yea, we establish
	17	the law.

| 4 | 1 | **What shall we say then that Abraham our father, as pertaining to the flesh, hath found?** For if Abraham were justified by works, he hath *whereof* |
| | 3 | to glory; but not before God. For **what saith the scripture?** Abraham believed God, and it was counted unto him for righteousness. |

	9	Blessed *is* the man to whom the Lord will not impute sin. *Cometh* **this blessedness then upon the circumcision** *only,* **or upon the uncircumcision also?** for we say that faith was reckoned to Abraham for righteous-
	10[2]	ness. **How was it then reckoned? when he was in circumcision, or in uncircumcision?** Not in
	5	circumcision, but in uncircumcision.

6	1[2]	**What shall we say then? Shall we continue in sin, that grace may abound?** God forbid.
	2	**How shall we, that are dead to sin, live any**
	3	**longer therein? Know ye not, that so many of us as were baptized into Jesus Christ were baptized into His death?**

| | 15[2] | For sin shall not have dominion over you: for ye are not under the law, but under grace. **What then? shall we sin, because we are not under the law,** |
| | 16 | **but under grace?** God forbid. **Know ye not, that to whom ye yield yourselves servants to obey, his servants ye are to whom ye obey; whether of sin unto death, or of obedience unto righteousness?** |

	CHAP.	VER.

What fruit had ye then in those things whereof ye are now ashamed? for the end of those things *is* death. — **6** **21**

8

Know ye not, brethren (for I speak to them that know the law), **how that the law hath dominion over a man as long as he liveth?** — **7** **1**

What shall we say then? *Is* **the law sin?** God forbid. Nay, I had not known sin, but by the law: for I had not known lust, except the law had said, Thou shalt not covet. — 7²

Was then that which is good made death unto me? God forbid. But sin, that it might appear sin, working death in me by that which is good; that sin by the commandment might become exceeding sinful. — 13

For I delight in the law of God after the inward man: but I see another law in my members, warring against the law of my mind, and bringing me into captivity to the law of sin which is in my members. O wretched man that I am! **who shall deliver me from the body of this death?** I thank God through Jesus Christ our Lord. So then with the mind I myself serve the law of God; but with the flesh the law of sin. — 24

5

For we are saved by hope: but hope that is seen is not hope: for **what a man seeth, why doth he yet hope for?** — **8** 24

What shall we then say to these things? If God *be* **for us, who** *can be* **against us?** He that spared not His own Son, but delivered Him up for us all, **how shall He not with Him also freely give us all things? Who shall lay any thing to the charge of God's elect?** *It is* God that justifieth. **Who** *is* **he that condemneth?** *It is* Christ that died, yea rather, that is risen again, who is even at the — 31² 32 33 34

CHAP.	VER	
8	35²	right hand of God, who also maketh intercession for us. **Who shall separate us from the love of Christ?** *shall* **tribulation, or distress, or persecution, or famine, or nakedness, or peril, or sword?** As it is written, For Thy sake we are killed all the day long; we are accounted as sheep for the slaughter. Nay, in all these things we are more than conquerors through Him that loved us.
	8	
9	14²	**What shall we say then?** *Is there* **unrighteousness with God?** God forbid.
		Therefore hath He mercy on whom He will *have mercy*, and whom He will He hardeneth. Thou wilt
	19²	say then unto me, **Why doth He yet find fault?** For **who hath resisted His will?** Nay but, O man,
	20²	**who art thou that repliest against God? Shall the thing formed say to Him that formed** *it*, **Why**
	21	**hast Thou made me thus?** **Hath not the potter power over the clay, of the same lump to make one vessel unto honour, and another unto dis-**
	24	**honour?** *What* **if God, willing to shew** *His* **wrath, and to make His power known, endured with much longsuffering the vessels of wrath fitted to destruction: and that He might make known the riches of His glory on the vessels of mercy, which He had afore prepared unto glory, even us, whom He hath called, not of the Jews only, but also of the Gentiles?**
	30	And as Esaias said before, Except the LORD of Sabaoth had left us a seed, we had been as Sodoma, and been made like unto Gomorrha. **What shall we say then?** That the Gentiles, which followed not after righteousness, have attained to righteousness, even the righteousness which is of faith. But Israel, which followed after the law of righteousness, hath not attained to the law of
	32	righteousness. **Wherefore?** Because *they sought it*
	10	not by faith, but as it were by the works of the law.

But the righteousness which is of faith speaketh on this wise, Say not in thine heart, **Who shall ascend into heaven?** (that is, to bring Christ down *from above*:) or, **Who shall descend into the deep?** (that is, to bring up Christ again from the dead.) **But what saith it?** The word is nigh thee, *even* in thy mouth, and in thy heart: that is, the word of faith, which we preach; that if thou shalt confess with thy mouth the Lord Jesus, and shalt believe in thine heart that God hath raised Him from the dead, thou shalt be saved. [10:6,7,8]

For whosoever shall call upon the name of the Lord shall be saved. **How then shall they call on Him in whom they have not believed?** and **how shall they believe in Him of whom they have not heard?** and **how shall they hear without a preacher?** And **how shall they preach, except they be sent?** as it is written, How beautiful are the feet of them that preach the gospel of peace, and bring glad tidings of good things! But they have not all obeyed the gospel. For Esaias saith, Lord, **who hath believed our report?** So then faith *cometh* by hearing, and hearing by the word of God. But I say, **Have they not heard?** Yes verily, their sound went into all the earth, and their words unto the ends of the world. But I say, **Did not Israel know?** First Moses saith, I will provoke you to jealousy by *them that are* no people, *and* by a foolish nation I will anger you. [14:3, 15, 16, 18, 19, 10]

I say then, **Hath God cast away His people?** God forbid. For I also am an Israelite, of the seed of Abraham, *of* the tribe of Benjamin. God hath not cast away His people which He foreknew. **Wot ye not what the scripture saith of Elias?** how he maketh intercession to God against Israel, saying, Lord, they have killed Thy prophets, and digged down Thine altars; and I am left alone, and they seek my life. But **what saith the answer of God unto him?** I have re- [11:1, 2, 4]

CHAP.	VER.	
		served to Myself seven thousand men, who have not bowed the knee to *the image of* Baal. Even so then at this present time also there is a remnant according to the election of grace.
11	7	**What then?** Israel hath not obtained that which he seeketh for; but the election hath obtained it, and the rest were blinded (according as it is written, God hath given them the spirit of slumber, eyes that they should not see, and ears that they should not hear;) unto this day.
	11	I say then, **Have they stumbled that they should fall?** God forbid: but *rather* through their fall salvation *is come* unto the Gentiles, for to provoke them to jealousy. Now if the fall of them *be* the riches of the world, and the diminishing of them the riches of the
	12	Gentiles; **how much more their fulness?** For I speak to you Gentiles, inasmuch as I am the apostle of the Gentiles, I magnify mine office: if by any means I may provoke to emulation *them which are* my flesh, and might save some of them. For if the casting away of
	15	them *be* the reconciling of the world, **what** *shall* **the receiving** *of them be*, **but life from the dead?** For if the firstfruit *be* holy, the lump *is* also *holy:* and if the root *be* holy, so *are* the branches.
	24	For if thou wert cut out of the olive tree which is wild by nature, and wert graffed contrary to nature into a good olive tree: **how much more shall these, which be the natural** *branches*, **be graffed into their own olive tree?**
	34² 35	For **who hath known the mind of the Lord?** or **who hath been His counseller?** Or **who hath first given to Him, and it shall be recompensed unto him again?** For of Him, and through Him, and
11		to Him, *are* all things: to whom *be* glory for ever. Amen.

ROMANS:—XIII., XIV. I. CORINTHIANS:—I.   337

	CHAP.	VER.
For rulers are not a terror to good works, but to the evil. **Wilt thou then not be afraid of the power?** do that which is good, and thou shalt have praise of the same: for he is the minister of God to thee for good.	13	3
		1
Let not him that eateth despise him that eateth not; and let not him which eateth not judge him that eateth: for God hath received him. **Who art thou that judgest another man's servant?** to his own master he standeth or falleth. Yea, he shall be holden up: for God is able to make him stand.	14	4
But **why dost thou judge thy brother?** or **why dost thou set at nought thy brother?** for we shall all stand before the judgment seat of Christ.		10²
It is good neither to eat flesh, nor to drink wine, nor any thing whereby thy brother stumbleth, or is offended, or is made weak. **Hast thou faith?** have it to thyself before God. Happy is he that condemneth not himself in that thing which he alloweth.		22
		4
	Romans	88

THE FIRST EPISTLE OF PAUL THE APOSTLE

TO THE

CORINTHIANS.

	CHAP.	VER.
NOW this I say, that every one of you saith, I am of Paul; and I of Apollos; and I of Cephas; and I of Christ. **Is Christ divided? was Paul crucified for you?** or **were ye baptized in the name of Paul?**	1	13³
Where is **the wise? where** is **the scribe? where** is **the disputer of this world?** hath not God made		20⁴
		7

22

CHAP.	VER.	
		foolish the wisdom of this world? For after that in the wisdom of God the world by wisdom knew not God, it pleased God by the foolishness of preaching to save them that believe.
		But as it is written, Eye hath not seen, nor ear heard, neither have entered into the heart of man, the things which God hath prepared for them that love Him. But God hath revealed *them* unto us by His Spirit: for the Spirit searcheth all things, yea, the deep things of God.
2	11	For **what man knoweth the things of a man, save the spirit of man which is in him?** even so the things of God knoweth no man, but the Spirit of God.
	16	But he that is spiritual judgeth all things, yet he himself is judged of no man. For **who hath known the mind of the Lord, that he may instruct Him?**
	2	But we have the mind of Christ.
3	3	For ye are yet carnal: for whereas *there is* among you envying, and strife, and divisions, **are ye not carnal, and walk as men?** For while one saith, I am of
	4	Paul; and another, I *am* of Apollos; **are ye not**
	5	**carnal? Who then is Paul, and who** *is* **Apollos, but ministers by whom ye believed, even as the Lord gave to every man?** I have planted, Apollos watered; but God gave the increase. So then neither is he that planteth any thing, neither he that watereth; but God that giveth the increase.
	16	**Know ye not that ye are the temple of God,**
	4	**and** *that* **the Spirit of God dwelleth in you?**
4	7³	And these things, brethren, I have in a figure transferred to myself and *to* Apollos for your sakes; that ye might learn in us not to think *of men* above that which is written, that no one of you be puffed up for one against another. For **who maketh thee to differ** *from another?* **and what hast thou that thou didst not receive?**

I. CORINTHIANS :—IV.-VI.

	CHAP.	VER.
now if thou didst receive *it*, **why dost thou glory, as if thou hadst not received** *it* ?		
Now some are puffed up, as though I would not come to you. But I will come to you shortly, if the Lord will, and will know, not the speech of them which are puffed up, but the power. For the kingdom of God *is* not in word, but in power. **What will ye? shall I come unto you with a rod, or in love, and** *in* **the spirit of meekness?**	4	21²
		5
Your glorying *is* not good. **Know ye not that a little leaven leaveneth the whole lump?**	5	6
But now I have written unto you not to keep company, if any man that is called a brother be a fornicator, or covetous, or an idolater, or a railer, or a drunkard, or an extortioner; with such an one no not to eat. For **what have I to do to judge them also that are without? do not ye judge them that are within?** But them that are without God judgeth. Therefore put away from among yourselves that wicked person.		12²
		3
Dare any of you, having a matter against another, go to law before the unjust, and not before the saints? Do ye not know that the saints shall judge the world? and if the world shall be judged by you, **are ye unworthy to judge the smallest matters? Know ye not that we shall judge angels? how much more things that pertain to this life?** If then ye have judgments of things pertaining to this life, set them to judge who are least esteemed in the church. I speak to your shame. **Is it so, that there is not a wise man among you?** no, **not one that shall be able to judge between his brethren?** But brother goeth to law with brother, and that before the unbelievers. Now therefore there is utterly a fault among you, because ye go to law one with another. **Why do ye not rather take wrong?**	6	1
		2²
		3²
		5²
		7²

CHAP.	VER.	
6	9	**why do ye not rather** *suffer yourselves to* **be defrauded?** Nay, ye do wrong, and defraud, and that *your* brethren. **Know ye not that the unrighteous shall not inherit the kingdom of God?** Be not deceived: neither fornicators, nor idolaters, nor adulterers, nor effeminate, nor abusers of themselves with mankind, nor thieves, nor covetous, nor drunkards, nor revilers, nor extortioners, shall inherit the kingdom of God.
	15[2]	**Know ye not that your bodies are the members of Christ?** **shall I then take the members of Christ, and make** *them* **the members of an harlot?** God forbid. **What?** **know ye not that he which is joined to an harlot is one body?** for two, saith he, shall be one flesh. But he that is joined unto the Lord is one spirit. Flee fornication Every sin that a man doeth is without the body; but he that committeth fornication sinneth against his own body.
	16[2]	
	19[2]	**What? know ye not that your body is the temple of the Holy Ghost** *which is* **in you, which ye have of God, and ye are not your own?** For ye are bought with a price: therefore glorify God in your body, and in your spirit, which are God's.
	16	
7	16[2]	But if the unbelieving depart, let him depart. A brother or a sister is not under bondage in such *cases*: but God hath called us to peace. For **what knowest thou, O wife, whether thou shalt save** *thy* **husband?** or **how knowest thou, O man, whether thou shalt save** *thy* **wife?** But as God hath distributed to every man, as the Lord hath called every one, so let him walk. And so ordain I in all churches. **Is any man called being circumcised?** let him not become uncircumcised. **Is any called in uncircumcision?** let him not be circumcised.
	18[2]	
	21	Let every man abide in the same calling wherein he was called. **Art thou called** *being* **a servant?** care not for it: but if thou mayest be made free, use *it* rather.

I. CORINTHIANS:—VII.-IX.

	CHAP.	VER.

For he that is called in the Lord, *being* a servant, is the Lord's freeman. likewise also he that is called, *being* free, is Christ's servant.

Art thou bound unto a wife? seek not to be loosed. **Art thou loosed from a wife?** seek not a wife.

	7	27[2]
		7

For if any man see thee which hast knowledge sit at meat in the idol's temple, **shall not the conscience of him which is weak be emboldened to eat those things which are offered to idols;** and **through thy knowledge shall the weak brother perish, for whom Christ died?**

	8	11
		1

Am I not an apostle? am I not free? have I not seen Jesus Christ our Lord? are not ye my work in the Lord? If I be not an apostle unto others, yet doubtless I am to you: for the seal of mine apostleship are ye in the Lord. Mine answer to them that do examine me is this, **Have we not power to eat and to drink? Have we not power to lead about a sister, a wife, as well as other apostles, and** *as* **the brethren of the Lord, and Cephas?** Or I only and Barnabas, **have not we power to forbear working? Who goeth a warfare any time at his own charges? who planteth a vineyard, and eateth not of the fruit thereof? or who feedeth a flock, and eateth not of the milk of the flock? Say I these things as a man?** or **saith not the law the same also?** For it is written in the law of Moses, Thou shalt not muzzle the mouth of the ox that treadeth out the corn. **Doth God take care for oxen?** Or **saith He** *it* **altogether for our sakes?** For our sakes, no doubt, *this* is written: that he that ploweth should plow in hope; and that he that thresheth in hope should be partaker of his hope. **If we have sown unto you spiritual things,** *is it* **a great thing if we shall reap your carnal things? If others be**

	9	1[4]
		4
		5
		6
		7[3]
		8[2]
		9
		10
		11
		12

CHAP.	VER.	
9	13²	**partakers of** *this* **power over you,** *are* **not we rather?** Nevertheless we have not used this power; but suffer all things, lest we should hinder the gospel of Christ. **Do ye not know that they which minister about holy things live** *of the things* **of the temple? and they which wait at the altar are partakers with the altar?**
	18	For though I preach the gospel, I have nothing to glory of: for necessity is laid upon me; yea, woe is unto me, if I preach not the gospel! For if I do this thing willingly, I have a reward: but if against my will, a dispensation *of the gospel* is committed unto me. **What is my reward then?** *Verily* that, when I preach the gospel, I may make the gospel of Christ without charge, that I abuse not my power in the gospel.
	24	**Know ye not that they which run in a race run all, but one receiveth the prize?** So run, that ye may obtain.
	20	
10	16²	**The cup of blessing which we bless, is it not the communion of the blood of Christ? The bread which we break, is it not the communion of the body of Christ?** For we *being* many are one bread, *and* one body: for we are all partakers of that one bread. Behold Israel after the flesh: **are not they which eat of the sacrifices partakers of the altar?**
	18	
	19²	**What say I then? that the idol is any thing, or that which is offered in sacrifice to idols is any thing?** But *I say*, that the things which the Gentiles sacrifice, they sacrifice to devils, and not to God: and I would not that ye should have fellowship with devils.
	22²	**Do we provoke the Lord to jealousy? are we stronger than He?**

But if any man say unto you, This is offered in sacrifice unto idols, eat not for his sake that shewed it, and for conscience sake : for the earth *is* the Lord's, and the fulness thereof : conscience, I say, not thine own, but of the other : for **why is my liberty judged of another** *man's* **conscience?** For if I by grace be a partaker, **why am I evil spoken of for that for which I give thanks?** Whether therefore ye eat, or drink, or whatsoever ye do, do all to the glory of God.

CHAP.	VER.
10	29
	30
	9

Judge in yourselves. **is it comely that a woman pray unto God uncovered? Doth not even nature itself teach you, that, if a man have long hair, it is a shame unto him?** But if a woman have long hair, it is a glory to her : for *her* hair is given her for a covering.

11	13
	14

When ye come together therefore into one place, *this* is not to eat the Lord's supper. For in eating every one taketh before *other* his own supper : and one is hungry, and another is drunken. **What? have ye not houses to eat and to drink in?** or **despise ye the church of God, and shame them that have not? What shall I say to you?** shall I praise you in this? I praise *you* not.

	25⁵
	7

For the body is not one member, but many. If the foot shall say, Because I am not the hand, I am not of the body ; **is it therefore not of the body?** And if the ear shall say, Because I am not the eye, I am not of the body ; **is it therefore not of the body? If the whole body** *were* **an eye, where** *were* **the hearing? If the whole** *were* **hearing, where** *were* **the smelling?** But now hath God set the members every one of them in the body, as it hath pleased Him. And **if they were all one member, where** *were* **the body?** But now *are they* many members, yet but one body.

12	15
	16
	17²
	19

Now ye are the body of Christ, and members in particular. And God hath set some in the church, first

CHAP.	VER.	
12	29⁴	apostles, secondarily prophets, thirdly teachers, after that miracles, then gifts of healings, helps, governments, diversities of tongues. *Are* **all apostles?** *are* **all prophets?** *are* **all teachers?** *are* **all workers of**
	30³	**miracles? have all the gifts of healing? do all speak with tongues? do all interpret?** But covet earnestly the best gifts: and yet shew I unto you a more
	12	excellent way.

14	6	Now, brethren, **if I come unto you speaking with tongues, what shall I profit you, except I shall speak to you either by revelation, or by knowledge, or by prophesying, or by doctrine?** And even things without life giving sound, whether pipe or
	7	harp, except they give a distinction in the sounds, **how shall it be known what is piped or harped?** For
	8	**if the trumpet give an uncertain sound, who shall prepare himself to the battle?** So likewise ye, except ye utter by the tongue words easy to be under-
	9	stood, **how shall it be known what is spoken?** for ye shall speak into the air.
	15	Wherefore let him that speaketh in an *unknown* tongue pray that he may interpret. For if I pray in an *unknown* tongue, my spirit prayeth, but my understanding is unfruitful. **What is it then?** I will pray with the spirit, and I will pray with the understanding also: I will sing with the spirit, and I will sing with the under-
	16	standing also. Else **when thou shalt bless with the spirit, how shall he that occupieth the room of the unlearned say Amen at thy giving of thanks, seeing he understandeth not what thou sayest?** For thou verily givest thanks well, but the other is not edified.
	23	**If therefore the whole church be come together into one place, and all speak with tongues, and there come in** *those that are* **unlearned, or unbelievers, will they not say that ye are mad?** But

if all prophesy, and there come in one that believeth not, or *one* unlearned, he is convinced of all, he is judged of all: and thus are the secrets of his heart made manifest; and so falling down on *his* face he will worship God, and report that God is in you of a truth. **How is it then, brethren?** when ye come together, every one of you hath a psalm, hath a doctrine, hath a tongue, hath a revelation, hath an interpretation. Let all things be done unto edifying.

14 26

What? came the word of God out from you? or came it unto you only? If any man think himself to be a prophet, or spiritual, let him acknowledge that the things that I write unto you are the commandments of the Lord.

36[3]

71

Now **if Christ be preached that He rose from the dead, how say some among you that there is no resurrection of the dead?**

15 12

Else what shall they do which are baptized for the dead, if the dead rise not at all? why are they then baptized for the dead? And **why stand we in jeopardy every hour?** I protest by your rejoicing which I have in Christ Jesus our Lord, I die daily. **If after the manner of men I have fought with beasts at Ephesus, what advantageth it me, if the dead rise not?** let us eat and drink; for to morrow we die.

29[2]

30

32

But some *man* will say, **How are the dead raised up? and with what body do they come?** *Thou* fool, that which thou sowest is not quickened, except it die: and that which thou sowest, thou sowest not that body that shall be, but bare grain, it may chance of wheat, or of some other *grain:* but God giveth it a body as it hath pleased Him, and to every seed his own body.

35[2]

So when this corruptible shall have put on incorruption,

CHAP.	VER.	
15	55²	and this mortal shall have put on immortality, then shall be brought to pass the saying that is written, Death is swallowed up in victory. **O death, where** *is* **thy sting? O grave, where** *is* **thy victory?** The sting of death *is* sin; and the strength of sin *is* the law. But thanks *be* to God, which giveth us the victory through our Lord Jesus Christ.
	9	

First Corinthians 113

THE SECOND EPISTLE OF PAUL THE APOSTLE
TO THE
CORINTHIANS.

CHAP.	VER.	
1	17²	AND in this confidence I was minded to come unto you before, that ye might have a second benefit; and to pass by you into Macedonia, and to come again out of Macedonia unto you, and of you to be brought on my way toward Judæa. **When I therefore was thus minded, did I use lightness? or the things that I purpose, do I purpose according to the flesh, that with me there should be yea yea, and nay nay?**
	2	But *as* God *is* true, our word toward you was not yea and nay.
2	2	But I determined this with myself, that I would not come again to you in heaviness. **For if I make you sorry, who is he then that maketh me glad, but the same which is made sorry by me?**
	16	For we are unto God a sweet savour of Christ, in them that are saved, and in them that perish: to the one we *are* the savour of death unto death; and to the other the savour of life unto life. And **who** *is* **sufficient for these things?**
	2	

	CHAP.	VER
Do we begin again to commend ourselves? or **need we, as some** *others*, **epistles of commendation to you, or** *letters* **of commendation from you?** Ye are our epistle written in our hearts, known and read of all men.	**3**	1²
But if the ministration of death, written *and* engraven in stones, was glorious, so that the children of Israel could not stedfastly behold the face of Moses for the glory of his countenance; which *glory* was to be done away : **how shall not the ministration of the Spirit be rather glorious?**		8 3
O *ye* Corinthians, our mouth is open unto you, our heart is enlarged. Ye are not straitened in us, but ye are straitened in your own bowels. Now for a recompence in the same (I speak as unto *my* children), be ye also enlarged. Be ye not unequally yoked together with unbelievers : for **what fellowship hath righteousness with unrighteousness?** and **what communion hath light with darkness?** And **what concord hath Christ with Belial?** or **what part hath he that believeth with an infidel?** And **what agreement hath the temple of God with idols?** for ye are the temple of the living God; as God hath said, I will dwell in them, and walk in *them ;* and I will be their God, and they shall be My people.	**6**	14² 15² 16 5
Do ye look on things after the outward appearance? If any man trust to himself that he is Christ's, let him of himself think this again, that, as he *is* Christ's, even so *are* we Christ's.	**10**	7 1
But though *I be* rude in speech, yet not in knowledge; but we have been throughly made manifest among you in all things. **Have I committed an offence in abasing myself that ye might be exalted, because I have preached to you the gospel of God freely?** I robbed other churches, taking wages *of them,* to do you	**11**	7

CHAP.	VER.	
11	11²	service. And when I was present with you, and wanted, I was chargeable to no man : for that which was lacking to me the brethren which came from Macedonia supplied : and in all *things* I have kept myself from being burdensome unto you, and *so* will I keep *myself*. As the truth of Christ is in me, no man shall stop me of this boasting in the regions of Achaia. **Wherefore? because I love you not?** God knoweth.
	22³ 23	I speak as concerning reproach, as though we had been weak. Howbeit whereinsoever any is bold (I speak foolishly), I am bold also. **Are they Hebrews?** so *am* I. **Are they Israelites?** so *am* I. **Are they the seed of Abraham?** so *am* I. **Are they ministers of Christ?** (I speak as a fool) I *am* more; in labours more abundant, in stripes above measure, in prisons more frequent, in deaths oft.
	29² 9	**Who is weak, and I am not weak? who is offended, and I burn not?** If I must needs glory, I will glory of the things which concern mine infirmities
12	13	Truly the signs of an apostle were wrought among you in all patience, in signs, and wonders, and mighty deeds. For **what is it wherein ye were inferior to other churches, except** *it be* **that I myself was not burdensome to you?** forgive me this wrong.
	17 18³ 19 6	But be it so, I did not burden you : nevertheless, being crafty, I caught you with guile. **Did I make a gain of you by any of them whom I sent unto you?** I desired Titus, and with *him* I sent a brother. **Did Titus make a gain of you? walked we not in the same spirit?** *walked we* **not in the same steps?** Again, **think ye that we excuse ourselves unto you?** we speak before God in Christ: but *we do* all things, dearly beloved, for your edifying.

Examine yourselves, whether ye be in the faith; prove

	CHAP. VER.
your own selves. **Know ye not your own selves, how that Jesus Christ is in you, except ye be reprobates?**	**13** 5
	1

Second Corinthians 29

THE EPISTLE OF PAUL THE APOSTLE

TO THE

GALATIANS.

	CHAP. VER.
AS we said before, so say I now again, If any *man* preach any other gospel unto you than that ye have received, let him be accursed. For **do I now persuade men, or God?** or **do I seek to please men?** for if I yet pleased men, I should not be the servant of Christ.	**1** 10²
	2
But when I saw that they walked not uprightly according to the truth of the gospel, I said unto Peter before *them* all, **If thou, being a Jew, livest after the manner of Gentiles, and not as do the Jews, why compellest thou the Gentiles to live as do the Jews?**	**2** 14
But if, while we seek to be justified by Christ, we ourselves also are found sinners, *is* therefore Christ the minister of sin? God forbid.	17
	2
O foolish Galatians, **who hath bewitched you, that ye should not obey the truth, before whose eyes Jesus Christ hath been evidently set forth, crucified among you?** This only would I learn of you, **Received ye the Spirit by the works of the law, or by the hearing of faith? Are ye so foolish?** having begun in the Spirit, are ye now made perfect by the flesh? Have ye suffered so many	**3** 1
	2
	3²
	4

CHAP.	VER.	
3	5	**things in vain?** if *it be* yet in vain. He therefore that ministereth to you the Spirit, and worketh miracles among you, *doeth he it* **by the works of the law, or by the hearing of faith?**
	19	For if the inheritance *be* of the law, *it is* no more of promise: but God gave *it* to Abraham by promise. **Wherefore then** *serveth* **the law?** It was added because of transgressions, till the seed should come to whom the promise was made; *and it was* ordained by angels in the hand of a mediator. Now a mediator is
	21	not a *mediator* of one, but God is one. *Is* **the law then against the promises of God?** God forbid: for if there had been a law given which could have given life,
	8	verily righteousness should have been by the law.
4	9	But now, after that ye have known God, or rather are known of God, **how turn ye again to the weak and beggarly elements, whereunto ye desire again to be in bondage?**
	15	**Where is then the blessedness ye spake of?** for I bear you record, that, if *it had been* possible, ye would have plucked out your own eyes, and have given them to
	16	me. **Am I therefore become your enemy, because I tell you the truth?**
	21	Tell me, ye that desire to be under the law, **do ye not hear the law?**
	30	But as then he that was born after the flesh persecuted him *that was born* after the Spirit, even so *it is* now. Nevertheless **what saith the scripture?** Cast out the bondwoman and her son: for the son of the bondwoman shall not be heir with the son of the freewoman. So then, brethren, we are not children of the bondwoman,
	5	but of the free.
5	7	Ye did run well; **who did hinder you that ye should not obey the truth?**

	CHAP. VER.
And I, brethren, **if I yet preach circumcision, why do I yet suffer persecution?** then is the offence of the cross ceased.	5 11
	2
Galatians 19	

THE EPISTLE OF PAUL THE APOSTLE
TO THE
EPHESIANS.

	CHAP. VER.
WHEREFORE He saith, When He ascended up on high, He led captivity captive, and gave gifts unto men. (Now that He ascended, **what is it but that He also descended first into the lower parts of the earth?** He that descended is the same also that ascended up far above all heavens, that He might fill all things.)	4 9
	1
Ephesians 1	

THE EPISTLE OF PAUL THE APOSTLE
TO THE
PHILIPPIANS.

	CHAP. VER.
SOME indeed preach Christ even of envy and strife; and some also of good will: the one preach Christ of contention, not sincerely, supposing to add affliction to my bonds: but the other of love, knowing that I am set for the defence of the gospel. **What then?** notwithstanding, every way, whether in pretence, or in truth, Christ is preached; and I therein do rejoice, yea, and will rejoice.	1 18
	1
Philippians 1	

THE EPISTLE OF PAUL THE APOSTLE

TO THE

COLOSSIANS.

CHAP.	VER.	
2	22	WHEREFORE if ye be dead with Christ from the rudiments of the world, **why, as though living in the world, are ye subject to ordinances,** (touch not; taste not; handle not; which all are to perish with the using;) **after the commandments and doctrines of men?**
	1	

Colossians 1

THE FIRST EPISTLE OF PAUL THE APOSTLE

TO THE

THESSALONIANS.

CHAP.	VER.	
2	19²	WHEREFORE we would have come unto you, even I Paul, once and again; but Satan hindered us. For **what** *is* **our hope, or joy, or crown of rejoicing?** *Are* **not even ye in the presence of our Lord Jesus Christ at His coming?** For ye are our glory and joy.
	2	
3	10	For **what thanks can we render to God again for you, for all the joy wherewith we joy for your sakes before our God; night and day praying exceedingly that we might see your face, and might perfect that which is lacking in your faith?**
	1	

First Thessalonians 3

THE SECOND EPISTLE OF PAUL THE APOSTLE

TO THE

THESSALONIANS.

NOW we beseech you, brethren, by the coming of our Lord Jesus Christ, and *by* our gathering together unto Him, that ye be not soon shaken in mind, or be troubled, neither by spirit, nor by word, nor by letter as from us, as that the day of Christ is at hand. Let no man deceive you by any means: for *that day shall not come*, except there come a falling away first, and that man of sin be revealed, the son of perdition; who opposeth and exalteth himself above all that is called God, or that is worshipped; so that he as God sitteth in the temple of God, showing himself that he is God. **Remember ye not, that, when I was yet with you, I told you these things?**

CHAP.	VER.
2	5
	1

Second Thessalonians 1

THE FIRST EPISTLE OF PAUL THE APOSTLE

TO

TIMOTHY.

FOR if a man know not how to rule his own house, how shall he take care of the church of God?

CHAP.	VER.
3	5
	1

First Timothy 1

THE SECOND EPISTLE OF PAUL THE APOSTLE

TO

TIMOTHY.

Second Timothy 0

THE EPISTLE OF PAUL

TO

TITUS.

Titus 0

THE EPISTLE OF PAUL

TO

PHILEMON.

CHAP.	VER.	
1	16	**N**OT now as a servant, but above a servant, a brother beloved, specially to me, but **how much more unto thee, both in the flesh, and in the Lord?** If thou count me therefore a partner, receive him as myself.
	1	

Philemon 1

THE EPISTLE OF PAUL THE APOSTLE

TO THE

HEBREWS.

	CHAP.	VER.

FOR unto which of the angels said He at any time, Thou art My Son, this day have I begotten Thee? And again, I will be to Him a Father, and He shall be to Me a Son?   **1**   5²

But to which of the angels said He at any time, Sit on My right hand, until I make thine enemies thy footstool? Are they not all ministering spirits, sent forth to minister for them who shall be heirs of salvation?   13 / 14 / 4

Therefore we ought to give the more earnest heed to the things which we have heard, lest at any time we should let *them* slip. For if the word spoken by angels was stedfast, and every transgression and disobedience received a just recompence of reward; **how shall we escape, if we neglect so great salvation; which at the first began to be spoken by the Lord, and was confirmed unto us by them** that heard *Him;* God also bearing *them* witness, both with signs and wonders, and with divers miracles, and gifts of the Holy Ghost, according to His own will? For unto the angels hath He not put in subjection the world to come, whereof we speak. But one in a certain place testified, saying, **What is man, that Thou art mindful of him? or the son of man, that Thou visitest him?**   **2**   4 / 6² / 3

While it is said, To day if ye will hear His voice, harden not your hearts, as in the provocation. For some, when they had heard, did provoke: howbeit not all that came out of Egypt by Moses. But **with whom**   **3**   17²

CHAP.	VER.	
3	18	**was He grieved forty years?** *was it* **not with them that had sinned, whose carcases fell in the wilderness? And to whom sware He that they should not enter into His rest, but to them that believed not?** So we see that they could not enter in because of unbelief.
	3	
7	11	And as I may so say, Levi also, who receiveth tithes, payed tithes in Abraham. For he was yet in the loins of his father, when Melchisedec met him. If therefore perfection were by the Levitical priesthood (for under it the people received the law,) **what further need** *was there* **that another priest should rise after the order of Melchisedec, and not be called after the order of Aaron?**
	1	
9	14	For if the blood of bulls and of goats, and the ashes of an heifer sprinkling the unclean, sanctifieth to the purifying of the flesh: **how much more shall the blood of Christ, who through the eternal Spirit offered Himself without spot to God, purge your conscience from dead works to serve the living God?**
	1	
10	2	For the law having a shadow of good things to come, *and* not the very image of the things, can never with those sacrifices which they offered year by year continually make the comers thereunto perfect. For **then would they not have ceased to be offered?** because that the worshippers once purged should have had no more conscience of sins.
	29	He that despised Moses' law died without mercy under two or three witnesses: **of how much sorer punishment, suppose ye, shall he be thought worthy, who hath trodden under foot the Son of God, and hath counted the blood of the covenant, wherewith he was sanctified, an unholy thing, and hath done despite unto the Spirit of grace?** For we know Him that hath said, Vengeance *belongeth* unto Me,
	2	

I will recompense, saith the Lord. And again, The Lord shall judge His people.

And what shall I more say? for the time would fail me to tell of Gedeon, and *of* Barak, and *of* Samson, and *of* Jephthae; *of* David also, and Samuel, and *of* the prophets: who through faith subdued kingdoms, wrought righteousness, obtained promises, stopped the mouths of lions, quenched the violence of fire, escaped the edge of the sword, out of weakness were made strong, waxed valiant in fight, turned to flight the armies of the aliens. | 11 | 32

| | 1

If ye endure chastening, God dealeth with you as with sons; for **what son is he whom the father chasteneth not?** But if ye be without chastisement, whereof all are partakers, then are ye bastards, and not sons. Furthermore we have had fathers of our flesh which corrected *us*, and we gave *them* reverence: **shall we not much rather be in subjection unto the Father of spirits, and live?** For they verily for a few days chastened *us* after their own pleasure; but He for *our* profit, that *we* might be partakers of His holiness. | 12 | 7

| | 9

| | 2

Hebrews 17

THE GENERAL EPISTLE

OF

JAMES.

MY brethren, have not the faith of our Lord Jesus Christ, *the Lord* of glory, with respect of persons. For **if there come unto your assembly a man with a gold ring, in goodly apparel, and there come in also a poor man in vile raiment; and ye have respect to him that weareth the gay** | 2 | 4

CHAP.	VER.	
2	5	clothing, and say unto him, Sit thou here in a good place ; and say to the poor, Stand thou there, or sit here under my footstool: are ye not then partial in yourselves, and are become judges of evil thoughts? Hearken, my beloved brethren, **Hath not God chosen the poor of this world rich in faith, and heirs of the kingdom which He hath promised to them that love Him?** But ye have
	6	despised the poor. **Do not rich men oppress you,**
	7	**and draw you before the judgment seats? Do not they blaspheme that worthy name by the which ye are called?**
	14[2]	**What** *doth it* **profit, my brethren, though a man say he hath faith, and have not works? can faith save him?** If a brother or sister be naked, and destitute of daily food, and one of you say unto them, Depart in peace, be *ye* warmed and filled ; notwithstanding ye give them not those things which are needful to the body ;
	16	**what** *doth it* **profit?** Even so faith, if it hath not works, is dead, being alone. Yea, a man may say, Thou hast faith, and I have works: shew me thy faith without thy works, and I will shew thee my faith by my works. Thou believest that there is one God ; thou doest well :
	20	the devils also believe, and tremble. But **wilt thou know, O vain man, that faith without works is**
	21	**dead? Was not Abraham our father justified by works, when he had offered Isaac his son upon**
	22	**the altar? Seest thou how faith wrought with his works, and by works was faith made perfect?** And the scripture was fulfilled which saith, Abraham believed God, and it was imputed unto him for righteousness : and he was called the Friend of God. Ye see then how that by works a man is justified, and not by faith
	25	only. Likewise also **was not Rahab the harlot justified by works, when she had received the messengers, and had sent** *them* **out another way?**
	11	For as the body without the spirit is dead, so faith without works is dead also.

JAMES:—III., IV.

Out of the same mouth proceedeth blessing and cursing. My brethren, these things ought not so to be. **Doth a fountain send forth at the same place sweet** *water* **and bitter? Can the fig tree, my brethren, bear olive berries? either a vine, figs?** so *can* no fountain both yield salt water and fresh. **Who** *is* **a wise man and endued with knowledge among you?** let him shew out of a good conversation his works with meekness of wisdom. But if ye have bitter envying and strife in your hearts, glory not, and lie not against the truth.

CHAP	VER.
3	11
	12²
	13
4	

From whence *come* **wars and fightings among you?** *come they* **not hence,** *even* **of your lusts that war in your members?** Ye lust, and have not: ye kill, and desire to have, and cannot obtain: ye fight and war, yet ye have not, because ye ask not. Ye ask, and receive not, because ye ask amiss, that ye may consume *it* upon your lusts. Ye adulterers and adulteresses, **know ye not that the friendship of the world is enmity with God?** whosoever therefore will be a friend of the world is the enemy of God. **Do ye think that the scripture saith in vain, The spirit that dwelleth in us lusteth to envy?** But He giveth more grace. Wherefore he saith, God resisteth the proud, but giveth grace unto the humble.

4	1²
	4
	5

Speak not evil one of another, brethren. He that speaketh evil of *his* brother, and judgeth his brother, speaketh evil of the law, and judgeth the law: but if thou judge the law, thou art not a doer of the law, but a judge. There is one lawgiver, who is able to save and to destroy: **who art thou that judgest another?** Go to now, ye that say, To day or to morrow we will go into such a city, and continue there a year, and buy and sell, and get gain: whereas ye know not what *shall be* on the morrow. For **what** *is* **your life?** It is even a vapour, that appeareth for a little time, and then vanisheth away.

	12
	14
	6

CHAP.	VER
5	13²
	14
	3

James 24

Is any among you afflicted? let him pray. **Is any merry?** let him sing psalms. **Is any sick among you?** let him call for the elders of the church; and let them pray over him, anointing him with oil in the name of the Lord: and the prayer of faith shall save the sick, and the Lord shall raise him up; and if he have committed sins, they shall be forgiven him.

THE FIRST EPISTLE GENERAL

OF

PETER.

CHAP.	VER.
2	20
	1
3	13
	1
4	17

FOR this *is* thankworthy, if a man for conscience toward God endure grief, suffering wrongfully. For **what glory** *is it*, **if, when ye be buffeted for your faults, ye shall take it patiently?** but if, when ye do well, and suffer *for it*, ye take it patiently, this *is* acceptable with God.

For the eyes of the Lord *are* over the righteous, and His ears *are open* unto their prayers: but the face of the Lord *is* against them that do evil. And **who** *is* **he that will harm you, if ye be followers of that which is good?**

Yet if *any man suffer* as a Christian, let him not be ashamed; but let him glorify God on this behalf. For the time *is come* that judgment must begin at the house of God: and if *it* first *begin* at us, **what shall the end** *be* **of them that obey not the gospel of God?** And

	CHAP. VER.
if the righteous scarcely be saved, **where shall the ungodly and the sinner appear?** Wherefore let them that suffer according to the will of God commit the keeping of their souls *to Him* in well doing, as unto a faithful Creator.	**4** 18
	2
First Peter 4	

THE SECOND EPISTLE GENERAL

OF

PETER.

	CHAP. VER.
THIS second epistle, beloved, I now write unto you; in *both* which I stir up your pure minds by way of remembrance: that ye may be mindful of the words which were spoken before by the holy prophets, and of the commandment of us the apostles of the Lord and Saviour: knowing this first, that there shall come in the last days scoffers, walking after their own lusts, and saying, **Where is the promise of His coming?** for since the fathers fell asleep, all things continue as *they were* from the beginning of the creation.	3 4
Seeing then *that* all these things shall be dissolved, **what manner** *of persons* **ought ye to be in** *all* **holy conversation and godliness, looking for and hasting unto the coming of the day of God, wherein the heavens being on fire shall be dissolved, and the elements shall melt with fervent heat?** Nevertheless we, according to His promise, look for new heavens and a new earth, wherein dwelleth righteousness.	12
	2
Second Peter 2	

THE FIRST EPISTLE GENERAL

OF

JOHN.

CHAP.	VER.	
2	22	I HAVE not written unto you because ye know not the truth, but because ye know it, and that no lie is of the truth. **Who is a liar but he that denieth that Jesus is the Christ?** He is antichrist, that denieth the Father and the Son.
	1	
3	12	For this is the message that ye heard from the beginning, that we should love one another. Not as Cain, *who* was of that wicked one, and slew his brother. And **wherefore slew he him?** Because his own works were evil, and his brother's righteous.
	17	But whoso hath this world's good, and seeth his brother have need, and shutteth up his bowels *of compassion* from him, **how dwelleth the love of God in him?** My little children, let us not love in word, neither in tongue; but in deed and in truth.
	2	
4	20	If a man say, I love God, and hateth his brother, he is a liar: for he that loveth not his brother whom he hath seen, **how can he love God whom he hath not seen?** And this commandment have we from Him, That he who loveth God love his brother also.
	1	
5	5	For whatsoever is born of God overcometh the world: and this is the victory that overcometh the world, *even* our faith. **Who is he that overcometh the world, but he that believeth that Jesus is the Son of God?**
	1	

First John 5

THE SECOND EPISTLE
OF
JOHN.

Second John 0

THE THIRD EPISTLE
OF
JOHN.

Third John 0

THE GENERAL EPISTLE
OF
JUDE.

Jude 0

THE REVELATION
OF
St. JOHN THE DIVINE.

	CHAP.	VER
AND I saw in the right hand of Him that sat on the throne a book written within and on the backside, sealed with seven seals. And I saw a strong angel proclaiming with a loud voice, **Who is worthy to open the book, and to loose the seals thereof?**	5	2
		1
And when He had opened the fifth seal, I saw under the altar the souls of them that were slain for the word of God, and for the testimony which they held: and they cried with a loud voice, saying, **How long, O Lord, holy and true, dost Thou not judge and**	6	10

CHAP	VER.	
		avenge our blood on them that dwell on the earth?
		And the kings of the earth, and the great men, and the rich men, and the chief captains, and the mighty men, and every bondman, and every free man, hid themselves in the dens and in the rocks of the mountains; and said to the mountains and rocks, Fall on us, and hide us from the face of Him that sitteth on the throne, and from the wrath of the Lamb: for the great day of
6	17	His wrath is come; and **who shall be able to stand?**
	2	
7	13²	And one of the elders answered, saying unto me, **What are these which are arrayed in white robes? and whence came they?** And I said unto him, Sir, thou knowest. And he said to me, These are they which came out of great tribulation, and have washed their robes, and made them white in the blood
	2	of the Lamb.
13	4²	And they worshipped the dragon which gave power unto the beast: and they worshipped the beast, saying, **Who** is **like unto the beast? who is able to make war with him?**
	2	
15	4	**Who shall not fear Thee, O Lord, and glorify Thy name?** for *Thou* only *art* holy: for all nations shall come and worship before Thee; for Thy judgments
	1	are made manifest.
17	7	And the angel said unto me, **Wherefore didst thou marvel?** I will tell thee the mystery of the woman, and of the beast that carrieth her, which hath the seven heads and ten horns.
	1	

Revelation 9

NEW TESTAMENT—Total 1024

NUMBER OF QUESTIONS IN EACH CHAPTER OF THE OLD TESTAMENT, AND TOTALS.

Chapter.	Genesis.	Exodus.	Leviticus.	Numbers.	Deuteronomy.	Joshua.	Judges.	Ruth.	1 Samuel.	2 Samuel.	1 Kings.	2 Kings.	1 Chronicles.	2 Chronicles.	Ezra.	Nehemiah.	Esther.
1	0	1	0	0	2	1	2	6	5	6	8	6	0	1	1	0	1
2	0	7	0	0	0	0	1	6	6	8	4	4	0	2	0	7	0
3	5	3	0	0	2	0	0	4	1	7	1	4	0	0	0	0	1
4	6	5	0	0	5	2	3	0	5	2	0	12	0	0	1	5	1
5	0	6	0	0	2	2	7	–	1	2	0	11	0	0	3	3	4
6	0	2	0	0	1	0	7	–	6	1	0	12	0	1	0	3	4
7	0	0	0	0	1	4	0	–	0	7	0	3	0	1	1	0	4
8	0	2	0	0	0	0	7	–	0	0	2	6	0	0	0	0	2
9	0	1	0	1	0	4	10	–	8	5	2	13	0	1	3	0	3
10	0	4	2	0	1	1	2	–	9	2	0	5	0	3	0	0	1
11	0	0	0	12	1	0	9	–	2	9	2	0	1	0	–	0	
12	3	1	0	4	1	0	3	–	6	7	3	2	0	1	–	0	
13	1	1	0	0	0	0	4	–	1	6	2	2	1	2	–	6	
14	0	5	0	6	0	0	6	–	5	5	3	4	2	0			
15	2	3	0	0	0	1	6	–	4	5	3	3	0	0			
16	3	3	0	7	0	0	1	–	4	10	4	1	0	1			
17	2	5	0	1	0	1	1	–	12	2	3	0	4	0			
18	9	2	0	0	1	1	11	–	4	4	5	12	0	9			
19	3	0	0	0	0	0	2	–	5	22	3	6	2	1			
20	5	0	0	3	4	0	5	–	13	3	4	7	0	5			
21	3	0	0	1	0	0	5	–	8	2	5	2	5	0			
22	1	1	0	9	0	4	–	–	4	2	12	0	2	0			
23	1	0	0	9	0	0	–	–	6	2	–	2	0	0			
24	7	0	0	2	0	0	–	–	5	6	–	1	0	2			
25	2	0	0	0	0	–	–	–	3	–	–	0	0	6			
26	3	0	0	0	0	–	–	–	12	–	–	–	0	0			
27	12	0	0	1	0	–	–	–	2	–	–	–	0	0			
28	0	0	–	0	0	–	–	–	7	–	–	–	0	1			
29	8	0	–	0	2	–	–	–	7	–	–	–	2	0			
30	5	0	–	0	2	–	–	–	6	–	–	–	–	0			
31	10	0	–	1	2	–	–	–	0	–	–	–	–	0			
32	5	4	–	2	6	–	–	–	–	–	–	–	–	8			
33	3	2	–	0	0	–	–	–	–	–	–	–	–	0			
34	2	0	–	0	0	–	–	–	–	–	–	–	–	0			
35	0	0	–	0	–	–	–	–	–	–	–	–	–	1			
36	0	0	–	0	–	–	–	–	–	–	–	–	–	1			
37	8	0															
38	5	0															
39	1	0															
40	2	0															
41	1																
42	4																
43	7																
44	11																
45	1																
46	1																
47	4																
48	1																
49	1																
50	1																
Total	149	58	2	59	33	21	92	16	157	125	66	118	19	47	9	24	21

OLD TESTAMENT (continued) :—

Chapter.	Job.	Psalms.	Proverbs.	Ecclesiastes.	Song of Solom.	Isaiah.	Jeremiah.	Lamentations.	Ezekiel.	Daniel.	Chapter.	Psalms.	Isaiah.	Jeremiah.	Chapter.	Psalms.
1	4	0	3	2	1	3	2	1	0	1	51	0	6	0	101	1
2	5	1	0	7	0	1	21	8	0	2	52	1	1	0	102	0
3	6	0	0	3	2	1	7	3	0	3	53	1	3		103	0
4	9	3	0	2	0	0	3	0	0	2	54	0	0		104	0
5	1	0	1	3	4	2	10	1	0	1	55	0	2		105	0
6	18	2	4	6	4	2	3	–	0	2	56	3	0		106	2
7	11	0	0	5	0	1	5	–	0	0	57	0	6		107	0
8	7	2	2	4	2	2	13	–	6	1	58	2	10		108	4
9	8	0	0	0	–	0	5	–	1	0	59	1	0		109	0
10	9	3	0	1	–	10	1	–	0	2	60	4	1		110	0
11	10	2	0	0	–	0	1	–	1	0	61	0	0		111	0
12	4	1	0	0	–	0	5	–	2	2	62	1	0		112	0
13	14	5	0	–	–	0	8	–	4		63	0	10		113	0
14	5	1	1	–	–	6	8	–	2		64	1	2		114	3
15	17	2	1	–	–	0	7	–	5		65	0	0		115	1
16	3	0	0	–	–	0	4	–	1		66	0	8		116	1
17	5	0	1	–	–	0	2	–	8		67	0			117	0
18	4	2	1	–	–	0	4	–	12		68	1			118	1
19	3	1	1	–	–	3	1	–	1		69	0			119	4
20	2	0	3	–	–	1	0	–	7		70	0			120	2
21	14	0	1	–	–	2	2	–	4		71	0			121	0
22	12	2	3	–	–	3	7	–	2		72	0			122	0
23	2	0	8	–	–	2	15	–	2		73	3			123	0
24	2	4	4	–	–	0	1	–	2		74	5			124	0
25	6	1	1	–	–	0	1	–	0		75	0			125	0
26	8	0	2	–	–	0	3	–	1		76	1			126	0
27	5	2	2	–	–	3	2	–	1		77	7			127	0
28	4	0	0	–	–	5	0	–	1		78	3			128	0
29	0	0	1	–	–	5	1	–	0		79	4			129	0
30	3	3	6	–	–	0	4	–	0		80	2			130	1
31	11	0	4	–	–	0	3	–	2		81	0			131	0
32	0	0	–	–	–	0	2	–	1		82	1			132	0
33	1	0	–	–	–	5	1	–	4		83	0			133	0
34	12	1	–	–	–	0	0	–	3		84	0			134	0
35	8	2	–	–	–	0	1	–	0		85	3			135	0
36	5	0	–	–	–	12	2	–	0		86	0			136	0
37	5	0	–	–	–	6	3	–	2		87	0			137	1
38	40	0	–	–	–	2	2	–	5		88	8			138	0
39	19	1	–	–	–	3	0	–	0		89	11			139	4
40	6	0	–	–	–	14	2	–	0		90	2			140	0
41	20	1	–	–	–	4	0	–	0		91	0			141	0
42	1	9	–	–	–	7	0	–	0		92	0			142	0
43	–	4	–	–	–	3	0	–	0		93	0			143	0
44	–	3	–	–	–	7	4	–	0		94	11			144	0
45	–	0	–	–	–	7	1	–	0		95	0			145	0
46	–	0	–	–	–	1	3	–	0		96	0			146	0
47	–	0	–	–	–	0	3	–	1		97	0			147	1
48	–	0	–	–	–	3	4	–	0		98	0			148	0
49	–	1	–	–	–	5	14				99	0			149	0
50	–	2	–	–	–	10	4				100	0			150	0
Total	329	–	50	33	13	–	–	13	81	16	Total	–	190	195	Total	163

OLD TESTAMENT (*continued*):—

Chapter.	Hosea.	Joel.	Amos.	Obadiah.	Jonah.	Micah.	Nahum.	Habakkuk.	Zephaniah.	Haggai.	Zechariah.	Malachi.		Chapters.	Questions.
1	0	2	0	4	7	4	3	5	0	2	7	12	Job..................	42	329
2	0	3	1	–	0	3	1	4	0	6	1	8	Jeremiah	52	195
3	0	2	9	–	1	2	4	3	0	–	1	7	Isaiah	66	190
4	0	–	0	–	4	3	–	–	–	–	8	0	Psalms	150	163
5	0	–	4	–	–	0	–	–	–	–	3		1 Samuel	31	157
6	2	–	6	–	–	9	–	–	–	–	1		Genesis...	50	149
7	0	–	3	–	–	2	–	–	–	–	4		2 Samuel	24	125
8	1	–	5	–	–	–	–	–	–	–	1		2 Kings....	25	118
9	2	–	3	–	–	–	–	–	–	–	0		Judges	21	92
10	1	–	–	–	–	–	–	–	–	–	0		Ezekiel	48	81
11	4	–	–	–	–	–	–	–	–	–	0		1 Kings	22	66
12	1	–	–	–	–	–	–	–	–	–	0		Numbers	36	59
13	2	–	–	–	–	–	–	–	–	–	1		Exodus	40	58
14	3	–	–	–	–	–	–	–	–	–	0		Proverbs ..	31	50
													2 Chronicles ..	36	47
Total	16	7	31	4	12	23	8	12	0	8	27	27	Deuteronomy .	34	33
													Ecclesiastes	12	33
													Amos....	9	31
													Zechariah.....	14	27
													Malachi ...	4	27
													Nehemiah...	13	24
													Micah ...	7	23
													Joshua .	24	21
													Esther ...	10	21
													1 Chronicles.... .	29	19
													Ruth .	4	16
													Daniel	12	16
													Hosea	14	16
													Song of Solomon	8	13
													Lamentations	5	13
													Jonah ..	4	12
													Habakkuk	3	12
													Ezra	10	9
													Nahum .	3	8
													Haggai	2	8
													Joel	3	7
													Obadiah	1	4
													Leviticus	27	2
													Zephaniah	3	0
													Total ...	929	2274

NEW TESTAMENT.

Chapter.	Matthew.	Mark.	Luke.	John.	The Acts.	Romans.	1 Corinthians.	2 Corinthians.	Galatians.	Ephesians.	Philippians.	Colossians.	1 Thessalonians.	2 Thessalonians.	1 Timothy.	2 Timothy.	Titus.
1	0	4	3	12	2	0	7	2	2	0	1	0	0	0	0	0	0
2	1	10	3	3	4	9	2	2	2	0	0	1	2	1	0	0	0
3	2	4	4	5	2	17	4	3	8	0	0	0	1	0	1	0	0
4	0	10	3	8	3	5	5	0	5	1	0	0	0	–	0	0	
5	5	6	7	4	7	0	3	0	2	0	–	–	0	–	0		
6	8	7	12	15	0	8	16	5	0	0	–	–	–	–	0		
7	9	3	15	19	10	5	7	0									
8	3	16	6	14	6	8	1	0									
9	6	8	6	16	4	10	20	0									
10	2	9	6	6	4	10	9	1									
11	8	7	8	8	1	11	7	9									
12	12	12	14	7	0	0	12	6									
13	11	3	9	6	2	1	0	1									
14	1	14	5	5	1	4	11										
15	7	7	2	0	1	0	9										
16	9	1	6	5	2	0	0										
17	8	–	6	0	2												
18	6	–	6	17	0												
19	9	–	3	4	4												
20	7	–	13	3	0												
21	12	–	2	10	5												
22	12	–	13	–	6												
23	3	–	4	–	3												
24	4	–	9	–	0												
25	6	–	–	–	2												
26	16	–	–	–	4												
27	10	–	–	–	0												
28	0	–	–	–	0												
Total	177	121	165	167	75	88	113	29	19	1	1	1	3	1	1	0	0

New Testament (continued):—

Chapter.	Philemon.	Hebrews.	James.	1 Peter.	2 Peter.	1 John.	2 John.	3 John.	Jude.	Revelation.		Chapters.	Questions.
1	1	4	0	0	0	0	0	0	0	0			
2	–	3	11	1	0	1	–	–	–	0	Matthew	28	177
3	–	3	4	1	2	2	–	–	–	0	John	21	167
4	–	0	6	2	–	1	–	–	–	0	Luke	24	165
5	–	0	3	0	–	1	–	–	–	1	Mark	16	121
6	–	0	–	–	–	–	–	–	–	2	1 Corinthians	16	113
7	–	1	–	–	–	–	–	–	–	2	Romans	16	88
8	–	0	–	–	–	–	–	–	–	0	The Acts	28	75
9	–	1	–	–	–	–	–	–	–	0	2 Corinthians	13	29
10	–	2	–	–	–	–	–	–	–	0	James	5	24
11	–	1	–	–	–	–	–	–	–	0	Galatians	6	19
12	–	2	–	–	–	–	–	–	–	0	Hebrews	13	17
13	–	0	–	–	–	–	–	–	–	2	Revelation	22	9
14	–	–	–	–	–	–	–	–	–	0	1 John	5	5
15	–	–	–	–	–	–	–	–	–	1	1 Peter	5	4
16	–	–	–	–	–	–	–	–	–	0	1 Thessalonians	5	3
17	–	–	–	–	–	–	–	–	–	1	2 Peter	3	2
18	–	–	–	–	–	–	–	–	–	0	Ephesians	6	1
19	–	–	–	–	–	–	–	–	–	0	Philippians	4	1
20	–	–	–	–	–	–	–	–	–	0	Colossians	4	1
21	–	–	–	–	–	–	–	–	–	0	2 Thessalonians	3	1
22	–	–	–	–	–	–	–	–	–	0	1 Timothy	6	1
23											Philemon	1	1
24											2 Timothy	4	0
25											Titus	3	0
26											2 John	1	0
27											3 John	1	0
28											Jude	1	0
Total	1	17	24	4	2	5	0	0	0	9	Total	260	1024

REMARKS
AS TO QUESTIONS IN THE BIBLE.

THE 929 Chapters in the Old Testament contain 2274 Questions. The 260 Chapters in the New Testament contain 1024 Questions. Total in the Holy Bible, 1189 Chapters and 3298 Questions.

All the Chapters in Joel, Obadiah, Nahum, Habakkuk, Haggai, Mark, and Luke contain 1 or more Questions.

Zephaniah is the only Book in the Old Testament without a Question. In the New Testament 5 Books are without—viz., 2 Timothy, Titus, 2 John, 3 John, and Jude.

Leviticus, with 27 Chapters, contains only 2 Questions.

There are only 3 Chapters out of 28 in Matthew without a Question.

The first Question in the Bible is in the 3rd Chapter of Genesis, and the last in the 17th Chapter of Revelation.

The 19th Chapter of Exodus to the 10th of Numbers inclusive contain only 10 Questions in 59 consecutive Chapters.

The 121st Psalm to the 150th inclusive contain 30 Chapters with only 7 Questions.

There are 6 Books in the New Testament containing only 1 Question each: these are— Ephesians, Philippians, Colossians, 2 Thessalonians, 1 Timothy, and Philemon.

Job contains the greatest number of Questions in any single Chapter of the Old Testament—viz., 38th Chapter, 40 Questions.

1 Corinthians contains the greatest number of Questions in any single Chapter of the New Testament—viz., 9th Chapter, 20 Questions.

The Book of Job averages the highest number of Questions in the Old Testament—viz., 7 8 each Chapter.

The Gospel of John averages the highest number of Questions in the New Testament— viz., 8 each Chapter.

In the Book of Revelation, with 22 Chapters, there are only 9 Questions.

From Ephesians to Revelation there are 17 Books with 92 Chapters, and only 71 Questions.

Job has just double the number of Chapters of John—42 against 21—but not quite double the number of Questions—329 to 167

There are only 2 Chapters out of 42 in Job without a Question.

There are only 2 out of 21 Chapters in John without a Question.

There are only 2 out of 16 Chapters in 1 Corinthians without a Question.

Out of 6 Chapters in Galatians there is only one without a Question.

There are 16 Chapters in Revelation without a single Question.

The average number of Questions in the Old Testament is 2·3 for each Chapter; and for the New Testament 3·9. Average total for the Bible, 2¾ Questions for each Chapter.

The New Testament has 50 per cent. more Questions for each Chapter than the Old Testament.

QUESTIONS	0	1	2	3	4	5	6	7	8	9	10	11	12	13	14	15	16	17	18	19	20	21	22	40
CHAPTERS { OLD	370	139	109	70	61	45	33	27	19	12	9	7	13	3	4	1		1	1	1	1	1	1	1
NEW	83	28	25	17	16	11	16	11	10	10	7	4	7	2	3	2	4	2		1	1			
	453	167	134	87	77	56	49	38	29	22	16	11	20	5	7	3	4	3	1	2	2	1	1	1

Old Testament Chapters with Questions .   559
Old Testament Chapters without Questions ..   370
New Testament Chapters with Questions 177
New Testament Chapters without Questions .   83

             736   453 = **1189**

www.ingramcontent.com/pod-product-compliance
Lightning Source LLC
Chambersburg PA
CBHW071226230426
43668CB00011B/1316